School Intervention

SCHOOL INTERVENTION

Volume I of a Continuing Series
in Community-Clinical Psychology

Edited by

WILLIAM L. CLAIBORN, PH.D
Assistant Professor, Department of Psychology,
University of Maryland

ROBERT COHEN, PH.D.
Director, Institute for Community Development,
Syracuse, New York

Behavioral Publications   New York
1973

Library of Congress Catalog Card Number 72-11596
Standard Book Number 87705-094-5
Copyright ©1973 by Behavioral Publications

BEHAVIORAL PUBLICATIONS,
2852 Broadway—Morningside Heights,
New York, New York 10025

Printed in the United States of America

Library of Congress Cataloging in Publication Data

Claiborn, William L
   School intervention.

   (Community-clinical psychology, v. 1)
   1. Personnel service in education--Addresses,
essays, lectures. I. Cohen, Robert, 1941-
joint author. II. Title. III. Series.
[DNLM: 1. Psychology, Educational. 2. Students.
W1 CO428F v. 1 1973. XNLM: [LB 1051 C585s 1973]]
LB1027.5.C547   371.4   72-11596
ISBN 0-87705-094-5

Contributing Authors

Steven J. Apter, Ph.D.
Division of
  Special Education
Syracuse University
805 South Crouse Avenue
Syracuse, New York 13210

Ralph Barocas, Ph.D.
Department of Psychology
University of Rochester
River Campus Station
Rochester, New York 14627

Richard E. Becker
Appalachian Mental Health
  Center
201 Henry Avenue
Elkins, West Virginia 25241

Albert A. Bell
Counseling Services Project
Philadelphia, Pennsylvania

Hershel Berkowitz, Ph.D.
Department of Psychiatry
University of Colorado
  Medical School
4200 East 9th Avenue
Denver, Colorado 80220

Eli M. Bower, Ph.D.
School of Education
University of California
Berkeley, California 94720

Harold Brecher
Counseling Services Project
Philadelphia, Pennsylvania

Anthony Broskowski, Ph.D.
Department of Psychiatry
Harvard Medical School
58 Fenwood Road
Boston, Mass. 02115

Jerome Carroll, Ph.D.
Director of Psychological
  Services
Eagleville Hospital and
  Rehabilitation Center
Eagleville, Pa. 19408

Gail Chandler, Ph.D.
Hamden Mental Health
  Service
3000 Dixwell Avenue
Hamden, Connecticut 06518

Richard DeCharms, Ph.D.
Professor of Education
and Psychology
Box 1183
Washington University
St. Louis, Missouri 63130

Lawrence Fisher, Ph.D.
Department of Psychiatry
University of Rochester
School of Medicine and
Dentistry
260 Crittenden Boulevard
Rochester, New York 14642

Linda H. Harris
905 West 25th Street
Minneapolis, Minnesota

Daniel Langmeyer, Ph.D.
Community Psychology
Institute
University of Cincinnati
Cincinnati, Ohio 45221

Len M. Lansky, Ph.D.
University of Cincinnati
Cincinnati, Ohio 45221

**Beryce W. MacLennan,
Ph.D.**
Mental Health Study Center
National Institute of Mental
Health
2340 University Blvd. East
Adelphi, Maryland 20783

Marshall W. Minor, Ph.D.
Counseling Services
Project
Philadelphia, Pennsylvania

W. Brendan Reddy, Ph.D.
University of Cincinnati
Cincinnati, Ohio 45221

Gerald Rubenstein, Ph.D.
Department of Psychiatry
School of Medicine
University of Rochester
260 Crittenden Boulevard
Rochester, New York 14620

James Stachowiak, Ph.D.
Professor of Psychology
and Head, Psychological
Clinic
University of Kansas
Lawrence, Kansas 66044

David D. Stein, Ph.D.
Assistant Professor of
Psychology
Albert Einstein College of
Medicine
Yeshiva University
2527 Glebe Avenue
Bronx, New York 10461

Contents

PREFACE

This book is a direct outgrowth of the First Annual Symposium on Current Issues in Community-Clinical Psychology: School Intervention, held at the University of Maryland in March, 1971. The symposium was planned to meet an emerging need for developing and disseminating useful approaches for mental health practitioners involved in working with major community social systems. The planners of the conference hoped to relate to this need by conducting a symposium in which innovative practitioners and interested mental health and school workers would come together to discuss the conceptual and strategical issues involved in school intervention. The specific objectives of the symposium were:

1) to acknowledge the importance of creative practitioners by inviting some of them to present their ideas and programs. This is in contrast to the traditional conferences which seem to reward academic erudition and methodological rigor at the expense of community relevance.

2) to provide a medium for practitioners in the area of community psychology to exchange ideas and information about methods and programs related to school intervention.

3) to stimulate persons who might work in school settings to develop new methods for looking at and modifying various components of the school system, including curriculum development, special instruction, supportive services and interpersonal relationships within the school.

4) to introduce students to a series of clinical approaches and models which digress from the orthodox one-to-one diagnostic and therapeutic relationships which professionals have relied on so heavily in the past.

With these objectives in mind, the co-sponsors of the symposium - the Department of Psychology of the University of

Maryland and the Institute for Community Psychology of Syracuse University (now the Institute for Community Development - an independent non-profit organization) - issued a nationwide invitation for people working in the area of schools and mental health to submit original contributions involving the application of psychological knowledge and methodology to school system problems.

More than one hundred and thirty papers were submitted for consideration. Because of the excellent quality of the papers it was difficult to select the limited number which would be presented at the symposium, but after consultation with staff members of the sponsoring organizations, eight papers were finally selected. In addition, Eli Bower and Richard DeCharms, noted authorities in working with schools, were invited to address the participants.

Approximately one hundred and twenty persons from schools, mental health facilities, medical centers, social service agencies and universities attended the symposium, which consisted of paper presentations, topical discussions and workshop sessions.

This book is basically a collection of edited papers submitted for the symposium, with introductory comments and a summation chapter written by the editors. The format of the book has been slightly revised from that of the symposium to provide continuity for the reader.

The first section of the book deals with the history of school intervention, as well as some of the philosophical issues involved in this field. The second part of the book contains information on training and preparation for new roles in school intervention. In the third part, some examples of innovative mental health programs are presented. The fourth section deals with evaluating school intervention programs and the final chapter is a summary of the key issues and concepts presented in the book.

The efforts represented by this book resulted from the commitments and dedication of many individuals. We would like to express our appreciation to Dr. C. J. Bartlett, Head, Department of Psychology, University of Maryland, Dr. Forrest B. Tyler, Director, Clinical Training Program, University of Maryland, Sharon Johnson, Barbara Henry, Dr. Dorothy Evans, Dr. Gerry Specter and especially to Abby Goodman and her friends.

W.C.
R.C.

INTRODUCTION

Those who are concerned with the development and well-being of children have become increasingly aware of the major impact which the schools have upon youngsters. Next to the family, school appears to be the greatest source of influence on the life of a child. (Joint Commission on Mental Illness and Health, 1961.) Debates about whether the school should go beyond teaching the intellectual skills of reading, writing and arithmetic have given way to discussions of how schools can best meet emotional and social needs. Schools have always had an effect on the mental health of children, but their impact has usually been unplanned and incidental. (Allinsmith and Goethals, 1962.) While some parents still object to the schools playing a socializing role (e.g. sex education), many others welcome the opportunity to share the awesome responsibility of "raising" their children in our complex society. Some parents seem eager to delegate the full burden of this task to the formal educational system, especially when their children are having difficulty.

For the schools, the implications of this increased acquisition of social responsibility are profound, and at times, overwhelming. Re-examination of purpose, structure and function is taking place in all parts of the educational system--from the preparation of teachers, to the planning of curriculum, to the relationships among students, teachers, administrators and the rest of the community. In almost all instances, the status quo has been found to be woefully inadequate to meet current demands. The need for revision (or as some would claim **revolution**) in all spheres of the educational system is apparent. The immediate availability of human and material resources needed for these changes, and the willingness of the current educational system to absorb innovations are not so obvious.

In the process of attempting to modify the delivery of educational services, mental health practitioners have begun to question their roles in relationship to the schools. (Cowen, et al., 1967; Goldston, 1965; Sarason, et al., 1966.) Traditionally mental health workers have functioned in a very narrow and fragmented manner. The Social Workers, Psychologists, and Psychiatrists, working in hospitals, mental health clinics or private practice worked with individual children, but with little or no

1

relationship with the schools which their clients attended. It almost seemed as if there were a taboo against intermingling educational and mental health agencies. Those mental health professionals who were employed by the schools, generally confined their activities to diagnosis and therapy with a small number of disruptive children.

In accordance with the re-appraisal of their general role in relation to the community, mental health practitioners found that their modes of functioning in relationship to the schools were neither efficient nor effective. Through examination of their weaknesses, several new directions for action emerged.

1. <u>Prevention</u>. Recognition of the enormous problem of mental disturbance is generally followed by acknowledgement of the challenge of creating conditions which promote and sustain mental health. In the long range, the most effective manner to deal with the emotional problems of children and adults will be to develop preventive approaches which will diminish the probability that emotional disorders will occur at all. (Caplan, 1964.)

Advocacy of the preventive model opened up a wide range of mental health intervention possibilities at a variety of levels. Preventive interventions have been attempted in such areas as (a) early identification of emotionally handicapped children (Bower, 1969); (b) prevention of emotional disturbance in public schools through the use of a mental health clinical services team which worked with school personnel and volunteer undergraduate student counsellors (Zax and Cowen, 1967); (c) introduction of a behavioral sciences curriculum in the elementary school classroom (Ojemann, 1961; Roen, 1967); (d) assisting teachers to become more effective mental health agents (Caplan, 1970; Knoblock, 1971; Morse, 1967; Ringness, 1968; Sarason, et al., 1966); and (e) improving the interpersonal climate in classrooms, schools and school systems through human relations training and organizational development work (Bennis, et al., 1969; Schmuck, et al., 1969).

2. <u>Social Systems Orientation</u>. Related to the concept of prevention is the notion that the mental health of the child is dependent on the interaction of many forces in the environment. It is not enough to "treat" the child alone, because the condition of the child is determined as much by the environment in which he exists as it is by the predisposing tendencies within the youngster. Thus, it may help to teach the emotionally troubled child new coping responses, but unless tension between the parents is reduced and teachers learn to support the child's positive behaviors, there is little chance that effective long-term rehabilitation will occur. Taking this one step further, it is

necessary to modify the sub-systems which influence the teachers
and parents if they are expected to respond affirmatively. Principals must communicate supportively with teachers; parents must
be able to find meaningful work and social activity; etc.

Acceptance of a social systems approach has led to a multitude of intervention programs ranging from teaching people to
be more effective teachers and parents (Gordon, 1970; Patterson
and Gullion, 1962) to working with entire school systems in
order to improve the quality of education (Sarason, 1970;
Schmuck, 1969).

3. <u>Manpower Resources</u>. The enormous scope of the mental
health problem has provoked some serious thinking by mental
health practitioners. Professionals have realized that their
own resources are inadequate to meet the needs for mental health
services. (Albee, 1959.) They have turned (sometimes reluctant-
ly) to the utilization of non-profesionally trained personnel,
who receive much of their education in the streets and on the
job, rather than in formal academic settings. Undergraduates,
housewives, grandparents, and adolescents and adults pursuing
"new careers" in the fields of teaching, education, social service, health and mental health, have contributed to the manpower
pool which delivers mental health services in school-related programs. These people have added qualitatively as well as quantitatively to our human service resources. (Guerney, 1969; Fishman, et al, 1969; Pearl and Riessman, 1965; Riessman, et al.,
1964; Riessman and Popper, 1968; Rioch, 1967.)

As mental health practitioners became involved in innovative
school intervention, they learned that there was great potential
for creating viable roles for themselves in school-related programs. Their new roles included expanded opportunity for direct
service with children and parents, development and evaluation of
exciting programs in and out of the classroom, consultation with
all levels of school personnel, and supervision of new careerists
who were providing valuable services. They also became painfully
cognizant of the new problems they would encounter as they moved
away from their traditional clinical roles: the inadequate training they had received in the area of community intervention; the
negative attitude toward mental health workers and other resistance expressed by school personnel; the complex and difficult-
to-manage environments in which they were asked to practice their
clinical skills; the reactionary political forces which strive to
maintain the status quo; and the sometimes overwhelming and de-
moralizing scope of the problem.

The chapters in this book address themselves to the movement
of mental health practitioners toward innovative school inter-

vention. These chapters review the conception and philosophical background, explore the potential impact, delineate the problems, and operationalize the approaches involved in promoting mental health in our schools.

REFERENCES

Albee, G. W. *Mental health manpower trends*. New York: Basic Books, 1959.

Allinsmith, W. and Goethals, G. W. *The role of the schools in mental health*. New York: Basic Books, 1962.

Bennis, W. G., Benne, K. D. and Chin, R. *The planning of change*. (2nd edition) New York: Holt, Rinehart and Winston, 1969.

Bower, E. M. *Early identification of emotionally handicapped children in school*. Springfield, Illinois: Charles Thomas, 1969.

Caplan, G. *Principles of preventive psychiatry*. New York: Basic Books, 1964.

Caplan, G. *Theories of mental health consultation*. New York: Basic Books, 1970.

Cowen, E. L., Gardner, E. A., and Zax, M. (Eds.) *Emergent approaches to mental health problems*. New York: Appleton-Century-Crofts, 1967.

Fishman, J. R., Denhan, W. H., Levine, M., Shatz, O. E. *New careers for the disadvantaged in human service: report of a social experiment*. Washington, D. C. Howard University Institute for Youth Studies, 1969.

Goldston, S. E. (Ed.) *Concepts of community psychiatry: a framework for training*. Washington, D. C.: Public Health Service Publication No. 1319, 1965.

Gordon, T. *Parent effectiveness training: the "no-lose" program for raising responsible children*. New York: Peter Wyden, 1970.

Guerney, B. G., Jr. (Ed.) *Psychotherapeutic agents: new roles for nonprofessionals, parents and teachers*. New York: Holt, Rinehart and Winston, 1969.

Joint Commission on Mental Illness and Health. *Action for mental health.* New York: Basic Books, 1961.

Knoblock, P. and Goldstein, A. P. *The lonely teacher.* Boston: Allyn and Bacon, 1971.

Morse, W. C. Enhancing the classroom teacher's mental health function. In E. L. Cowen, E. A. Gardner, and M. Zax, (Eds.) *Emergent approaches to mental health problems.* New York: Appleton-Century-Crofts, 1967. pp. 271-289.

Ojemann, R. H. Investigations on the effects of teachnng an understanding and appreciation of behavior dynamics. In G. Caplan (Ed.) *Prevention of mental disorders in children.* New York: Basic Books, 1961. pp. 378-396.

Patterson, G. R. and Gullion, M. E. *Living with children: new methods for parents and teachers.* Champaign, Illinois: Research Press, 1967.

Pearl, A. and Riessman, F. *New careers for the poor. The nonprofessional in human service.* New York: The Free Press, 1965.

Riessman, F., Cohen, J. and Pearl, A. (Eds.) *Mental health of the poor.* New York: The Free Press, 1964.

Riessman, F. and Popper, H. (Eds.) *Up from poverty.* New York: Harper and Row, 1968.

Ringness, T. A. *Mental health in the schools.* New York: Random House, 1968.

Rioch, M. J. Pilot projects in training mental health counselors. In E. L. Cowen, E. A. Gardner and M. Zax (Eds.) *Emergent approaches to mental health problems.* New York: Appleton-Century-Crofts, 1967. pp. 110-127.

Sarason, S. B. *The culture of the school and the problem of change.* Boston: Allyn and Bacon, 1971.

Sarason, S. B., Levine, M., Goldenberg, J. D., Cherlin, D. L. and Bennett, E. M. *Psychology in Community Settings: clinical, educational, vocational, social aspects.* New York: John Wiley and Sons, 1966.

Schmuck, R. A., Runkel, P. J., and Langmeyer, D. Improving organizational problem-solving in a school faculty. *Journal of Applied Behavioral Science.* 1969, 5, 455-482.

Zax, M. and Cowen, E. L.   Early identification and prevention
of emotional disturbance in a public school.   In E. L.
Cowen, E. A. Gardner and M. Zax (Eds.) *Emergent approaches
to mental health problems.* New York: Appleton-Century-
Crofts, 1967.   pp. 331-351.

SECTION   I

BACKGROUND AND PHILOSOPHY

1. THE COMMUNITY AND THE SCHOOL

Dr. Bower's many years of experience have provided him with a healthy dose of skepticism about the elegant platitudes which community psychologists have offered to justify their existence. In the lead off chapter for this book, Dr. Bower indicates his view of community psychology, tracing several of its origins. According to Dr. Bower, little had been accomplished to date; theory and concepts are quite weak. He adds, further, that in the mental health movement, power and knowledge are not the same thing. The politician, at least, has social responsibility by virtue of the vote, while community psychologists and psychiatrists offer solutions to mental health problems yet are able to avoid the responsibility for the consequences. They want to "play in someone else's ballpark" without having to pay the gatekeeper.

Arguing that primary institutions are largely responsible for "making people," Dr. Bower suggests that psychology has had relatively little impact on them. In order to survive, psychology and psychiatry in the community must build their "platform" on or close to these primary institutions and be seen by these institutions as aiding their goals and processes. This point we will see emphasized throughout the chapters in this book; perhaps conceptually obvious, it is difficult to implement. Mental health training seems not to prepare the professional for work in a setting in which the concerns, goals and processes of the institution are honored and accepted.

On a different level, Dr. Bower makes the point that even mental health establishments are often not interested in developing new ways of relating to primary treatment or innovative prevention programs. Perhaps unless professional guild conflicts are resolved, ideas for progress in mental health programs will continue to meet overwhelming obstacles and resistance.

Having chosen schools as the most efficient, economical and potentially successful focus for detection of early disorder, Dr. Bower reviews the question of who should do the detecting. He argues persuasively that the logical source for early detection is the teacher. The "defective" child must learn to make it in the school system as well as in other primary institutions

including the family, peer groups, neighborhoods, etc. The
teacher is on the front line, the only agent readily able to
make the referral for primary prevention screening of pre-school-
ers and kindergarten children. He suggests that a child development specialist could search for the strengths within the child,
the family and the neighborhood and communicate these strengths
to the parents and teachers. This information can then be used
by the teachers in curriculum building and in defining what additional help might be needed.

Some of Dr. Bower's ideas can be discerned in the programs
and implicit philosophies developed in the following chapters.

COMMUNITY PSYCHOLOGY AND COMMUNITY SCHOOLS

Eli M. Bower
University of California, Berkeley

Community psychology, like Pirandello's six actors searching for an author, is many characters searching for a playable theme. Themes abound in community psychology as will be pointed out later, but playing them is another matter. Some sound polyphonic; others diffuse and a few are off-key. The day-to-day, on-the-job realities of community psychology may exist here and there in these United States; when visible, it is usually someone flying by the shiny seat of his pants. But for those of us looking for the words and music, community psychology is yet to be discovered.

Everyone seems to know the territory. It is back away from treatment and hospital facilities to where life is lived, in homes, schools, offices, churches, synagogues and coffee houses. But what does a community psychologist do in or about life in this territory? Where are the specific leverages from which psychological knowledge and practice can produce measurable positive change toward mentally healthy living?

Cook, in his preface to a book on community psychology (1970), writes, "Community psychology is something more than psychologists working in community mental health. Community psychology is similar to, yet different from, community psychiatry or community social work." So we know it is more than something, that it is similar to, yet different from something else. In all fairness to Cook, he does go on to say outright that the community specialist is a "participant-conceptualizer" in community systems. It is difficult to visualize exactly what a "participant-conceptualizer" does but I'm sure there are those who could work out the details for hard nosed fiscal sceptics.

One action or type of action implicit in the concept of community psychology is preventive intervention at the community level. Bennett (1965) defines it as "The community it-

self is being taught to collaborate in creating health-giving environments." Teaching communities ought to be quite a
trick. I'm for an ounce of prevention against sixteen ounces
of cure any day but what does a community psychologist prevent and how? How is the community being taught to create
health-giving environments and where can we observe such teaching and learning?

The magic by which one defines one high-level abstrac-
tion with another is not the exclusive abracadabra of mental
health workers or educators. My own biased view, however, is
that mental health workers do it better than any other group.
The complexities of human minds are no small matter to understand or symbolize. "Words and magic," wrote Freud (1926)
"were in the beginning one and the same thing and even today
words retain much of their magical power." Man's relationship with man is built up or down with words and concepts.
Mental illnesses themselves are concepts inferring for the
most part non-visible conditions inside the mind--however one
defines mind. Mental health workers are caught up in this
type of activity and undoubtedly some of it rubs off.

Nevertheless, community-minded mental health workers, be
they psychiatrists, social workers, nurses or psychologists,
seem to know where they want to go but apparently are not
quite sure what they want to do. If he is to be a change
agent, who is he to change, in what direction and how is this
to be accomplished? Or if one buys Scibner's (1968) notions
of what community psychology is made of, it comes out like the
seasons -- to be four separate but interdigitated kinds of
psychologists. These she calls: 1) social movement--psychol-
ogists who identify themselves with the goals and aims of political and social movements and work in those movements; 2)
social action--psychologists who work in community-based programs for human betterment such as poverty, drug addiction and
delinquency programs; 3) new clinical-- psychologists who go
beyond face-to-face psychotherapy; and 4) social engineer--
psychologists who try to change systems and perhaps a few
social action psychologists who get in their way. While all
this gets psychologists into the big picture of community life
it is still doubtful that any of these concepts give the psychologist more than one leg to stand on or jump from.

Community psychologists ought to find more powerful and
specific preventive roles for their services in community
mental health centers. Such centers, as many of you know,
were authorized and financed by Federal funds beginning in
1963. As a member of the National Institute of Mental Health
(NIMH) at the time, one of our major tasks was to come up with

a model or models by which community mental health could be differentiated from what was going on before. We prescribed five basic services and several other important but non-mandatory services. Four of the mandatory services were direct services to people who were ill or who had troubles. The other was called "mental health education and consultation." Commenting on this one service, Brewster Smith and Nick Hobbs (1966) suggested that the addition of this service opened "wide vistas for imaginative experimentation." Eight years later the portals of these wide vistas for imaginative experimentation have yet to be approached by community-minded psychologists.

I could go on with additional definitions, new territories and goals for community psychology but it would become, if it hasn't already become, boring and repetitious. The idea is there but the follow-through is muddled. To some, getting into the community is to become like other community workers.

There is a question whether psychologists who leave their Binet and Rorschachs behind to become special actionists, engineers or mental health consultants should be involved in such goings on. One might well heed Dunham's (1965) advice to community psychiatrists. If any psychologist thinks he or she can organize and move a community toward a more healthy state, why not run for political office? Despite oft quoted aphorisms, power and knowledge are not the same thing. The goal of the average politician is to know his constituency and thereby to be elected. He may be guided by knowledge as he perceives it-- or as his constituents see it which is perhaps the knowledge that counts. A community-minded psychiatrist or psychologist might advise a community-minded politician how the mental health of the community might be improved but the politician is left alone to accept the responsibility or blame when the citizens vote or do not vote for him.

Community psychology or psychiatry or mental health (or any other appellation you wish to use) is basically a mental health person playing in someone else's ball park. We know that people are made or not made inadequately in our primary institutions--our health, family, play and educational institutions and that these are run by non-psychologists. We also know as Albee (1968) and others pointed out many times, that current manpower shortages in community treatment and rehabilitation programs are pitiful.

More importantly, community psychologists are trained and educated very often in ways which may make them good psychologists but poor partners to workers in primary institutions.

I'm all for psychologists becoming change agents, social move-ment or social engineering psychologists but I would be more impressed and happy to find one training program wherein psy-chologists were learning how to help recreation specialists extend the experience of healthy play to children or another wherein they were learning how to help teachers plan more ef-fective educational experiences for all children. These would need to be specific arenas of training and assumed to be pre-sent as a matter of course in community mental health. Much is assumed under the broad rubric of "consultation." If it isn't psychotherapy or just plain talk it must be consultation. In my experience of more than a third of a century I have seen very few consultants who could score with consistent profes-sional effectiveness in primary institutions. This is not to lessen the impact of the few good training programs which do succeed in adding a significant measure of professional com-petency to intuitively-minded community psychologists, psychi-atrists and social workers. But this represents only a begin-ning. What community psychology needs is specific but solid platforms in community programs from which they can begin to put their psychology to good use. The platforms need to be built upon or close to primary institutions and to be seen by them as aiding and abetting their goals and processes. I will say the same thing again at a later time because in my experi-ence this is the single most critical issue in community psy-chology. This comes from standing around over a half hundred years and trying to make sense of the passing professional phe-nomena. Reflection upon the past as prologue to meaning led me back to my first major work assignment.

This was in an institution for emotionally disturbed and delinquent children which in addition to aging me rapidly pushed me just as rapidly to consider alternatives to treat-ment. This experience was sandwiched between two other in-stitutional experiences, one perched in the lofty and occasion-ally exciting altitudes of higher education; the other at sea and at sea level awaiting "short sharp shocks" from below and above. In the peaceful interludes I was able to contemplate how ineffective and energizing our attempts had been to help our institutionalized charges. Most puzzling and perplexing to me was trying to understand how children could become so maladaptive, unhappy and disorganized in such as short period of living. Despite a good sized, competent staff, it was ap-parent that our best efforts had no significant impact on any-thing but our own egos. Here and there a brief, healthy con-nection and some gain, but short-term follow-up studies were consistently depressing. Looking backward, I would judge us to be about as successful as doing nothing except that we weren't doing nothing.

Later, in the dull apprehensive moments at sea, it occurred to me that my attempts to help emotionally disturbed
children fit into a cyclical irrationality. Part of the cycle
was the effective way in which the children had been disorganized and destroyed; the other was our valiant efforts to remedy and rectify processes which, being beyond our reach, we
only succeeded in enhancing. Nevertheless, we and others tried
and are trying today. Perhaps programs like Project Re-Ed
and some of the behavior programs do better than we did. But
the treatment and rehabilitation of a young life is a difficult
and God-like task. It seems reasonable to assume that if we
can be so effective in producing the disorganized, depressed
and delinquent child we could be just as masterful in creating
integrated, ebullient and competent children. The dialectic
was unassailable; at least so it seemed sitting out in the Pa-
cific with wild thoughts of utopia and survival.

Since the end of my mandatory servitude at sea I have considered ways of implementing this wild dialectic. Specifically
I have moved to what was do-able, feasible, and supportable.
The place to do battle would be the school since most, if not
all, key adults in the life of the children could be involved.
Along the way, I have borrowed the best I could find from my
colleagues and put it in some playable theme for community psychologists.

SCHOOLS--A POINT OF CONCENTRATION

After the tragic events of November 1963, many citizens
were moved to examine the life and death of Lee Harvey Oswald.
There were many indications that the boy needed help; at one
point his mother had been asked to bring her son to a school
mental health service but she never did. Many members of Congress began to think of legislative programs to prevent other
Lee Harvey Oswalds. One such Congressman, Sam Gibbons, of
Tampa, Florida had served for many years in the Florida Legislature where one of his major interests had been the treatment
and care of children and adults in Florida's institutions. He
was aware that such institutions did little to reduce or prevent the problem they were supposed to solve. In some cases,
he felt such institutions just made the problem worse. He too
began to reflect and consider if preventive approaches had
been made to pathological and criminal behavior.

He asked a research librarian in the Library of Congress
to look into it. She did and found my name plastered on several articles and books on the subject. Since they had been
authored in California, he called me there only to find me
practically a neighbor. We discussed what might be done about

the problem in a free society. He supplied the political realities and I the behavioral science fantasies. We could not,
under any system of free government and taxation, force the
Lee Harvey Oswald family and others like them to obtain treatment. Moreover, it was virtually impossible to make mental
health facilities and manpower available wherever and whenever
needed. Under the circumstances, the Congressman felt that
pre-school and early school programs should have personnel who
might help those children and families with beginning problems.
A bill was introduced in the 89th Congress, 1st session
(HR 11322)[1] by Congressman Gibbons, cited as the Elementary
and Pre-School Development Act, which would provide specialists
at about or just beyond the masters level who would be trained
to assist pre-school and school personnel with children who
had individual learning or behavior problems. Such specialists
were also trained in the use of every conceivable resource for
families and children needing such help.

The bill also provided a ratio of one Child Development
Specialist for no more than 350 children below grade 4 and
funds for educational institutions to train such personnel.
Such training was focussed on developing a preventive specialist who could work primarily with key adults (teachers and
parents) and who would not be immobilized or pinned down by
individual cases as befalls most mental health workers in
schools. The bill contained a sizable appropriation for support and training since Mr. Gibbons felt that all States, including those pressed for funds ought to participate. Hearings were held on the bill in October 1965 by the House Sub-
committee on Education but there, as far as I know, the Child
Development Specialist bill rests to be reborn perhaps under
a new administration.

It may be of interest to all community-minded mental
health workers and educators to note the posture of some of
our professional associations during the hearings on this bill.
Would it surprise you to discover that several large psychological and educational organizations opposed the bill? One
wanted the name, Child Development Specialist, changed to correspond more closely to a name used by its membership. Another
felt that because the training was less than doctoral level, it
would fall into the hands of less competent colleagues. Two
others suggested the legislation was unnecessary since their
membership could now do what was requested by the bill. A letter to the Congressman from the American Psychoanalytic Association, Victor H. Rosen, M.D., President, pointed out that
they were heartily in favor of the principle of the bill but

---

[1]Renumbered HR 7403 in the 90th Congress

wondered "if it would be possible to acheive the same desirable goal through an extension of already existing programs
for training psychiatrists, psychologists, psychiatric social
workers, etc., so that more such personnel can be made available to the various school systems..." Dr. Rosen also raised
the desirability of having such a program carried out under
the Office of Education since "it was felt that this approaches
a medical problem which might better be handled through authorized medical channels..."

So it went and so it goes today. Professions and professional organizations, with few exceptions, are no longer in
the business of solving problems but tending and patrolling
professional fences. There is, in most professions, a dis-
placement of goals from solving community and individual problems to self-maintenance and protection. As community psychologists, by whatever name, attempt to move into new roles and
old institutions, they will face the same array of professional
vigilance, altruism and heavily patrolled organizational
fences, often electrified.

Yet, what seems to be a defeat may be, in one way, a small
victory. Apparently the small pebble tossed into the placid
preventive lake by HR 11322 did set off a few vibrations along
some frontiers. A few universities became interested in training preventive specialists. The National Institute of Mental
Health became interested in supporting such experimental training programs and did. Programs were launched in 1968 at Florida State University, George Peabody College, the University
of Chicago, University of Michigan and Kent State University.

I visited with recent graduates of the program at Florida State University in the fall of 1970. While it was apparent that this was still a program in development, feedback
by Child Development Specialists who were out in the schools
was heartening and hopeful. They knew what they were not there
to do--act as a vice-principal, curriculum consultant and general flunkey--and knew how to fight to maintain their identity
and their helping role. In several instances the communities
had been one jump ahead of them and were more protective and
cooperative than the Child Development Specialist expected.
One young lady who had gone to work in a city half-way across
the State was having such a fine learning and service experience that she fairly bubbled over in recounting it. In her
happy narration it was clear that she came to her job well-prepared by a host of intangibles called personality, intuition,
joie de vivre, interpersonal competency or just plain guts.
The training she received was well integrated with a wholesome
and insightful person who was doing a large community, the

State of Florida and herself a great deal of good.

The Child Development Specialist is only one significant step on a long road. As he or she makes her way in the community, they must devise strategies which change in some significant way how a primary or KISS[1] institution effects children. This is the program content or platform for action.

It is not enough to have a well-meaning, iridescent Child Development Specialist or community psychologist wandering about like Diogenes looking for mental health. One is or can be a child advocate only to the extent to which one can change the institutions which children undergo. One needs to examine institutions like the school, their goals and operations and find points of leverage for change which gets you where you want to go and is not seen a ego aversive to the institution. To tell a mother who is racked by doubt and anxiety to learn to love her child or ask a teacher with 35 hell-on-wheels students to understand one child is well and good; it does not, however, place the mother or teacher in the picture as they see it. Community psychologists are child advocates only to the extent that others who work with children can be made more effective and comfortable.

While there are many points of possible action, I will present a specific conceptual approach, the vertical and horizontal outreaching of the action and what the immediate payoff might be. All of this is related to my earlier notion of a Child Development Specialist and what the position had to offer to community mental health. None of this is a wild revolutionary idea suddenly thrust upon us from a distant galaxy. I have no wish for the "new" qua new. I want what is good for children despite its medieval heritage or its shiny new face. Above all it must fit, be seen positively by parents, teachers and communities and workable within present budget limitations. One such possible preventive institution is the school.

Children and school go together like fish and chips. To a child with a learning or behavior problem the school is a micro-society from which he can't escape. From society's point of view the education of children is one of the most prodigious and critical undertakings of the nation, the State and the community. In the year 1970, there are more than 58 million children and youth in school, spending roughly five hours a day for about 180 days a year in an instructional relationship. Multiplying these apples, onions and radishes, one comes out with the more than 5 billion hours of planned professional

---

[1]Key integrative social system

interpersonal interactions per year. How can we make these planned interactions go on more positively for more children?

The school seems to be, at present, the only social institution which has a ghost of an epidemiological chance of touching all children and all families. Some behavioral scientists and educators feel that by age 5 or 6 it may already too late to do much about the direction in which a child's life is going. But then it may also be too late for some children when they are resting **in utero**. Whatever else may be said about the school (and in some large cities, much can be said) it is a potential **linking** point between the two primary or KISS institutions intended to civilize children. There is also a great deal of research to support the operational validity of teacher ratings of the mental health status of children. Teachers have daily contacts with children in a normal group setting over a period of at least one year. The natural backdrop of age-appropriate behavior and experiences with different children each year give teachers a professional sense of when a child is right, questionable or needs individual attention. This is not to say that teachers are clinicians or don't go off the deep end here and there. In some ways the teaching profession has never lived down the early Wickman (1928) study. Since those days, much has happened.

About 12 years ago, the State of California risked a sizable amount of funds and professional time (Bower, Tashnovian & Larson, 1958) to find out if "emotionally handicapped" children could be identified early in their school life and if so, whether something could be done to head off or redirect this kind of development. Our research indicated that it was relatively easy to identify children with beginning learning and behavior problems within the school system using teacher-, peer-, and self-perceptions. At this point some of our mental health colleagues began to shake their heads, "Remember," they cautioned, "the old Wickman study in which considerable doubt was raised about the ability of teachers and schools to recognize the serious, much less the beginnings of, emotional and social disturbances in children and youth. How do we know," they asked, "that the children the teachers have identified are **really** and **truly** the mental health and juvenile delinquent problems of our society? In other words, how reliable and valid are teachers in this hazardous kind of prediction?"

Let me resurrect Wickman's (1928) study for those of you too young to have been exposed or too old to remember. I do so not to honor the past but to assist the future. What Wickman did was to compare the ratings of 511 teachers and 30 mental hygienists on the seriousness of 50 behavior traits of children. What set the fulminating cap sizzling was his finding that the ratings of the teachers and the mental hygienists had zero correlation. Wickman himself was not at all dismayed by this result and was most emphatic and forceful in pointing out that the directions to each group has been significantly different. The teachers had been asked to rate the behavior of students as problems they faced in the classroom, in the here and now. The mental health people were directed to rate the traits on the basis of their eventual effect on the future life of the child. When the smoke cleared, teachers had rated as teachers, mental hygienists as mental hygienists and the twain did not meet. Each group was looking at the children pretty much from its own professional biases and job-related firing line as indeed it should.

So what happened? Two educators (Schrupp & Gjerde, 1953) examined 12 texts in psychology and educational psychology and found that only two books gave a clear and accurate statement of the study and its findings. Most of the presentations indicated that the disparity between the mental health judges and the teachers showed that teachers were way off the beam. The basic assumption in all cases was that the mental health experts were right and the teachers were wrong. Nobody called it the other way and only rarely did an investigator say something about the problem of comparing papaya to pinochle.

In the study mentioned earlier, we paid clinicians to do individual studies of children selected out as "emotionally handicapped" and found pretty good agreement. When there was some disagreement, the weight of evidence often lay on the side of the teacher. The perceptual differences between teachers and other behavioral specialists is a myth which has surrounded possible action programs like the magic fire around Brunnhilde. The myth is that someone, somewhere, somehow can assess behavior and/or mental health as a characteristic or state of being independent of the social context and social institutions in which the individual is living and functioning. A study by Cohen (1963) compared the predictive skill of a teacher, a clinical psychologist and a child psychiatrist in assessing and predicting the achievement level of 56 kindergarten children when they got into first grade. Each professional person related to the children as he would in his normal professional practice. The teacher did what kindergarten teachers do, the clinical psychologists tested and observed and the child psychiatrist employed a standard play observation stiuation. All three did a good job of predicting how each of the kindergarteners would do in the first

grade but the teacher did the best. The psychiatrist predicted more underachievement than actually occurred. In assessing his misfires, he found that some of the clinical anxiety which he picked up in some of the children and which he
expected to lead to underachievement actually led to high
achievement.

This is, of course, the nub of the problem--the evaluation of intrapsychic states separated from their social and
individual implementation tells you nothing. The teacher, of
all the professionals, may not know much about levels of anxiety but she can't help notice which children are hyperactive
and how they manage it. Each child mediates his own feelings,
cognitive abilities, personality traits and physical self in
his own way. The nature of this mediation is what teachers
are constantly observing. What it comes to is that teachers'
judgments provide the most economical and efficient perceptual platform for intercepting children moving in the wrong direction.

If the point of concentration for community psychology is
to be the school (or the home, the playground or the well-ba-
by clinic), one needs to focus on behaviors relevant to the
school. The teacher tends to judge a child on the basis of
his ability to perform the role of a student. Occasionally
quiet children who look like they might be learning something
get through the teacher's net. This is especially true of
girls who are more often seen as better students compared to
boys. In fact, **they are** in the early grades. In the study of
emotionally handicapped children, mentioned earlier (Bower, et
al., 1958) teachers were asked to rate each child in their
class on dimensions of aggression and withdrawal. The surprising result is that more students are scored as being overly
withdrawn or timid than overly aggressive or defiant. However, if you were to ask teachers which children they wanted
help with, they would give the aggressive ones priority for
a rather simple reason. One aggressive student can disrupt
an entire clsss; a quiet child disturbs no one but himself.
Note also in Table 1 that more than 10 percent of the students
are overly aggressive or withdrawn most of the time; that
boys are about twice as overly aggressive most of the time
than girls; and girls are about twice as overly withdrawn or
timid most of the time than boys.

The percentage of students who cannot seem to play the
student role comes out much the same in a variety of studies.
In a Mental Health Survey of Los Angeles County done by the
Department of Mental Hygiene in 1960, the teachers were asked
to rate children on the basis of the following questions:

Table 1

Is this child overly aggressive or defiant?

	Male		Female		Total	
	No.	%	No.	%	No.	%
Seldom or never	1579	54.0	1945	73.0	3524	63.0
Not very often	709	24.2	404	15.1	1113	19.9
Quite often	469	16.0	239	9.0	708	12.7
Most of the time	169	5.8	78	2.9	247	4.4
TOTAL	2926	52.3	2666	47.7	5592	100.0

Is this child overly withdrawn or timid?

	Male		Female		Total	
	No.	%	No.	%	No.	%
Seldom or never	1700	58.1	1367	51.2	2067	54.8
Not very often	732	25.0	699	26.2	1431	25.6
Quite often	351	12.0	406	15.2	757	13.6
Most of the time	144	4.9	197	7.4	341	6.1
TOTAL	2927	52.3	2669	47.7	5596	100.0

1) Is this child disturbed enough to be referred for psychiatric help; 2) Is this child disturbed, perhaps not seriously enough to require psychiatric help but a problem enough to require more than his "share" of the teacher's time and attention. In kindergarten categories nominees for 1 and 2 add up to 6.1 percent. In first grade this jumps to 9.3 percent, rises to 10.1 percent in the second grade, hits a peak at 11.0 percent in the fourth and fifth grades and begins to drop in junior and senior high schools as many of the problem kids drop out. By the twelfth grade, teachers report only 1.9 percent of students in category 1 and 3.3 percent in category 2. The rest of the kids are out in the community raising hell.

The difficulties boys and girls have in school vary with the structure, the demands and the professionl perception of the teachers. A high school teacher sees the students more nearly as "subject matter" depositories; the elementary school teacher, especially the early elementary teachers, sees children as members of an extended family. For example, many kindergarten and first grade teachers object to formal rating or judging of their students in much the same manner as a mother avoids choosing favorites or black sheep among her children. The elementary teacher has a different frame of reference than the high school teacher, yet both are sensitive to the child who needs help (Bower, 1960). A teacher's major concern when a child is overly aggressive or is unable to learn because of his apathy is that she cannot teach him and therefore is unable to carry out her professional responsibility. This disturbs her and therefore makes the child a disturbing student. Similarly, when a child in a play group or nursery school cannot adhere to rules of games, or cannot take turns, the teachers and the group will identify him as a problem **in that setting** and, if the behavior continues, will tend to isolate him or evict him. A child who gives little or no emotional response to a mother (as in childhood autism or related disorders) will become even a greater problem in a family setting since emotional responsiveness is what makes a mother, and even at times a father, act like a warm, loving parent. The child "makes" the parent as the parent "makes" the child; the student "makes" the teacher as the teacher "makes" the student. It seems necessary to reemphasize that competent or incompetent behavior can only be evaluated or judged in relation to the primary or KISS institution in which the behavior takes place. A play group requires rule-awareness behavior; a school requires cognitive attention; in a family one needs to be able to accept anger and demonstrate love. Life, for children, is lived within these primary institutions, each of which requires of all its participants specific functioning skills and behavior appropriate to its goals.

One can define the effectively growing child as one who has learned the competencies to make it through the KISS institutions--family, play, neighborhood or peer groups and school.

A STRATEGY AND PLAN FOR ACTION FOR A COMMUNITY PSYCHOLOGIST

The basic strategy of this approach is to develop a pre-school spring screening or anticipatory helping program for all families whose children are entering kindergarten. This will be integrated with a one-year and in some cases two-year kindergarten program in which screening will continue and during which specific interventions will be planned for those who need it. It will also be moved down into pre-school programs in communities where they exist.

This screening approach will differ in some ways from traditionally conceptualized screening. First it will be geared in theory, practice and in all communications toward helping **all children** to be more **effective** in school. Full-time personnel with case work or school psychologist backgrounds will be "given" positive titles and positive orientations. The titles might be something like "child development consultant," "school-home liason worker," or "supervising teacher." The initial screening and staffing with all families prior to the entrance of their children into kindergarten will include the prospective kindergarten teacher. The purpose of the initial contact is to get some rough and ready data on each child and his family, but more importantly, to set the school screening personnel and the family into a positive relationship. Indeed, one of the goals of this initial get-together is to search for strengths in the child and his family, neighborhood and school ecology which can be identified, communicated and discussed with the parents. In time, this data will be used by the teacher in curriculum building for the child when he comes to school in the fall.

If it seems apparent that some type of additional experience might be helpful to the child, such possibilities would be presented and discussed with the parents. In the Sumter, South Carolina program it was found that specific children needed some growth help prior to school entrance. One such group of kids needed school-related enrichment, adaptive skills and peer-group experiences. These were enrolled in a six week preparatory summer program. In this summer program it was discovered that such children responded better to gradually introduced enrichment in a less stimulating room than the usual "give 'em all you've got" approach. Another group with apparent speech difficulties was intercepted via a parent education and speech skills program planned and administered by the Health Department. Another group of children of families who could not afford private kindergartens or nursery schools, children of working parents or parents with transportation problems were guided into a new program developed by the City Recreation Department with the help of the Project staff. These and other "intercept" programs were developed as needed. As these developed, it soon became apparent that the Screening Project was changing the nature and function of several family-serving, child-helping agencies. The Screening Project provided the impetus for many of these agencies to swing into action in a preventive enhancing manner with children and parents. Such changes in practice and agency goals were not temporary but became an integral part of the agencies' new concept of themselves. Nothing was asked of any of these community programs that was inconsistent with their goals or their budgets.

The Sumter program had the task of providing transitional preventive programs between home and first grade. Most California communities provide first-rate kindergarten programs as part of public education. This greatly expands the possibilities of gathering more accurate and valid screening data and provides a greater variety of preventive approaches, the results of which can be monitored during the kindergarten year. In some cases, it is possible and desirable to develop a two-year kindergarten program so that entrance into first grade will be a salutory rather than an automatic action. Laura

Weinstein (1968), at George Peabody College in Nashville, re-
searched the thesis that there is an optimal absolute age at
which children should be admitted to first grade. In her investigation, she found that it is the age of the child relative to his classmates that seems to make the difference! Almost all researchers on this problem have found that younger
children who entered first grade did significantly poorer in
school work and academic achievement and that this state of
things held up throughout the 12 public school years. Weinstein also takes note of the fact that this consistent and
significant finding has been blurred by studies in which speci-
ally screened children who are admitted to first grade do well.
Even here the evidence is far from convincing.

Children who start the first grade below the mean age of
their classmates are **more likely** to be seen as emotionally disturbed by school personnel and more likely to be referred to
a residential treatment center. This is probably more true
for boys than girls and more true for children coming to bat
with one or two strikes already on them because of environmental or emotional problems.

The results of breaking the lock step of entrance into the
first grade are documented in one study by two investigators
(Miller & Norris, 1967) who found that the differences between
younger children and their classmates disappeared by the end
of the second grade. Why? In this school system, new students were grouped by maturity and ability levels and did not
enter a traditionally-organized program until they reached the
fourth grade. This, of course, freed the system so that the
child could be placed with comparable groups and reduced the
pressure for grade level acheivement.

Why then is this knowledge not plowed into programming? In
part there is the inertia of social institutions and all sorts
of legislative and pseudo-legislative (I'm sorry, Mrs. Einstein,
but since your son Albert was born at 11 pm on December 31 he
will have to start school this September, not next September)
fol-de-rol which schools use to maintain their own social san-
ity. Parents and schools face a mountain of legislative and
administrative regulations if they are to change the processes
of school entrance. Yet, the mountain is easily conquered if
one believes the view from the top is worth the effort.

Here and there, a few school districts have rushed into
developing full-scale individualized school entrance programs.
only rarely, however, have such programs managed to concleptu-
alize their efforts as a home-school-community effort. Blain
(in Bower, 1960) cites a school system in Pennsylvania where

tests were used in predicting the probable success of pre-
school children. Where children had a low probability of
success, parents were advised to wait before enrolling them.
Some did, some didn't. The children whose parents waited
as advised did significantly better. The children whose parents did not wait did significantly worse. The lesson to be
learned here is that school entrance is not a simple step from
home to school one bright September morning. For many mothers,
it is a giant step into freedom. For others, it marks the beginning of an achievement-oriented relationship between child
and parents calculated to get the budding student into college.
For all parents, this simple step is fraught with emotional
tensions, worries, anticipation, doubts and crises. After
struggling for five years to play the most difficult, most potentially guilt-ridden role of our society, parents see their
efforts go on public display for competitive judging. The
first years of schooling not only represent a major crisis for
the child but also represent a major crisis for the parents.
Parents begin to unconsciously ask such questions of themselves
as--Have we given him what is necessary to make it? Should
we have listened to Aunt Jane, Benjamin Spock or our own intuition? Should we have given him more time and concern? With
our genes and chromosomes how come he's only doing a little
better than average? What it comes down to for many parents is
a test of themselves. Under such circumstances, anything the
school might do to build positive mediational relationships
should fall on eager ears.

REFERENCES

Albee, George W.   Conceptual models and manpower requirements in psychology. *American Psychologist*, XXIII, 1968, pp. 317-320.

Bennett, Chester C.   Community psychology: Impressions of the Boston Conference on the Education of Psychologists for Community Mental Health. *American Psychologist*, XX, 1965, pp. 832-835.

Bower, Eli M.   *Early identification of emotionally handicapped children in school.*   Springfield, Ill.: Charles C. Thomas, 1969.

Bower, Eli M., Shellhammer, T.A., and Daily, John M.   School characteristics of male adolescents who later became schizophrenic. *American Journal of Orthopsychiatry*, October 1960, XXX, 4.

Bower, Eli M., Tashnovian, Peter and Larson, Carl.   A process for early identification of emotionally disturbed children. Sacramento, California: State Department of Education, 1958.

Cohen, T.B.   Prediction of underachievement in kindergarten children. *Archives of General Psychiatry*, 1963, IX.

Cook, Patrick (Ed.).   *Community psychiatry and community mental health.*   San Francisco: Holden-Day, 1970.

Dunham, Lawrence.   Community psychology--The newest therapeutic bandwagon. *Archives of General Psychiatry*, XII, 1965. pp. 303-313.

Freud, Sigmund.   *Introductory lectures on psychoanalysis.*   London: Allen and Unwin, 1926.

Mental health survey of Los Angeles County.   Sacramento, California: State Department of Mental Hygiene, 1960.

Muller, W.D. and Norris, R.C.   Entrance age and school success. *Journal of School Psychology*, 1967, VI, pp. 47-60.

Schrupp, M.H. and Gjerde, C.M. Teacher growth in attitudes toward behavioral problems in children. *Journal of Educational Psychology,* April, 1953, XLIV. pp. 203-214.

Scribner, Sylvia. What is community psychology made of? *APA Newsletter,* II, 1968. pp. 4-6.

Smith, M. Brewster and Hobbs, Nicholas. The community and the community mental health center. *American Psychologist,* XXI, 1966. p. 499-509.

Weinstein, Laura. School entrance age and adjustment. *Journal of School Psychology,* 1968-69, VII, 3.

Wickman, E. K. *Children's behavior and teachers' attitudes.* New York: Commonwealth Fund, 1928.

2. THE AUTHENTIC CONSULTANT

This chapter on the role of consultants in the school system provides more challenges to our ways of thinking than solutions. Perhaps Dr. Rubenstein's major thesis is that the consulting process is without solutions and must be confronted as is. Dr. Rubenstein begins by examination of some aspects of change: change is a process, not an end in itself; it is often obtained when the end point is forsaken; change can often be illusory.

Dr. Rubenstein notes that teachers are, as the rest of us, a product of their system and obviously invested in the status quo. This point, also made by Dr. Chandler from a different perspective, is often forgotten by consultants. Teachers will continue to exist within the structure in which they work. Consultants who forget this may be surprised as to the resistance from teachers to change. The job of the teacher is often fragmented, prohibiting the individual teacher from becoming totally involved with the relationship with her pupils. Finally, the institution has strong resistance to change coming not only from upper level administration, but also from colleague teachers, parents and students.

Dr. Rubenstein's suggestion for the solution to some of these problems is that the consultant become authentic, meaning that he attempt to resolve the conflict and disparity between cognition and affect. To approach authenticity, Dr. Rubenstein suggests the consultant ponder several questions, the point of which seem to be that consultants need to be personally isomorphic with their values and goals and need to act in ways which are living examples of the ends to which they are striving.

The problems of change and consultation are complex and paradoxical. The consultant relationship may be successful if the consultant can keep his and his consultee's perspective and "differentiate between when one is realistically needed and when one needs to be needed."

31

TOWARDS AUTHENTICITY IN THE CONSULTING PROCESS

Gerald Rubenstein
University of Rochester

Introduction

Psychologists involved with school consultation programs, in general, and with school mental health programs, in particular, are under rapid-fire from several quarters. The new left sees consultants as tools of the establishment for maintaining the status-quo; minority groups see the consultant as facilitating the selecting and sorting machinery of the school; politically conservative groups see the mental health consultant as fostering a "laissez-faire" ethic relative to problems of discipline and control; old-guard teachers see him as raising problems which didn't exist until "mental health" came into vogue; radical educators see the consultant as advocating too little; administrators argue that he advocates too much; parents feel that he adds to the problems of an already over-burdened youth culture and finally our own colleagues see us as fad-prone, political and "ascientific."

In attempting to become all things to all people, the school consultant has a tendency to simply become impotent. In our otherwise worthwhile effort to facilitate positive mental health within schools, we have also (albeit unknowingly) generated a good deal of, as yet, unleashed anger and hostility. In our real commitment to establish programs, effect change, generate new knowledge and data and supervise trainees how routinely and how well do we reflect the very principles we are trying to promote? Is our professional behavior within a school system consistent not only with the psychological values we, as individuals, hold to be important but is it consistent with the very issues on which we are asked consult?

This chapter will explore the possibility that the art and science of consultation, as it has been traditionally conceptualized and especially as it related to the implementation of mental health programs in a school setting, should at some level undergo significant alteration. This is not to imply change for

its own sake, or even that there is a present "something" that
the consultant can change into, but simply that it is time to
reflect upon some of the more cogent issues and assumptions underlying the consultant-consultee relationship, and, if necessary, generate viable alternatives. The primary focus of this
chapter will be centered on pragmatic issues related to the interpersonal style of the consultant in a school setting, with
some emphasis on why traditional procedures are no longer oper-
ative. The last section will explore a style of consultation
and a specific technique derived from it which might well have
interesting implications for mental health consultation.

It should be kept in mind that this exposition presents a
rather singular point of view. It is derived from experiences
the author has had as both a school psychologist within schools
and as a "mental health" consultant to schools. It is in part
a presentation of the realities he has come to accept but also
affords the reader a glimpse of the author's frustrations,
failures, frailties and fantasies. It is hoped that although
some thoughts which can be somewhat alienating are suggested,
the motivations for such a tactic will become clear. A second
consideration is that this chapter focuses on only one highly
specialized style of consultation which is not only constrained
by the individuals involved and by the nature of the "contract,"
but that it also presumes an on-going, long-term commitment to
both program-specific and agency-specific consultation.

*   *   *

In order for the mental health consultant to maximize his
effectiveness and his impact within a school setting, it is
suggested that he might rely more upon his own authenticity by:
(1) coming to terms with the realities of the school setting
as he experiences it; (2) being sensitive to his perceptions
of these experiences as they are tendered by his prejudices,
needs, and values; (3) communicating these perceptions, with
their selective qualities, to his consultee; and (4) consistently focusing on an issue (or issues) which not only has a
sense of urgency surrounding it and which is not intimately tied
to a large number of other issues, departments, or agencies,
but which is also not readily amenable to parochial or "pac-
kaged" solutions (form a committee, "let George do it," "check
it out with our lawyer," "we can't give them time off," "the
primacy of due process," etc.).

A sense of urgency provides a source of motivation as well
as a channeling of energy toward a reasonable resolution of the
problem. Isolated problems, though rare, do not have to be ex-
tracted from a morass of personal or interdepartmental rivalries. Most important of all is the definition of the problem

in terms which do not allow for the implementation of "standard operating procedures (SOP)" that tend to put off, deny, rationalize   or project the problem into a myriad of other forms making the immediate dynamics easier to handle, but, nevertheless, do not make the problem any more amenable to eventual solution or resolution.

The points just raised present several questions and at least two working propositions which might be routinely asked or applied by mental health consultants.

1. Am I sensitive to my own needs which at some level entered my decision to focus my professional energies on the school?

2. To what extent do I see the school as facilitating or inhibiting positive mental health and how does my value system and occupational choice enter into my attitudes in this area?

3. How do my entree tactics contribute to the emotional-social well-being of the system as a whole and to my consultee in particular? (Have I made my reasons for being there explicit?)

4. How do my own educational experiences shape my attitudes about schools? Keeping in mind the professional hierarchy is in many ways dependent upon some of the less wholesome attributes of schools, how then does my own professional success, or lack of it, contribute to the kind of impact I would like to have on schools?

5. To what extent am I able to divest myself of my traditional consulting garb so that my consultee might step out of his traditional role (not only his role as consultee but that of administrator or teacher as well)? And how comfortable am I when he does this?

Proposition I: To the extent that the consultant focuses on or uses the perceived reality of his client, he cannot justify his working relationship as that of an adjunct professional within the system, because by accepting his client's reality for his own, he has become an integral part of his client's system and is no longer able to effectively and accurately perceive the dynamics of that system. At all stages of the consulting process, the consultant might best act as a "reality tapper," that is, to reflect back to teacher and/or administrator the untenable assumptions and misperceptions which prevent them from

altering the life space and style of the school or classroom
they are working within. Simple direct questions and statements
such as "Who says?" "Why not?" "I cannot accept that" can do
much to alter the set, expectancies, and values of school personnel.

Proposition 2: If a sense of institutional existential
crisis is not achieved, then solutions will tend to be variations on old themes which simply serve to decrease anxiety and
perpetuate the consulting game. This sense of existential crisis occurs with the realization that conventional solutions are
not workable and when neither consultant, nor teacher, nor administrator can choose a reasonable course of action.

A RATIONALE FOR AUTHENTICITY

The consultative style described in this chapter was constructed with the conviction that if significant educational
change is to come about, then not only must new consultative and
educational techniques be generated, developed, and validated
but simultaneous with these activities, the very assumptions on
which consultation and public education are predicated must be
exhumed, exposed, and critically examined. When necessary,
these assumptions must be revised to account for recent research
findings, new educational and psychological models, and for
changes in value orientations. "Psycho"-logical discontinuities
or inconsistencies between educational programs and what is
known about human nature and techniques for altering that nature
can only eventuate in the failure of the educational system.

The psycho-educational ethic which permeates educational
programming at all levels is based on a teaching-learning model.
This model can be expressed in a variety of forms, but invariably it rests on the naive assumption that what teachers teach,
students learn. Thus, whenever educational failure manifests
itself in a system (school or individual), the sources of such
failure "simply" have to be located within the model. Much
valuable energy has been dissipated in making attempts at lo-
cating the sources of dysfunction within this model. Thus, we
find many school personnel and consultants bandying about such
concepts as "behavioral objectives," "educational priorities,"
"cultural pluralism," "educational goals," "teaching strategies,"
"learning styles," and "models for assessment or evaluation."
These constructs not only predominate discussions which seemingly eventuate in educational decisions, but they also have a tendency to cloud the issues and perpetuate the mystique of educational innovation. Since these constructs can often appear in
the guise of empirical statements, they can be perpetually in-
tertwined to form a patchwork of different designs, patterns,

and styles of varying complexity and texture. Thus, programs
which are based upon these constructs can appear under different
labels, but the generic mix remains basically unchanged. This
patchwork successively masks many of the untenable assumptions
upon which these programs are based, but fortunately, it works
only as long as consequent failures can be attributed to other
sources of dysfunction (genetic factors, family crises, social
or emotional deprivation, etc.). Thus, rather than examining
these difficulties and ameliorating them, educators with the
avid support of consultants have instead tended to create new
mixtures of "objectives," "priorities," "sub-cultures," "goals,"
"strategies," "styles," and "models." This maneuver allows the
educator and the consultant to maintain the sanctity of the teaching-learning model without questioning the assumptions upon
which it is based.

Perhaps one way of focusing attention on these untenable
assumptions (which foster this vicious cycle of educational innovation) is by exploring the literary fantasy world of children.
This not only affords us a fascinating view of the symbolically
projected and displaced concerns of the young, but it might also
demonstrate some of their devices and techniques for conceptualizing their world.

In psychology we are faced with a radical challenge: to
what extent are we willing to revise our assumptions about the
teaching-learning process in light of what we know to be true
about real, live teachers and learners. Are we willing to pick
away or even burn the strawmen of education and psychology? One
of these strawmen, like the scarecrow who sought out Oz, has the
unique capacity of separating out his feelings from his thoughts:
he can feel but he does not think. Like Dorothy, psychologists
and educators have also fantasized a tin man: a man who parti-
cipates in experiments or classroom activities without letting
his feelings confuse his thoughts. But sadly enough, this is
where the analogy ends, for psychologists and educators do not
have their Dorothy to pull the curtain off this facade. Thus,
the entertainment in the laboratory and the classroom flows on
and when we leave all that goes with us is the echo of the subject's and the student's hollow, vacant words. We know nothing
more about the subject or the student than what the script provided for, for like the actor, the only thing they actively interact with is their role and the audience (the experimenter or
teacher). They are fully functioning actors, subjects, and students but partially functioning human beings. This dichotomy
between thinking and feeling exists both in our models of human
nature (psychology) and in our models of how to change that
nature (education); it is rationalized in psychology and ignored
in education.

Practically the whole folklore of Western culture
asserts that thought and feeling are utterly different
things. . . Psychologists have, of course, always been
of "two minds" regarding the nature of perceiving, thinking, and remembering; for while as theorists they have
striven to separate these cognitive processes from feeling and will, they have gone on living on the assumption
that every man perceives, thinks, and remembers in terms
of his economic interests, his religious and racial biases, and his personal ego defenses (Murphy, 1964, p.
302-303).

Thus, Symonds (1958) can reasonably ask if the educational
ideal is:

. . . a retreat from the heat and passion of the
world to a place where contemplation and meditation
can permit learning to proceed without the distortion
of strong emotion (p. 61).

Or is it

. . . the excitement and anticipation of starting something new, the struggles, hopes, and doubts
that accompany the process, the final feeling of tri-
umph at the successful completion of one's task or
the feeling of gloom and discouragement that accom-
panies failure (p. 61).

The manifest effect of perpetuating this dichotomy between
cognitive and affective processes has been an increasing concern
with the "cognitive responsibilities" of the school and a con-
commitant decrease in the school's responsibilities for the
affective domain. Thus, the accumulation of "facts" has become
more important than their utilization; content has conquered
structure, structure has achieved precedence over process, and
the teacher-student relationship has been relegated to textbook
formulations and frustrated in the classroom by structural and
curricular constraints.

As long as educators and mental health consultants fail to
recognize the importance of the student's affective processes
and continue to foster the acquisition of knowledge which is external to the student, they will fail to produce individuals who
are "fully functioning." Until those responsible for training
and supervising teachers recognize that "what a teacher is, is
more important than what she teaches" (Menniger, 1963. p. 243)
--until they realize that the acquisition of knowledge which
does not also satisfy needs is forgotten more readily than it is
acquired--until teachers recognize that they are teaching think-

ing and feeling human beings, not partially functioning tin
men--until they acknowledge that:

> The development of intelligence is based on the
> gratification of certain emotional needs, and so long
> as the teachers and administrators refuse to recognize
> the function of the school system in fulfilling or
> frustrating or distorting these needs, (until then)
> the school system (will) remain a clumsy, inefficient,
> disappointing institution, in spite of all the time
> and money we continue to lavish upon it and in spite
> of the high hopes for it which we all continue to cher-
> ish (Menninger, 1942, p. 239).

The manifest effect of this divisiveness is that people in
schools are continually denied the opportunity to develop a
wholesome and meaningful affective life style. In place of
affective development, school systems have imposed upon people
within their realm a number of roles which allow for the sterile
channeling of affect into innocuous, if not destructive, patterns of behavior.

The consultant who is insensitive to these phenomena and
who goes about "doing his thing" oblivious to the artificiality
of interpersonal functioning as well as the suppression of affective expression cannot be a promoter of positive mental
health.   The impact of being in an environment for six hours a
day, five days a week, forty weeks a year, for twelve years,
which routinely denies part of one's existence must take its
toll on intrapersonal and/or interpersonal functioning. Either
students and teachers fight the system, express their feelings
verbally or behaviorally, and become "radical educators," "de-
linquents," "underachievers," or "crazy" in the eyes of the
power structure or they adapt (become adjusted-socialized) by
introjecting the value system of the environment they are in
in order to survive. Thus, typical strategies which develop involve both students and teachers in evolving elaborate plans to
"beat the system" by not "rocking the boat" or by reinforcing
and rationalizing traditional teacher-student roles. The consultant who does not get caught up in this "gaming" experience
is afforded the best possible opportunity for effecting change,
although he is also perpetually placed in the most precarious of
positions.

MENTAL HEALTH CONSULTATION:
RATIONALIZING FAILURES - SEARCHING FOR SUCCESSES

Enhancing or altering human nature is essentially a psycho-
educational process. The complexity of this process is not only
a function of the level of change which is required (cognitive,

surface behavior, ego-functioning, value-shifts, attitudinal
alterations, or unconscious changes) but of the nature of the
learner and teacher as well. If this axiom is granted than we
can see how, although the task of educating children is perplexing, confusing, and at times frightening, that the task of re-
educating or retooling teachers around mental health issues can
in many ways be nothing less than impossible. The reason for
this impossibility can be found couched in an ironic by-product
of the elaborate academic complex we call schools. The entire
thrust of most of the activities which take place in school are
designed to facilitate change or growth, and yet the people who
are most responsible for such change are least able to alter
their own behavioral repertoires.

The reasons for this phenomenon would appear to be five-
fold:

1. Teachers are products of the system we are attempting
to alter. As such, their attitudes, values, teaching styles, and
and conceptualizations of the teaching-learning process have
been shaped and differentially reinforced by their own academic
experiences. Thus, they perceive their present, on-going educational experiences in terms of the standards, expectations,
and objectives which they learned as a by-product of their own
schooling. Information which is dissonant with these experiences will tend to be rejected. Many teachers, especially those
who have been involved with the system for a long period of time,
have difficulty accepting the possibility that students reject
their efforts because they, the students, see the act of learning as an act of submission. This kind of insight is difficult
to generate because to present it and have it accepted means
that one must also accept the possibility that one has spent a
lifetime acquiescing to the same system.

(Note: Do you, the reader, have difficulty accepting this pos-
tulate? If so, why? Reread question 4 above if you do.)

2. Teachers have a real and understandable investment in
perpetuating the system as it presently exists. It was suggested that the changes the consultant must undergo to become more
authentic could be temporarily debilitating in terms of one's
individual response to the increased anxiety which such change
engenders. Are we not raising an equally threatening alternative for teachers when we conduct in-service workshops around
mental health issues. To accept the validity of a child-center-
ed, affectively-based orientation, the teacher must forsake his
traditional white, tight fitting garb for one which is multi-
colored and multi-formed. The school setting as it is presently
structured provides a very real security base, with its explicit
role prescriptions, for teacher, student, administrator, and

parent. Average expectable behaviors are the norm. The scripts
are world famous and all know their lines well. What would
happen if school systems were to suddenly implement the following proposals:

        a. Declaration of a five year moratorium on the
use of all textbooks.
        b. Have "English" teachers "teach" math, math
teachers English, social studies teachers science, and
science teachers art, and so on.
        c. Transfer all elementary school teachers to
high school and vice versa.
        d. Dissolve all "subjects" "courses" and espec-
ially "course requirements."
        e. Limit each teacher to three declarative sen-
tences per class, and five interrogatives.
        f. Prohibit teachers from asking any questions
they already know the answers to.
        g. Require teachers to take a test prepared by
students on what the students know.
        h. Prohibit the use of the following words and
phrases: teach, syllabus, covering, IQ, make-up test,
disadvantaged, gifted, excelerated, cost, grade, score,
human nature, dumb, college material, and administrative necessity. (Postman and Weingartner, 1969, pp.
137-140).

    Suggestions for altering classroom atmosphere which require
even relatively subtle changes in teacher behavior are frequently met with a defensive wall (that could insultate China!) which
might then take weeks to break down.

    3. <u>Teachers are both the subjects and objects of study in
many forms of mental health consultation.</u> As in traditional
psychotherapeutic experiences, we find teachers who are frequently quite reluctant to reflect upon their own behavior, explore
the impact of their behavior on those around them, and focus on
their own techniques for managing anger, guilt, anxiety, etc.
But, is this not the essence of behavior change? Even the impli-
mentation of a behavior modification program requires that teachers not only reflect upon their own behavior, but that they
quantify it for public perusal. It is, therefore, highly questionable to think that telling, directing, lecturing, suggesting, showing, providing reading materials, etc. will in any
significant way increase the probability of generating teacher
behavior change in the school setting.

    4. <u>Many teachers experience a dichotomy betweeh their pro-
fessional responsibilities and their responsibilities to themselves as human beings.</u> As in several of the helping profes-

sions, the teaching role is frequently at odds with other aspects of a person's total functioning. Teachers are part "organizational men" and part "assembly-line workers" responsible to those above and below them but also alienated from themselves and others around them. The nature of their work requires that they concern themselves with piecework production and with "parts" rather than with "wholes." As was suggested earlier this results in a separation of thoughts and feelings and a kind of fragmentation which is then easily communicated to and reinforced in their students. Two by-products of this separation between thinking and feeling are alienation and a sense of meaninglessness.

> Alienation as we find it in modern society is almost total; it pervades the relationship of man to his work, to the things he consumes, to his fellows and to himself (Fromm, 1962, p.59).

> Where there is meaning, there is involvement. When something has meaning, one is committed to it. Where there is meaning, there is conviction. Such commitment and conviction is something different from conformity, or merely playing a part, or living as a cog in a machine, or losing ones individuality in what Kierkegaard has called the "featureless crowd." When meaning is lacking in ones work as a teacher, the self is uninvolved. The substance is lacking, and teaching is just an empty formality (Jersild, 1955, p. 84).

5. <u>Any change which is generated within teachers as a group is frequently punished by the existing power structure of the school, and those behaviors which perpetuate the status quo are routinely reinforced.</u> The task of implementing mental health programs within the school system not only involves generating a variety of changes (cognitive, attitudinal, and behavioral) within teachers but also necessitates that these changes be acted out at some level within the school system. Many systems have elaborate, yet subtle, socialization schemas, which are based upon a variety of schedules of reinforcement sanctioning only certain forms of role-appropriate behaviors. Being called by one's first name or being called out of the teacher's room by a student, meeting with students after hours and away from the school, going into a student bathroom, admitting one's faults to students, relating to fellow teachers on a personal rather than a professional basis, etc. are all examples of behaviors which frequently receive negavive sanctions. Thus the frustrating problem of generating change is not only related to moblizing and channeling anxiety into new and appropriate repertoires, but it is also a process which is caught up in person-

institution interactions with the press of the institution frequently working against change.

The task then is how to work within the system in spite of these inherent resistances and defenses. This is a difficult goal because ultimately, it involves more than just structural changes, procedural changes, alterations in student populations, and/or staff or curricular changes which can be affected through administrative edict, union negotiations, alterations in board policy, or economic conditions. It involves the most complex and difficult of change--human change, which can only be effected through human dialogue, interaction, or encounter.

A crucial prerequisite for the successful implementation of any mental health program is the support of both line and staff personnel. Ultimately, for a classroom based mental health orientation to have a significant impact, not only is the active support of teachers necessary, but a security base from which they can operate is also needed. This security base is difficult to establish when teachers are caught between the "yin" of a cognitively-oriented school press and the "yang" of emotionally-laden classroom interactions. This situation is further exacerbated when we realize that our traditional vehicles for communicating mental health concepts are not particularly effective tools within the school setting. It is, therefore, necessary to generate some new consultative styles and techniques in order to both communicate mental health concepts and to generate a security base so that teachers are comfortable in implementing them.

AN ALTERNATIVE . . .

One alternative consultive style has been implied throughout this chapter. This style suggests that the consultant operate and present himself in a manner which is consonant with the ways he would like others to work. By doing this, he not only provides a healthy model to be emulated, but he also maximizes on his time spent within the system. The consultant who bases his style on his own authenticity uses every encounter with the system he is relating to as a potentially growth facilitating experience. Ultimately, every decision must rest with the system. No responsibilities can be shared or divided up unless the system has contracted to become a dependent, passive, tentacle of the consulting agency. This style also has important implications for the manner in which in-service programs are conducted.

The form and content of in-service teacher education must be isomorphic. The consultant working with groups of teachers around any issue must be cognizant of the fact that the way he does what he does can be just as crucial as whatever it is that he does. The consultant who suggests a workshop topic and who assumes responsibility for implementing it runs the same risk that teachers encounter when they organize their classrooms for learning. Every decision which is made for the group reduces by one degree of freedom the potential for significant growth experiences within that group. How can the group leader discuss freedom in the classroom if he has previously decided when, where, and why the group is meeting. What is conveyed about sensitivity to feelings when the consultant continues to administer evaluative instruments to a group of people who are passively communicating their apprehension to him? What is learned about the dynamics of casual behavior (antecedent and consequent patterns) when the group leader neglects to point out that the bored look on the faces of the people in his group are somehow related to what he is doing or saying. And should not the consultant realize that creative teaching cannot be lectured about; that a minimal amount of group dynamics can be learned in an auditorium with 110 people present; that freedom to learn is necessarily constricted when attendance, assignments, and final exams are required; that we cannot ask teachers to do what we ourselves cannot invest energy into.

A technique which evolves from this style and which closely meets the criterion of isomorphism involves the consultant in structuring self-directed teacher groups. Implicit in such a technique are a large number of meaningful values which are entirely consonant with the aims of education in its deep sense:

1. Focuses on here and now learning.
2. Enhances responsibility for own learning.
3. Facilitates reliance on self and peer group rather than on expert.
4. Focuses on independent learning in the context of a peer group.
5. Focuses on content as well as feelings.
6. Nothing is imposed: learning proceeds in the direction which is valued by the learner.
7. Generates operant-type behaviors.
8. Stresses individuality and self-worth.
9. Does not preclude involvement of outside specialists, if the group reaches such a decision on the basis of realistic needs.
10. Facilitates learning about processes (group development, problem solving, production of new knowledge, etc.)

The role of the consultant with a self-directed group is similar to that of the model or anti-model of teaching proposed by Rogers (1961, pp. 273-278). The consultant's primary respon-

sibility is simply to structure an environment so that self-
directed learning can proceed. It may be argued that certain
minimal kinds of prerequisite learnings are necessary before
such a group experience can be undertaken. Further precautions
should be noted relating to the kinds of anxiety and stress
which are often engendered by such a group experience. This
experience would certainly not be recommended for teachers or
schools which are not otherwise healthy to begin with. In such
cases, another kind of working model should certainly be articulated if the consultant still wishes to involve himself around
mental health issues.

The consultant attempting to establish self-directed groups
must at all times behave in a fashion which is consistent with
this style. Answering substantive questions, setting too many
limits, illusions to "right" solutions, issuing evaluative
statements, etc. all tend to foster a potentially destructive
dependency relationship. Such a relationship will usually have
to be worked through before self-directed learning experiences
can proceed.

Although only one research study evaluating the effectiveness of this kind of approach with teachers has been attempted,
with results which are only somewhat encouraging, it will nevertheless serve as a valuable case in point. The study involved
the development and evaluation of a series of audiotapes designed to promote self-awareness, enhance interpersonal functioning
and generate skills presumed to be fundamental in creating meaningful therapeutic and educational relationships. Although applicable to the training of both professionals and paraprofes-
sionals who provide helping services, the program was designed
specifically for elementary school teachers.

Jersild suggests that many teachers feel that they need
some kind of help if they are to make full use of their personal and professional potentialities. He goes on to suggest
that:

> Just as it is within an interpersonal setting
> that one acquires most of the attitudes involved in
> one's view of oneself, so it is likely that only in
> an interpersonal setting can a person be helped to
> come to grips with some of the meanings of these at-
> titudes (1955, p.84).

The question **arises** then, can a program be developed in
which small groups of teachers can work together toward greater
understanding, toward a blending of their professional responsibilities and personal commitments, toward enhanced interpersonal functioning, toward a deeper appreciation of the role that

feelings play in interpersonal relationships and in learning processes, and toward a deeper understanding of their impact on students and peers? Futhermore, can this kind of undertaking be successful without the guidance of trained group leaders?

The GAGED-IN program which was developed in response to these questions, is a "modified instrumented group" program. It attempts to create an environment in which it is safe to explore the nature of one's own individual "cages"--those "cages" which exist within and those which are created in the context of inter-personal functioning.

The program itself is composed of a series of intrapersonal (e.g., relaxation exercises, sensory awareness experiences, etc.) and interpersonal exercises which are designed to create a learning environment into which a participant can project personal and/or professional concerns. In this environment, the participants deal with such issues as their interpersonal relations (their impact on others and their receptivity of others), their values and the basis for their perceptions and motivations. The focal point of the program relates to the participants capactiy for giving and receiving help. Concern is directed not so much towards actual techniques "helping" as it is on the conditions of helping effectively (positive regard, genuineness, and empathic understanding).

The exercises are presented on audiotape and are designed specifically for use by small groups (5 to 7 participants) of elementary school teachers. The exercises establish limits which regulate or maintain substantive issues within certain specifiable areas but within these limits the group is free to explore the issues in any manner it deems appropriate.

"CAGED-IN" is an acronym which stands for "Controlled Audio-taped Group Experience for Directing Individual Naturalism." Several elements of this description need elaboration:

1. Controlled. The program has a variety of mechanisms which structure the activities and at the same time free the participants within that structure. The experience runs for five days and is "programmed" to last one hour each day. The group is told that they can in fact, order the movement of their group in any way which seems appropriate. Some groups abide by the initial structuring, whereas others stretch the experience out for six to eight days. Other groups spend longer periods of time on individual sessions: some running as long as three and one half hours. Control is also provided in the nature of the exercises they are asked to participate in. These exercises are presented with varying degrees of ambiguity. This ambiguity provides the group with some limits but also permits them to re-

interpret the exercise in a form which they are not only comfortable with, but which is possibly more meaningful to them than the original set of directions.

2. <u>Audiotape</u>. The program is presented on tape. This allows the group the freedom to behave as autonomously as possible. It prevents them from establishing dependence on a group leader. It also allows them to confront such issues as responsibility (for adhering to the limits), leadership, and concern over dependency itself.

3. <u>Group Experience</u>. The group creates a microcosm which replicates many of the significant dimensions of the participant's real worlds. To the extent that the participants perceive these similarities, the transfer of interpersonal skills will much more readily be effected.

4. <u>Directing Individual Naturalism</u>. This statement is actually a contradiction in terms, for that which is natural and inherent must eminate from within and cannot be directly controlled by outside intervention. It is perhaps more appropriate to describe the process of directing, in terms of simply providing an environment which is structured to allow for and to facilitate the occurrence of more "natural" behaviors.

Although research with this technique has generated a number of quantitive analyses relating to the impact it has on teacher verbal behavior in the classroom, the perception of teachers by students, and on intragroup processes relating to involvement and anxiety, for our purposes it might be most useful to examine only the qualitative data this program has produced.

Tables 1, 2, and 3 present selected sentence completions which were obtained from 36 elementary school teachers who participated in the original studies of the CAGED-IN program.

These sentence completions were obtained at the conslusion of each session and at the end of the entire program. These reflections about professional, intrapersonal, and interpersonal concerns were all derived from leaderless group experiences (i.e. a "professional expert" was not in attendance). Although the direct effect of such an experience on classroom mental health is still questionable (the hard data is ambiguous, yet promising), the experience certainly did have some impact on the institutional press.

Table 1

Content Analysis: Professional Reflections

1. Methods by which I can share, if possible, some of these experiences with my children in school.
2. Concrete experiences to use in the classroom to increase sensitivity and awareness.
3. I would like to explore ways of creating a natural, free atmosphere. . . to instill some sort of spontaneity.
4. How can I use some of the techniques in my class that we used in our group in order to get more cohesiveness in the class.
5. Realizing that I was actually using some of the things that I had picked up (in this group) in the classroom.
6. Become aware of the way I talk to children and use of "key phrases" everyday.
7. To bring my "at-home personality" to my "work personality" and blend the best of each.
8. Realizing that primary teachers were aware they scolded their children, perhaps too much.
9. I feel I can let more of my own personality weaknesses, strengths, etc. (show) to my kids.
10. I became more interested in what was going on inside my students.
11. Realizing how some of my comments in the classroom affect others.
12. A sharing of ideas and feelings about our role as teachers.
13. To make the cohesiveness and feelings we felt as a group carry through to other people we work with.
14. Realizing that teachers are quite creative in their writing and thinking.

Table 2

Content Analysis: Intrapersonal Reflections

1. Realizing how hard it is to find words to describe yourself.
2. (I thought today's session) was like a confessional. Most significant part of the session was:
3. A statement someone made to me: I think you sometimes don't think too much of yourself. The statement pertained to the adjective I used concerning my weight.
4. The ideas which came from discussion (such as really listening to others without using any preconceived notions). Each paired exercise brought out two different interpretations, both of which were valid in their own particular context and

both of which proved helpful to me.
5. The discussion of values that you yourself feel are important.
6. Thinking of myself as a person, being able to be a little more open and involved.
7. Learning how parental attitude influenced our attitude.
8. The beginning where awareness of self was carried out.
9. Time for physical awareness--great.
10. Amazingly in the relaxation period my chest and nasal passages completely cleared. It was a great feeling - I'm a heavy smoker.

Table 3

Content Analysis: Interpersonal Reflections

1. . . . the wonderful rapport and atmosphere (which was) developed. Not only did we have to be completely open about ourselves, but the others had to be the same with us. It made me feel much closer to the others in the group, even though at times I felt somewhat embarrassed with what they had to say to me concerning my strengths. I also found that what I interpreted as a weakness in me, others felt was a strength.
2. I think I have a good idea of how people feel about me and how I can better help other people.
3. (Most significant part was) being able to force myself to be open and trust the others to accept me.
4. Basically people have the same needs and feelings, including and especially children.
5. I have gotten some rewarding feedback on myself as well as the others in this group. . . I think I might be able to get to know other people better and their feelings by pursuing some of the things we talked about.
6. People want to be loved and accepted and need to know they are.
7. A very special bond can be developed with certain people you really didn't think of developing anything with.
8. I feel that the session today was the best so far because of our level of honesty. We never could have spoken this freely on Monday or before.
9. Most people are afraid to admit their strengths and use them fully.
10. As sensitive as I thought I was, I now realize how much deeper my sensitivity must go to really understand and help others.
11. (Most significant part was) breaking through to another person who I felt was very cold and distant.
12. . . . .Many things that are problems to me are problems

to others--or at least similar.

13. I feel I have gotten to know these people much better.

14. Most c haracteristics named were quite superficial; however, upon discussing them more internal (I don't know if that's the right word) and underlying ones were discussed which were far more revealing of the true person.

15. Revealing my problems in relationships to groups of people.

16. I still feel uncomfortable speaking in a group, although it is certainly not as terrifying for me as before the course (the CAGED-IN Program).

17. Realizing the amount of negative responses used and how it affects you and others.

IN CONCLUSION . . .

The essential points in this chapter are simple although their simplicity should not override their meaningfulness. To what extent does the style of the mental health consultant reflect the principles he is trying to promote? To what extent is the consultant's behavior isomorphic with both his values and goals? And finally, to the extent that he is sensitive to they dynamics of the system he is consulting to, how does he utilize this information to maximize on his own input and impact?

The consultative style suggested in this chapter is a difficult one to adopt. The difficulty stems from the argument that this style does not generate role-specific behaviors, but that it only relates in a somewhat global sense to a set of processes within which the consultant can find much freedom (and ambiguity). In the final analysis, these processes might only be a reflection of a state of mind; a state of mind where one has the courage to be authentic, to reflect upon the accuracy of one's perceptions, to "tune-in" to one's needs, values, and biases and make the appropriate accommodations, to strive for a congruency among one's words, actions, and values, and most of all to differentiate between when one is realistically needed and when one needs to be needed.

REFERENCES

Argyris, C. *Intervention Theory and Method: A Behavioral Science View*. Reading Mass.: Addison-Wesley, 1970.

Jersild, A. *When Teachers Face Themselves*. New York: Teachers College Press, 1955.

Menninger, K. *Love Against Hate*. New York: Harcourt, Brace, and World, 1942.

Menninger, K., Maymen, J., and Druyser, P. *The Vital Balance*. New York: Viking Press, 1963.

Murphy, G. Personality: A biosocial approach to origins and structure. In E. A. Southwell and M. Merbauk (Eds.). *Personality: Readings in Theory and Research*. California: Brooks/Cole, 1964.

Perls, F. *In and Out the Garbage Pail*. Lafayette, California: Real People Press, 1969.

Postman, N. and Weingartner, C. *Teaching as a Subversive Activity*. New York: Delacorte Press, 1969.

Symonds, P. *What Education has to Learn from Psychology*. (Third Edition) New York: Teachers College Press, 1958.

Webb, E., Campbell, D., Schwartz, R. and Sechrest, L. *Unobtrusive Measures*. Chicago: Rand McNally, 1966.

SECTION II

TRAINING AND PREPARATION

FOR SCHOOL INTERVENTION PROGRAM

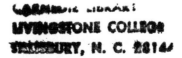

3. COLLABORATIVE APPROACH

The collaborative approach to school consultation taken by Dr. Berkowitz is characterized by an open sharing of ideas and trial and error exploring of hypotheses. The psychologist and teachers meet together, each eschewing formal, mystical, defensive roles. According to Dr. Berkowitz, this form of consultation is effective and provides essential internal support for teachers who often felt harassed and unsupported.

Psychologists are often unsuited to the role of consultant: by lack of training, experience, and practice at conceptualizing the positive interrelationship among the school, child and teacher. Traditional referrals to psychologists from school systems have concerned only the pathological. The psychologist consults with teachers who are failing, sees children who are failing and works in schools which are failing. Using primary or early secondary approaches to prevention stressed by Dr. Berkowitz, the consultant has a chance to work with students, teachers and administrators in a system which is succeeding; consultation intervention builds on strength and confidence rather than pathology.

A consultant who takes time to learn and is willing to risk himself in developing relationships with the school system and teachers, should find the processes outlined by Dr. Berkowitz the basis for an encouraging model.

A COLLABORATIVE APPROACH TO MENTAL HEALTH

CONSULTATION IN SCHOOL SETTINGS

Hershel Berkowitz
University of Colorado

During the past decade, there has been an increasing emphasis upon the prevention of mental illless and upon involvement in community institutions on the part of mental health professionals of all disciplines (Caplan, 1964; Joint Commission, 1961; Newman, 1967; Sarason, Levine, Goldenberg, Cherlin, and Bennett, 1966). In particular, the needs of children and the importance of early intervention and assistance have been emphasized; the schools have been viewed as ideal institutions upon which to focus endeavors in these areas. During the same period of time, there has been a reciprocal increase in interest on the part of the schools themselves in making greater use of mental health services. This interest has arisen in part out of a steadily growing involvement in broader aspects of education and child development on the part of educators and the public at large. In part, it has been stimulated by an increase in the complexity of the educators' task which has resulted from the significant growth in social change, stress and unrest which our society has experienced at an accelerated rate during this period of time.

As a consequence, and with the facilitation of generous Federal funding during the early 1960's, there has been a burgeoning increase in collaborative attempts by educators and mental health clinicians around a variety of endeavors. Joint programs have been developed for the early identification of disturbed or problem children, special classes have been established for the emotionally disturbed child, and innovative programs have been implemented in order to motivate potential high school dropouts to remain in school. Many comprehensive mental health centers have established contractual arrangements to provide mental health services to school districts and other districts have greatly enlarged their own mental health staffs.

In many instances, these collaborative attempts have been mutually rewarding for educators and clinicians alike, and have been of significant benefit to the children being served. In other instances, however, the results have been less positive; on many occasions a mutual disaffection has occurred. Clinicians have withdrawn from the schools, seeing them as "resistive" and inhospitable institutions with which to work; educators have seen clinicians as unhelpful, even at times regarding their contribution as hindersome or disruptive. While there are obviously many individual and specific reasons for the failure of particular collaborative attempts between clinicians and educators, there are also, it would appear, some more general problems in the relationship between the two professions.

On the clinician's side these problems arise from a general lack of familiarity with the school environment or culture and a lack of empathy for the skills, strengths and problems of the educator. For the most part, clinicians reenter the school setting after leaving it at the age of seventeen or eighteen. To the extent that the clinician's most recent experience in the schools has been in the role of student, one might expect a host of biases, misconceptions and distortions to arise which would make it difficult to empathize with the educator's perspective and intent.

These distortion are, if anything, likely to be reinforced during the course of the clinician's graduate education and experience in the clinic work setting. Students of education and their teachers are held in low repute in most university academic settings, and there is little communication between them and faculty or students from other disciplines, the mental health disciplines included (Conant, 1964; Sarason, Davidson and Blatt, 1962).

With some notable exceptions (Blom, 1969; Sanford, 1965) there has been little speculation in the course of clinicians' training upon the contributions which the educational process might make in the area of mental health To be more specific, clinicians spend little time thinking or conceptualizing about such issues as the crucial role of mastery experiences in the child's development and the unique part which the classroom plays in providing such experiences in a carefully controlled gradated manner. Nor is much thought given to the role played by non-parental identification figures in a child's life and again, to the unique position of the school in providing such figures. Again, the role of the school in helping to structure peer relationships and the role which these extra-familial relations play in development has received little attention in the thinking of clinicians. Given this conceptual bias, it

is not surprising that many clinicians are unaware of the significance of events transpiring within the classroom.

   In the clinic setting, a negative outlook towards educators is often further reinforced. All too often, teachers are
viewed by clinicians as incompetent or unhelpful to children,
in part perhaps, because when communication does occur between
clinic and school, it is most often around a difficult child
with whom the school is, in fact, experiencing failure. Since
the majority of referrals to mental health clinics are school
related (Berkowitz, 1968), clinicians rarely receive referrals
concerning children who are succeeding in school or who are
being helped by teachers. On occasions where a child is, in
fact, experiencing success in school, but not in other areas,
it is unlikely that any but the most superficial contact will
be maintained with the school, where, after all, the clinician's assistance is not needed. As a consequence, the clinician's contact is often, in reality, with the teacher who is
failing with a particular child; very rarely does he have communication with a teacher around experiences of success and
accomplishment.

   Even in the absence of such negatively biasing factors,
the clinician's experience in his own institutional base, the
clinic or graduate school, will poorly prepare him to work in
the schools. As a number of authors have indicated (Berkowitz,
1968; Bower, 1964; Sarason et al,1966) the goals and milieu of
the school are different from that of the clinic. The task of
the teacher is a complex and difficult one, and while there
are many points of common interest and overlapping knowledge
and skill between teacher and clinician (Blom, 1969) there are
also many points of difference. The techniques and knowledge
of the mental health profession, developed in the context of
small group or individual interaction, frequently with an emphasis more on affect than on cognition, are often not directly
translatable into the large group situation of the classroom
where issues of cognition receive the highest priority. All
too often, educators have been correct when they have accused
mental health workers of attempting to transform teachers into
therapists by urging upon them behaviors and attitudes which
were simply inappropriate for the accomplishment of the teachers' task.

   On the other hand, teachers have also had a less than
accurate view of the clinician. The schools have, in general,
been experiencing a period of increasing crisis in recent years.
Confronted with increased and often unrealistic and conflictual community pressures in a number of areas, with a broader
awareness of the problems of children, and with a rapidly-
growing dropout rate, educators have often turned to the mental

health profession in desperation, at times seeking almost magical solutions to truly overwhelming problems. Individual teachers, seeking help with frustrating and difficult classroom problems, often entertain equally unrealistic wishes of the clinician, frequently placing him in the initially flattering role of lofty and powerful expert, and then experiencing bitter disappointment when this expertise fails to immediately alleviate the problem at hand. These expectations, too, have a culturally-supported component, given our society's tendency to view the mental health worker as a dabbler in the occult, a reputedly omniscient figure who can expose others' thoughts and feelings at will.

Given the prevalence of such mutually unrealistic expectations on the part of both educators and clinicians, the most immediate task for the clinician seeking to work with the schools becomes one of establishing a relationship which can become the basis for a positive mutual learning experience for both himself and his educational colleagues. The first step in accomplishing this aim is for the clinician to acknowledge to himself the possible unrealistic nature of his expectations and the necessity for his seeking to utilize his contract with the schools as an opportunity to learn something of the realistic parameters operating in this new situation. It is likely to be helpful if the clinicians would enter the schools with a set towards gaining an appreciation of the difficult task confronting the teacher, who is attempting to afford an optimal learning situation to a group of twenty-five or more children, often of diverse skills and backgrounds, in a situation in which he himself often receives little support or assistance. This task requires a capacity to attend to a variety of interpersonal stimuli, while continually dividing attention between background and foreground. The teacher must focus on the activities of an individual or small group, while at the same time, maintaining awareness and responsivity to even subtle inputs from other children in the classroom. When some of the children in class do not find learning gratifying or have needs which are not readily met in the classroom context, the teacher's task becomes even more difficult. In most classes there is at least one child who would be difficult to assist or relate to even in the context of the one-to-one situation so prevalent in the clinic. Learning about the kinds of skills and techniques which are necessary for mere survival in the face of such a complex and, at times, overwhelming task will greatly facilitate the clinician's development of an appreciation for the strengths and resources of teachers. It will help him to view them more as peers and colleagues and less as subordinates or technicians. This kind of appreciation can be gained by talking to teachers about their work, by observing them in the classroom and even more immediately, by the clinician's own experience if he himself were to have the temerity to spend some time trying to teach on occasion!

The above should not be construed as suggesting that the clinician should adopt the role of a passive learner as he enters the schools. Such a position is not likely to be tolerated for long; teachers are likely to become most impatient around a clinician who devotes his time exclusively to observations and talk when they themselves are seeking to deal with real and pressing problems. School personnel have many experiences with experts of one stripe or another from nationally-renowned educational consultants to local psychologists. These experts most often come to the schools, observe and then make recommentdations, leaving the school and the teacher to deal with the same difficult problems that confronted them to begin with.

For this reason, the clinician would do well to assume a stance in which he communicated his interest in learning, but also his willingness to learn ways of helping in the course of his contacts with the school staff. Within the limitations of his time and ability, he should be willing to meet with personnel, to see students or parents, to observe in the classroom, even to carry out those tasks which on the surface may not make much sense to him. He must be willing to take the risks of self-exposure, the exposure of his own doubts and weaknesses, if he expects the school personnel to take the same risks themselves. By engaging in these activities, the clinician will develop a keener sense of the problems facing the people in the school, and will also begin to establish a kind of mutual trust, openness, and respect which is a necessary foundation for any successful collaborative endeavor.

The specific nature of the collaborative endeavor which results from the sort of process described above, is one which will necessarily vary as a function of the needs, resources, and prospensities of the particular school and clinician involved. The present author and his colleagues have been working with a variety of school settings in the Denver, Colorado metropolitan area over the past six years and have developed a consultative approach which they have found useful. Mental health personnel involved in these endeavors have been staff members and trainees from the disciplines of psychology, psychiatry, social work, and education, in the University of Colorado Medical School's Department of Psychiatry. They have been motivated by a desire to explore primary and secondary preventive approaches to problems of mental illness, by a wish to develop models for the more effective delivery of mental health services, and by a basic interest in the schools themselves.

Entry into the schools has most often resulted from would-be
consultants seeking out contact with school personnel and offering to explore mutually rewarding avenues of collaboration.
Most often the settings contacted in this way have been those
which had a prior relationship, based upon direct service in-
volvements, with the Department's psychoeducational facility
for children, the Day Care Center.

In most instances, the pattern for the establishment of
the consultation has been a familiar one (e.g., see Sarason et
al, 1966 and Newman, 1967). While the exact sequence of events
has varied from setting to setting, the prospective consultant
has usually become initially involved through a case-related
contact with a member of a school building staff. This contact
has been followed, with some variation, by meetings with members of the particular school district's administrative staff,
with individual building principals and with the principal and
staff of the school in which the consultation finally occurred.
In each case, the would-be consultant has discussed his possible interests and skills with the school personnel involved,
emphasizing his desire to explore ways of being helpful around
those problems which were of most concern to the schools them-
sleves. In the course of these discussions, the consultants
have emphasized the importance of involving teaching staff members in any planning or program development which might be expected to have an eventual effect of any kind in the classroom.
If the planned-for consultation was to take place at the building level, which was most often the case, the consultant involved would usually arrange to spend approximately one day per
week in the school concerned, usually over at least a year's
period of time. This time has been spent in becoming acquainted
with the setting and staff and in helping to delineate issues
and develop possible solutions to the particular problems concerning the school.

This process has usually begun with a variety of contacts,
both formal and informal, between consultant and building personnel. Care has been taken to establish on-going communication with the building's principal and special services personnel in most instances. While the consultant has usually addressed at least one initial faculty meeting, most initial communication with the teaching staff has occurred informally, in
the teachers' lounge and lunchroom, in the halls, and in the
classrooms themselves. Much of this initial communication has
centered around the staff's and consultant's mutual attempts
to delineate roles with regard to one another. In particular,
school personnel have attmepted to ascertain what skills the
consultant might be able to offer, and to explore ways to make
use of his services. The consultant, on the other hand, has
attempted to learn something about staff members' philosophies,

skills, styles and concerns and has engaged in reciprocal attempts to find ways to be of help with the problems presented
to him. Thus, as has been discusssed earlier, classroom observations have been conducted, parents have been interviewed,
and children have been tested or otherwise evaluated in the
course of these explorations. Where formal planning groups or
committees have existed in the school, the consultant has attempted to attend them and faculty meetings have been attended
as often as possible.

Almost invariably, clusters of concerns or problems have
begun to emerge in the course of the consultant's interaction
with the staff. These problems, common concerns of a number of
staff members, have been identified by the consultant and have
lent impetus to his suggesting that there might be some value
in establishing ongoing group meetings in which concerned personnel might address and attempt to resolve them.

While the idea of such problem solving meetings has been
accepted with varying degress of readiness from school to school,
school, invariably problem solving groups have been implemented
and have then become the core of the ongoing consultative endeavor in each setting. The building's principal and other
administrators have been crucial figures in these meetings,
either by participating in an ongoing manner, or by sanctioning the activities involved. The membership of these problem-
solving meetings or groups has usually been composed of those
teachers and other personnel who sought out the assistance of
the consultant involved, and who have been concerned about similar issues or problems. Thus, in one setting, a consultant
met on an ongoing basis with a group of primary grade teachers
who worked in separate classrooms but who shared similar concerns about the management and teaching of disturbed and difficult children in their classes. Another group involved teachers at the same grade level who were functioning as a teaching
team in an open classroom situation and who were concerned a-
bout children in their class who had learning problems and
about their own difficulty in working together as a team. In
another instance, a group of counselors, teachers and administrators had been working individually with a consultant around
students in their high school who were performing poorly, failing to attend classes and involved in drug abuse. It became
clear that, although they had been working to some degree in
isolation, the staff members did, in fact, have concerns about
these students in common, and they began to meet and plan as
a group. This activity resulted in their beginning to assess
the true extent of the problem confronting them, and in the
consequent development of an extremely innovative, and to date,
successful alternative educational program for the kinds of
students who had been of concern.

In all of these instances, the consultant involved had had some contact and first-hand experience with the children and problems involved, and during the course of discussions, often shared the information which he had gathered and his own views and ideas. His chief role, however, was one of facilitating a problem-solving process on the part of school personnel, encouraging them to explore issues and to share their ideas and feelings with one another. The discussions were most often task oriented, focused upon issues that were of concern to the personnel involved in the course of their attempts to carry out their professional tasks in the school. While expression of feelings was encouraged by the consultant, these feelings were usually job related and the exploration of more private and personal concerns was not solicited; usually such exploration was overtly discouraged.

The philosophy which formed the explicit basis for these groups was that the open sharing of ideas and concerns was useful and that problems were solved most often through a trial and error process of exploring alternative hypotheses. In general, the notion was that such a sharing of thoughts was usually mutually facilitative for those involved, that many heads were better than one, and that the wisdom of the group was greater than that of any individual member in it.

While there were, in some instances, feelings among some of the school personnel that these problem-solving sessions demanded too much time, in general, they were viewed positively and attended with enthusiasm on the part of most members. In addition to coming up with useful solutions to a variety of specific issues, the groups seemed to serve other purposes also. perhaps even more important. They afforded the personnel involved an opportunity to interrelate in a constructive manner around many of the issues that were concerning them individually. Such an opportunity is seldom afforded teachers and other school personnel and usually there is little encouragement in schools for such problem-solving activities. In point of fact, schools often seem to operate under the belief that personnel in general and teachers in particular can successfully carry out their task in the isolation of the classroom, and that contact, support or involvement with others is not necessary or even helpful. The problem-solving sessions thus provided the personnel involved with an experience in mutual support and assistance which was unusual but which became, for the most part, a valued and institutionalized activity.

The groups also promoted, in most instances, an increase in openness of interchange among the personnel of the school which generalized to other interactions with one another. In

one elementary school setting, the teachers had been quite
fearful of any kind of questioning or disagreement with the
principal who tended to maintain a somewhat authoritarian stance
towards his staff. In the course of one of the early problem-
solving sessions, the teachers discussed the fact that the principal had told them in the course of a faculty meeting that
they were responsible for maintaining order in their classroom,
and that when, during the course of the year, they found themselves in difficulty with problem children, they were reluctant
to send them to the office or to ask for help in working with
them. In the course of the meeting, they stated that they felt
that to do so would be to shirk their responsibility or to show
themselves to be weak teachers, and that they felt the principal would condemn them for such weakness. With the group's permission, the consultant explored this matter with the principal
in a tentative way and then invited him to discuss the matter
with the teachers. In the course of their discussion together,
the principal and teachers were able to resolve this issue, but
more importantly, each became sensitive to the others' concerns
and more willing to share and listen to one another's ideas.
This kind of interaction began to generalize during the course
of the year, the teachers began to perceive the principal differently and to be more open with him. On his part, the principal began to take on a much less authoritarian and much more
empathic stance with his faculty. This shift in relationship
enabled principal and faculty to resolve many of the difficulties which had previously frustrated both parties in their
attempts to work together. One very specific outcome of the
consultation in this particular setting was that the teachers
and principal agreed upon the need to develop a system to provide for individualized instruction for students. They began
to focus their meetings around the development of such plans
and the final program designed involved the use of non-graded
classrooms and team teaching. Teachers' wishes and feelings
played a crucial role in the development of these plans, even
to the placement of classrooms in the building, the curriculum
to be employed, and the composition of teams. The result was
an extremely smooth, unproblematical, and successful introduction of a non-graded program which has continued to function
over several years' time and despite a change in principals.

REFERENCES

Berkowitz, H. The child clinical psychologist in the schools: consultation. *Psychology in the Schools,* 1968, 5, pp. 118-124.

Berkowitz, H. A preliminary assessment of the extent of interaction between child psychiatric clinics and public schools. *Psychology in the Schools,* 1968, 5, pp. 291-295.

Blom, G. E. The psychoeducational approach to learning disabilities. *Seminars in Psychiatry,* 1969, 1, 3, 318-329.

Bower, E. M. Psychology in the schools: conceptions, processes, and territories. *Psychology in the Schools,* 1964, 1, pp. 3-12.

Caplan, G. *Principles of Preventive Psychiatry,* Basic Books, New York, 1964.

Conant, J. B. *The Education of American Teachers,* New York: McGraw-Hill, 1964.

Joint Commission on Mental Illness and Health, *Action for Mental Health,* New York: Wiley, 1961.

Newman, Ruth. *Psychological Consultation in the Schools,* New York: Basic Books, 1967.

Sanford, Nevitt, "Ego Process in Learning" in The Protection and Promotion of Mental Health in Schools, Lambert, N., (ed.), USPHS #1226, 1965, pp. 22-30.

Sarason, S. B. *The Culture of the School and Problem of Change,* Boston: Allyn and Bacon, 1971.

Sarason, S. B., Davidson, K., and Blatt, B. *The Preparation of Teachers,* New York: Wiley, 1962.

Sarason, S. B., Levine, M., Goldenberg, I., Cherlin, D., and Bennett, E. M. *Psychology in Community Settings,* New York: Wiley, 1966.

4. A BRIDGING PROGRAM

In contrast to in-school consultative services, the chapter by Dr. Apter concerns how to put together a program that is outside of the school system, but meets a need that is perceived by teachers and administrative staff alike. Dr. Apter has constructed six factors which provide a useful review for the development of any new programs. The factors are: 1) inclusion of community people in planning; 2) avoiding interference of academic research and training; 3) a willingness of university people for long personal involvement; 4) developing a program that accurately reflects the real need and provides appropriate service; 5) making realistic plans and 6) providing sufficient coordination for follow through and evaluation.

Dr. Apter illustrates each of these six points in the development of this summer camp program. As can be seen in some cases, it is a painful process. He suggests that as a rule of thumb, things don't go as planned in the beginning. A point understated in this chapter is that Dr. Apter and others spent many hours in meetings and more meetings which at times must have seemed futile or not worth the effort. Also evident in this chapter and worth remembering is that there are *a priori* no right ways to do things. In a sense, each program has to find out and feel for itself ways in which the program will work. Points of reference as illustrated by these six factors help the worker by providing check points against which to evaluate his work.

STARTING A SCHOOL INTERVENTION PROGRAM:

A SIX-FACTOR ANALYSIS OF THE BRIDGE PROGRAM

Steven Apter
Syracuse University

Traditionally, University-based psychological programs for school intervention have met with less than overwhelming success. Their failures can be traced to a variety of factors inherent in the structure of the model often employed to initiate and carry out these programs. This chapter is aimed at describing and analyzing the development and eventual launching of the BRIDGE Program: a comprehensive, year-round, psycho-educational program for emotionally disturbed children within the Syracuse, New York Public School District. Before doing that, however, it would seem appropriate to try to describe the traditional model of school intervention and to identify the elements of that model that have led to the failure of University-based school intervention programs in the past.

A typical University-based school intervention program might be looked at in terms of six crucial characteristics, of which the absence of any one is sufficient to doom the program to failure. These six factors could be described as:

1. The inclusion of community people, especially school personnel, in program planning
2. The refusal to allow research and academic interests to become paramount
3. The willingness of University faculty to go into the field and make personal contact with community people, especially school personnel, at all stages of the project
4. An ability to accurately define a community need and/or an appropriate service
5. An ability to make realistic plans (to secure staff, funding, etc.)
6. Provision of adequate coordination and follow-up services

Perhaps it would be most useful to examine each of these six factors individually, in order to understand how the absence of each of them has led to the failure of school-intervention programs in the past. Having done that, it might be possible to look at the development of the BRIDGE Program, to analyze it in terms of the six factors listed above, and finally to evaluate the model by which the BRIDGE Program has developed, identifying both its strengths and its weaknesses.

In terms of the first factor then, persons in charge of developing and implementing University-based programs for school intervention have become notorious for their failure to include community people in the planning stages of these projects. Frequently, this apparent lack of concern for community viewpoints at the planning stage has resulted in a number of unfortunate consequences. Usually, by the time community people, especially school personnel, are informed of the program, there is no legitimate channel for their opinions. As a result, they are confronted with an already complete program which they are compelled to administer, regardless of any objections they might have. Thus, school personnel, most notably teachers, are often left with the feeling that they are merely the last link in a very long chain, charged with doing all the "dirty work" for some academician's pet project; a project they might view very negatively. It is not very hard to understand how school personnel in this type of position might act in ways that would passively undermine the goals of the program, or even become actively involved in placing barriers in the project's path. It is certainly very easy to see how their attitudes about future programs would become increasingly negative if their opinions were never taken into account in the planning process.

There are probably a great many reasons for the traditional failure to include community inputs in program planning. One of the most important factors, however, may very likely be related to the second factor in the above list, and might be described as the rather selfish nature of many University projects. Over the course of many years, it has become a well-known fact that Universities have often been far more concerned with developing programs of research likely to lead to fame and fortune for the University, than with developing and providing badly needed services for the community. Many school intervention projects then have been designed and initiated much more for the research programs built into them, than for the services they ostensibly provided. Schools have always been rich sources of research data, but have attempted to strike bargains with research-minded academicians by asking for needed services in return for access to their ready-made subject pools. It was not at all difficult for University people to present their programs in ways that emphasized the services they would offer in order to make their

way into the school. Once they were there, however, it was
just as easy to carry out their programs in ways that clearly
emphasized their research at the expense of the services they
had promised. It wasn't long before school personnel realized
what was happening and their feelings could often be summed up
in one word--"used." Not only did these kinds of programs usually offer inadequate and incomplete services to the children
involved, but also their duplicity made it exceedingly difficult
for programs more sincerely concerned with offering services to
find their way into the school system.

Many University-based programs of school intervention have
been doomed to failure by the typical unwillingness of University faculty to go into the field and make personal contact with
people who might be involved at all levels of their program.
This is a problem that often exists at all stages of a given
program: planning, implementation and follow-up. Although innumerable reasons for the lack of personal contact can be con-
jured up, there seems to be no real justification for the absence of this personal contact factor. For the many excuses always seem to boil down to one central fact; i.e., University
program developers are really not interested in what community
people, especially school personnel, might be able to add to
University-based school intervention projects.

This lack of interest is unfortunate for a number of reasons. First of all, it quickly makes itself known to those
whose inputs are not desired and thus makes enemies out of persons who might have become strong and trusted allies. Secondly,
it causes a huge gap to begin forming within the program being
planned. Thus, for example, the failure to include school personnel's inputs at all stages in planning, development and implementation of new school intervention programs has brought
about both the active sabotage of many programs as well as the
slow, torturous death of many others.

The failure of University faculty to make meaningful personal contact with school personnel often leads to still another
important failure factor: the inability to accurately define a
current need and an appropriate program to fill that need. Thus
the gaps that are formed as the result of a lack of personal
contact can be seen as the distance between what the University
program offers and what the community really needs.

It is relatively easy to understand how the inability to
define the appropriate need and/or services would often lead
directly to the absence of the fifth crucial factor, the ability to make realistic program plans. If the persons responsible
for a school intervention program had no idea how many children
they might be serving, it would be impossible for them to make

logical plans to secure the needed staff, necessary funds, etc. Even programs that have been carefully thought out, with the help of school personnel at all phases, have suffered because of an inability to deal with hard, cold reality problems. This failure to provide realistic answers to very real problems has been the crucial factor in the failure of many University-based school intervention programs.

One final factor, often responsible for the failure of many programs, might be seen as a failure to provide adequate coordination of the program while it was ongoing and/or sufficient follow-up after the program had ended. All too many seemingly perfectly planned programs have floundered miserably during their implementation due primarily to the lack of someone to keep all the loose ends tied together. Even the perfectly planned system will disintegrate rapidly without someone to quickly identify and correct each of its malfunctions. Follow-up activities present the same kinds of difficulties and also carry important implications for future programs. Thus, failure to provide adequate follow-up services can destroy the current program and, at the same time, make people more reticent about future programs.

It seems then, that we have been able to identify six elements of University-based school intervention programs. The absence of any one of these six elements has often led to failure in the past. Although this list is undoubtedly not an exhaustive one, the six factors included do each seem to have some bearing on the success or failure of many University-based school intervention programs.

The BRIDGE Program is a comprehensive year-round psycho-educational program for emotionally disturbed children which was developed jointly by the Institute for Community Psychology of Syracuse University, The Syracuse, New York School District, and the Mental Health Association of Onondaga County. A brief history of the development of this program would indicate that the idea for such a service arose initially late in 1967 with planning for the program really being undertaken by the Institute for Community Psychology. Assistance of major proportion was given both by the Mental Health Association of Onondaga County and, by the Spring of 1969, by the Syracuse School district.

A long series of meetings with both individuals and representatives of agencies concerned with the treatment of emotionally disturbed children culminated, in the early Spring of 1970, in a proposal for development of a year-round psycho-educational program for children with severe emotional disturbance.

The proposed program, which was a collaborate effort of the Institute for Community Psychology and the Mental Health Association of Onondaga County, would focus on children with emotional and behavioral problems who were either having considerable difficulty functioning in the school system or had already been excluded from school participation. With the hope that the support and services offered by this program would enable children to increase their level of school functioning, the program would be directed toward helping these children develop the skills and abilities needed for effective personal and social growth and adjustment.

In an attempt to develop as comprehensive a service as possible, the proposed program would consist of three major components: 1) an after school activities program for children, 2) a parent counseling program during the school year, and 3) a Summer psycho-educational camp program for the children. The entire program would have the over-all focus of helping the child with as many aspects of his life as possible.

In the Spring of 1970, eleven children between the ages of seven and ten were identified and selected from the Syracuse School District, and the BRIDGE Program was officially underway. The first Summer camp season was held at a rented facility in upstate New York during June and July of 1970. Activity-based programs with the children, counseling programs for the family, and coordination with school personnel are the three facets of the BRIDGE Program that have existed on a regular basis since September of 1970.

In many ways, those persons responsible for the planning of the BRIDGE Program have attempted to base it on a model which maximizes the existence of the six crucial characteristics mentioned above and thus minimizes the chances of failure which might stem from their absence. Perhaps an examination of the BRIDGE Program with regard to each of those six factors, will make it possible to evaluate this new model.

First of all, the BRIDGE Program attempted in many ways to involve the community in the program planning stage. The idea for a comprehensive year-round psycho-educational program for emotionally disturbed children was initiated as the result of the clear documentation of that need in a report prepared by the Committee for Emotionally Disturbed Children of the Mental Health Association of Onondaga County in 1967. Following the release of this report, the Institute for Community Psychology began a series of meetings designed to assess community needs in relation to the proposed program. Meetings were held with people concerned with child welfare in both the University and general community. Especially important in this regard were a series of meetings held with the Assistant Superintendent for Pupil Personnel and the Director of Special Education, both of the Syracuse School District. Eventually, through the efforts and cooperation of these two people, the BRIDGE Program was able to set up a direct referral system from teachers and guidance counselors in the Syracuse School District to the staff of the BRIDGE Program.

At the same time, our conversations with elementary school principals, teachers, and social workers were the source of many productive new ideas which we were able to incorporate into the program being planned. Discussions with people employed at innumerable community agencies concerned with child care helped us gather all sorts of information necessary to the proper planning of a program for emotionally disturbed children. By the time the BRIDGE Program had become a reality, our inclusion of community inputs during the planning stages had provided us with both new and important program ideas, as well as with a very broad and influencial base of support.

With regard to the second of the six factors, although the Institute for Community Psychology, the organization primarily responsible for the planning and development of the BRIDGE Program, believes in the need for psychological research and program evaluation, an attempt was made to prevent academic and research interests from assuming a position of primary importance during the planning of the BRIDGE Program. The factor of primary importance throughout all phases of the BRIDGE Program development was the service to be provided for emotionally disturbed children. Training of college students and para-professionals concerned with the care of emotionally disturbed children, as well as research and academic interests were secondary issues. Although they were always mentioned in official proposals they were always regarded as extra attractions to be added to the basic service that the BRIDGE Program would provide.

An attempt was made to maintain this ordering of priorities in informal conversations as well as in official documents. As a result, we were able to enlist the aid of many people who were more than happy to be part of a University-based program focusing primarily on a real community need, rather than a grand scale research project.

As the BRIDGE Program developed, repeated attempts were made to maintain personal contact with those who had provided so much assistance in the early planning stages, and also to initiate contact with still other people who might be at all concerned, in any way, with the project.

As the planning of the BRIDGE Program progressed, our contact with many community people continued. We worked especially closely with the Mental Health Association of Onondaga County, a group of concerned citizens who have volunteered their time and efforts to study and improve mental health services for children, hospitalized patients, discharged patients and the community in general. Our association with this group was an especially productive one, for it was their sincere belief in the need for and appropriateness of our program that led them to help us secure the funds we needed for our first year of operation. Without their aid, the BRIDGE Program might still be in the planning stage.

The extensive nature of our planning period and the degree to which we gathered specific evidence of the need for a comprehensive program for emotionally disturbed children, enabled us both to define a very clear community need and then to develop a service designed to precisely fill that very need. For example, our discussions with people who worked in Syracuse elementary schools every day made us realize that there were many very young children who, due to emotional disturbance, had become so disruptive in class that their status in school could only be seen as "marginal" at this time. Board of Education personnel indicated to us that this problem was prevalent throughout the system. Members of both these groups agreed that the problem was a severe one; that the Syracuse School District was not able to handle it completely by itself; and that the School District, the specific school, the teacher and especially the child himself, were in great need of a service that would offer some assistance for children with these kinds of difficulties.

Innumerable discussions with members of the Mental Health Association, and a long series of meetings with persons concerned with the care of emotionally disturbed children both within the Syracuse University and City of Syracuse communities led us to form certain ideas about the kind of program needed. Through all the above channels, it became clear to us that the program to be offered would have to be psycho-educational in nature, i.e., the children we wanted to serve would need academic help in addition to personal counseling. The program would have to be offered on a year-round basis; too many programs designed to aid children with special needs had suffered from a lack of continuity between the school year and Summer vacation. Finally, it seemed clear that the program to be offered would have to be a very comprehensive one; the children we wanted to serve would need help with many aspects of their lives...we'd have to work with their families and their schools as well as with the children themselves.

With regard to the fifth crucial factor, the BRIDGE Program has attempted but not entirely successfully, to make realistic staffing and funding arrangements. Although it has been possible to staff the BRIDGE Program with a number of talented college students interested in developing their skills in working with emotionally disturbed children, funding plans have not been completed so easily. Thus, although we were able to obtain sufficient donations from individuals and small organizations to support the first year of operation, we have, as of this date, been unsuccessful in securing the needed funds for our next year of operation.

The sixth and final factor concerning the program coordination and follow-up has also been met with partial success. Thus, although we have been able to contact all the schools and the majority of our families, there remain one or two families with whom we have been unable to initiate any meaningful follow-up contact. Coordination of the entire program has been difficult at times, and even though we have made significant improvments in this area, the problems haven't entirely disappeared.

In summation then, the model upon which the BRIDGE Program was built appears to have been reasonably successful in minimizing the chances of failure stemming from the absence of the first four factors. Although some success has also been made with regard to the last two factors, there seem to be considerably more problems still remaining in those two areas. One possible reason for this differential success rate may be that the first four factors are more directly under the control of the administrative staff of the BRIDGE Program, than are the last two factors. The importance of these last two factors can not be over-estimated, however, as the absence of either of them can certainly doom the program to failure. Thus, despite years of hard work, and many successes in working with disturbed children (and thus filling a severe community need), the BRIDGE Program is now faced with ultimate failure due to the absence of only one of the six factors...an inability to secure adequate funds.

With regard to its generalizability to other school intervention programs, the model upon which the BRIDGE Program was based would seem to be an appropriate one. Judging from our experience though, it would be wise for persons attempting to implement such a model, to pay very careful attention to the last two factors. The ability to insure the existence of those two factors would really stack the cards in favor of the proposed program.

5. CONSULTANT TRAINING

The mental health professions have developed now traditional ways of training therapists, diagnosticians, and more recently, case-centered consultants. Dr. Fisher raises the prospect
of training a consultant uniquely in terms of kinds of functions
or roles they will take in their work. Using his own classification of agency-oriented and program-oriented consultation, he
distinguishes between assumptions and the roles appropriate for
each kind of consultation. It follows that training experiences
should vary depending upon the consulting role to be assumed.
Dr. Fisher feels that a mental health background and experience
is most appropriate for agency-oriented consultations while other backgrounds may offer uniquely valuable skills in program
consultation.

In a section of the chapter oriented toward the teacher of
the new consultant, Dr. Fisher raises several points concerning
problems of supervision that are either unique or emphasized in
the training of consultants. For example, he mentions that it
is virtually impossible to obtain firsthand knowledge of a student's initial consultation agency contact. The consequences of
the student's behavior on his supervisor's relationship to the
community are potentially great. Dr. Fisher feels that it is
important, therefore, to have the student maintain a written
record of his activities and to seek "supervision of the supervision."

Dr. Fisher's thoughtful comments should be valuable to both
the student and the instructor in establishing or evaluating
training in community or school consultation.

TRAINING IN SCHOOL CONSULTATION

Lawrence Fisher
University of Rochester

With the increasing number of professionals seeking entrance into local school systems for purposes of "consultation," it is probably safe to say that many school systems are being inundated with the multitude of would-be assisters. Such individuals usually run the gamut from extensively trained professionals interested in providing a variety of services to the school, to the so-called "experts" in a particular approach to mental health, teacher group work or reading curricula.

To say the least, the school principal or central office administrator is now being placed in an extremely precarious position. After years of shouting for help from the community as a whole and from local agencies and university centers in particular, school personnel are in many areas being forced to set up offices for the purpose of coordination and evaluation of consultation services provided by non-school personnel. This has been necessitated in order to develop some level of awareness of which consultants are where, as well as to protect the system from unqualified or unskilled parties. It is unquestionably quite reasonable to state that, in some instances at least, consultants have left the school setting in far worse shape than when they entered it.

This situation again points up the need for more thorough and comprehensive training of mental health professionals in the area of school consultation. To be emphasized in the present paper is not so much the particular requirements regarding competence in content areas, but the necessity for the development of specific consultation skills peculiar to the school setting. There are undoubtedly many individuals who could plan and design a series of in-service programs for teachers, but very few who could gain entree to the school and be **effective** in the delivery of the program. It is the writer's belief that we have for too long focused our attention on the factual issues of program development and application of underlying psychological concepts to the classroom, to the exclusion of adequate training in the subtleties of what a consultant's interpersonal position is within the school setting (Cohen, 1964).

It is therefore of crucial importance for community oriented training programs to include the kinds of opportunities which will provide the trainee with experience in dealing with and assessing the social hierarchy and interpersonal issues within a particular school as well as the broadly based administrative system under which many schools function. The notion here is that the more accurate a consultant is in his appraisal of these issues in the consultation process (Rhodes, 1960), the greater the probability that he will be effective in the delivery of his consultation program. There is nothing like spending two months planning the evaluation of the school's new arithmetic program to find yourself asked to delay implementation for six months or a year because the teachers were so angry at the administrator for bringing you in without consulting them, that they refused to cooperate. Or, to cite another example, there is nothing like being attacked during the middle of your in-service course, because the teachers see you as an arm of the vice-principal who just doubled their lunch room duty schedule.

The opinions and practices espoused in this chapter were developed from our experience in a new school consultation training program established through the Community Mental Health Center of the Department of Psychiatry of the University of Rochester School of Medicine and Dentistry. Briefly, the program is comprised of a multidisciplinary team which focuses substantial amounts of time on the development of school programs based on a variety of school and community issues. For the most part, the programs are quite variable and are established solely through the expressed needs of the school rather than created beforehand and offered to the school as a specific program. While mental health oriented in general, the training program is not solely restricted to the delivery of mental health services but instead, is sufficiently broadly based to include educational, medical, and organizational services as well. In addition, those involved in the program see the school in the context of the community in which it is situated. Therefore, services can often be delivered to a variety of parties serving the school population rather than identifying the school as the sole focus of concern. For example, in one instance a member of our team thought it wise to deliver information and service on drug usage to a newly initiated program outside the school, rather than through the school. Such flexibility has often provided us the opportunity to work on many fronts simultaneously to tackle a community based problem.

In the following paragraphs, I would like to present two models of consultation which have particular relevance for training. Next will be a discussion of the applicability of the models to a variety of training issues, followed by a discussion of additional concerns in the supervision of trainee consultants. Last, I would like to present a number of unresolved supervisory issues which we have found particularly troublesome. All of these issues represent the kinds of problems one must begin to face in the development of a new consultation training program.

MODELS OF CONSULTATION

One of the major concerns of the consultation training supervisor is whether or not his trainee is sufficiently prepared to handle his forthcoming experience in the community. Part of this concern is due to the lack of a clear way of relating the kind of consultation program to the level of training required by the consultant. Although there are many useful classification systems in the literature (Bindman, 1969), none, to the author's knowledge, is successfully linked to a consultation training orientation which includes both content oriented and interpersonal issues. In order to meet this need insofar as our own program is concerned, we have devised a scheme which proved quite useful in aiding in decisions regarding the placement of trainees in programs commensurate with their level and area of training.

As conceptualized, the classification scheme breaks school consultation down into two broad models: agency-oriented and program-oriented consultation. These two models should be seen as a re-working of Caplan's (1970) useful four model system of client-centered case consultation, consultee-centered case consultation, program-centered administrative consultation, and consultee-centered administrative consultation. Roughly, what we have called program consultation is a combination of Caplan's client-centered case consultation and program-centered administrative consultation. What we have designated as agency consultation is a mixture of Caplan's consultee- centered case consultation and consultee-centered administrative consultation. To follow is a brief description of the philosophy of each of the models, the position of the consultant, and the underlying assumptions of the approach. Following, will be a demonstration of the usefulness of the scheme with regard to a variety of issues of concern to the consultation supervisor.

Agency Oriented Consultation

Philosophy. This form of consultation reflects the consultant's interest in entering the school with no preconceived ideas

as to the type ofprogram he wishes to initiate. The consultant enters the school, spends a substantial amount of time and
energy assessing the structure of the school (usually in the
teacher's lounge over coffee), and with the school personnel,
he develops a role for himself based upon the particular interests, problems and attributes of that school. In essence,
the consultant acts as a facilitator insofar as he assists the
school in determining in what way he can make best use of his
time in the school. He serves to help the organization (1) to
become better able to meets its responsibilities, both internally and externally; (2) to advance its skills in handling
educational and administrative issues; and (3) to develop new
programs to meet new needs.

   Position of the Consultant. Under this framework the consultant positions himself as an objective observer who is not
caught up in the internal workings and politics of the system
or supersystem. He should see himself as a problem-specifier,
a critical reviewer, and a diagnostic evaluator. **He is never
a problem-solver.** His goal is always to help the agency to
solve its own problems on its own terms. He acts as a facilitator or catalyst for such action. He brings nothing with him
to the agency but the agency's request for assistance and his
desire to help. He emphasizes himself as a person and not an
institution or consultation agency. He presents himself honest-
ly and fosters feelings of understanding and helpfulness. He
is never overtly directive.

   Assumptions. The model implies a long-term commitment
aimed at agency change. Since the goal is service to the agency
rather than to the population it serves, the role assumes some
form of structural alteration.

   The model assumes a component of action in an effort to
foster change. This aspect, however, is geared to well-thought-
through development of services rather than to change for change's sake alone.

   The model assumes detailed assessment by the consultant
of the possibilities for the effectiveness of his services and
his willingness and honesty to bow out if he sees himself unable to effect change or service.

   The model assumes a commitment to a given philosophy with
the willingness to stick to that philosophy even in the face of
stress and confrontation. The idea here is to come in with a
specific mode of operating in an effort to provide some structure to the consultant's functioning. Dropping this or any
other model in mid-stream often creates the risk of losing one's

perspective. It has been our experience that agencies can be
quite seductive in this respect, such that one can keep tabs
on his own functioning only by assuming a philosophy and stick-
ing to it. This notion begins to make more sense in terms of
helping the consultant realistically assess which tasks he can
deal with and which tasks he cannot. This approach does not
imply rigidity. It simply helps the consultant create an
approach for self-direction and to use it as a tool to meet
needs.

Program Oriented Consultation

Philosophy. In this model, the consultant enters the
school district or individual school for the sole purpose of
initiating a specific program. To illustrate, such programs
could center around drug education for students, classroom
management issues, specific program evaluation, etc. The point
to be made in this model is that the consultant has a given
interest and he offers his skills and experiences to the school
around a particular theme.

Position of the Consultant. He is seen as an expert in a
given area and he assumes the responsibility for providing expert and well-defined service. He avoids getting involved in
other than those services for which he has contracted. While
program-oriented consultation can be used as an introduction to
an agency-oriented program, the consultant in this situation
must always be on guard against the pitfalls of accepting new
roles which extend beyond his initial contract. In this sense,
then, the consultant fills a "problem solver" role insofar as
he provides recommendations, procedures, and techniques around
specific issues.

Assumptions. The model assumes a short-term or time-speci-
fied commitment around specific issues and goals which are de-
lineated beforehand. In addition, it assumes that the consultant has some understanding of the system he is entering before
the formal program is initiated. Although not as much detail
and specification of the school's functioning is required in
this approach as is required in the agency-oriented model, this
is not to say that efforts in this direction are not often profitable and frequently crucial.

A Merging of Extremes

The program and agency consultation models mentioned above
must be viewed as two extremes on a continuum of approaches.
These seem to run from the more directive to the more open-ended,

but as far as it is possible to assess, there are few consultation roles that fit exactly into these extreme categories.
Most are somewhere in between. Being realistic, many consultants assume some of both roles in that over time the agency
consultant becomes defined within a given program, and the program consultant may be asked to broaden his base to include a
variety of other functions. It should be emphasized that these
models are useful only as a guideline for **approaching** an agency
or school, instituting contact, and entering the initial stage
of the consultation process. The models may not be as useful
after programs are underway and people are freer and more trust-
ing of each other to discuss needs openly.

Applications to Training

There has been a time-honored controversy regarding the
level of graduate training required before training in psychotherapy can begin. A similar, but perhaps more germane, controversy exists in consultation training. At what level of
training should the student be introduced to the school as a
consultant? A second concern is related to the students' area
of training i.e., clinical psychology, school psychology, experimental psychology, etc. What kind of professional training and background is required as a prerequisite for consultation training?

It has been quite apparent that teachers and school personnel in general have become rather sophisticated individuals
with often extensive experience in working with a variety of
consultants. Many urban schools have exposed their teachers
to a variety of nontraditional experiences from sensitivity
training to special in-service programs utilizing experimental
instructional methods. The revolution in education has not
remained with the so-called upper crust, but has filtered down
to almost all classroom teachers. (In some schools one must
be careful even in the use of the term, "classroom.") Such
sophisticated individuals will be especially sensitive to the
naive consultant who is entering not only an area of little
experience, but in some cases an area outside the "general"
domain of his training. The question must be raised as to the
appropriateness of training non-child and non-**mental** health
oriented professionals in this area.

The agency-program dichotomy can provide substantial assistance in relating to these issues. Because agency-oriented
consultation often requires a variety of rather advanced observational skills, as well as content oriented knowledge, the
introduction of a relatively naive undergraduate or graduate

student into this role can often prove disastrous. In effect, such a placement requires the young, inexperienced student to thoroughly assess a huge, dynamic, multi-faceted, interpersonal system, and to handle himself and his reactions, at times, with the skill of an expert therapist. Amorphousness and lack of structure may also prove debilitating to the young student, who at least at the outset should have some framework within which to function.

We have made the general decision that agency-oriented consultation should only be assumed by trainees at advanced levels of training. In addition, their background should fall within the mental health area. This generally would include psychiatry, psychology, and social work, although individuals with group experiences from education, sociology, and related areas would also be included. In essense, we have decided that formal clinical expertise is required of any individual who aspires to tackle the issues involved in agency-oriented consultation.

A limited number of agency-oriented programs have been assumed by several of our Child Psychiatry Fellows and Child Psychology Postdoctoral Fellows. The details are often program-specific, but, generally speaking, requests from a given school or pre-school are funneled directly to the trainee. These requests are received in light of past experience with the school and an initial meeting is called between the trainee and the school to explore program possibilities. In most situations the request is secondary to the need, and often the real and more more meaningful issues become subtley apparent to the sensitive trainee. Promising consideration of the request pending staff time, etc., the trainee returns to discuss the experience and, given the pooled opinion and experience of all staff members, a decision is made as to whether or not the trainee should proceed. It should be emphasized that the trainee carries the consultation from the first contact on. Although a request may come through a staff member, the initial contact is made by the trainee alone, so as to provide him with a supervised experience of independently entering a school and initiating a relationship.

Although problems with this approach are apparent, it has proven useful insofar as it provides the trainee with an opportunity for independent functioning quite similar to the kind he will face when he leaves the university setting and initiates his own programs. In addition, the supervision enables the trainee to step back and see what he is being asked to do, how the messages are being delivered, and by whom. In one instance, a request around a classroom management meeting for teachers ended up as a series of group meetings between teachers and administrative personnel, eventually leading to substantial changes in the administrative organization of the pre-school. The trainee consultant, in this instance, was not tied to the delivery of a specific program and was able to flexibly adapt to the needs of the school as perceived by the appropriate individuals within that school. Holding off his decision and making use of his supervision enabled him to better assess what were obviously a series of multiple and mixed messages.

Under the program-oriented consultation rubric, however, individuals from a wide variety of backgrounds and levels of training can be most effective if given responsible and appropriate supervision. Although it is not entirely clear as yet whether an individual with limited training and experience can function in such a setting without others directly involved, such issues are presently under study. With our limited experiences so far, however, we would see no reason why individuals with reasonable levels of maturity and interpersonal sensitivity could not operate as primary, program-oriented consultants once a role was specifically defined and a decision made to go ahead. A good procedure in this regard is for the supervisor to make the initial contact and to assist until the role definition seems reasonably acceptable to school personnel and consultant. At that point, the supervisor can withdraw from the scene, as far as the school is concerned, remaining intimately involved with the new primary consultant. In addition, we have found that the more inexperienced the trainee consultant is in formal intervention programs, the more circumscribed and well-delineated his consultation role should be. For example, given a choice between a drug education program for high school students and a role geared toward the organization of high school students around their student government, we would be most inclined to place the inexperienced trainee in the drug program.

Briefly, let me now present a few examples of the kinds of roles persons in training from a variety of areas can play in what we broadly conceptualize as mental health oriented programs. All of the following fall within the general category of program consultation as opposed to agency consultation.

A group of medical students, concerned about the rising drug usage by high school students, came up with the idea of providing a series of drug education programs to a number of local schools. With guidance from a number of medical school faculty around possible approaches and preparation as to what to expect from the students themselves, these medical students delivered the program to a number of suburban and inner city schools. The program consisted of a number of formal meetings and informal group discussions with interested students. Although its effectiveness is difficult to assess, the attempt did offer relevant information to large segments of the community. In addition, it enabled these medical students to taste some of the rewards and frustrations of working in a non-clinical setting. Their comments following the experience were most encouraging. Some of them felt that they had begun to see the "relevance" of their expertise to the broader issues facing society as a whole. The issue of "relevance" is by no means irrelevant in facing our responsibilities as educators.

Another example has to do with an experience with experimental and developmental psychology graduate students and the need for program evaluation by a variety of community agencies and schools. Although still in the preliminary stages, the program seeks to use the research design, statistical, and assessment skills of these students to deal with the realistic, concrete problems of field research and evaluation. To be specific, we have been asked to assess the impact of a number of programs of pre-school and day care centers on the children and families they serve. With supervision, such students can play a major role in the development of agency-specific assessment procedures and the creation of reasonable and workable research designs. At the same time, these students will be faced with the real problems of non-laboratory environments and lack of classically required control groups. These students will be also challenged by the difficult task of dealing with pre-school educators, laymen from the community, and parents. Such an experience often forces the student to translate his academic jargon into workable terms understandable to the community at large. Here, too, the relevance of academic training to community problems becomes apparent.

Further examples of program consultation utilizing individuals from many disciplines may also be cited: having college and graduate student secondary majors design and possibly deliver curricula on mental health, sex education, or drug abuse programs; having sociology students prepare and coordinate administration of procedures designed to assess the reaction of a given community to the introduction of a new school program; having psychiatry residents work with individuals or groups of public health nurses on mental health issues as related to the children of a given school.

Again, the point to be remembered is that a consultation program to the formal school environment or to the agencies which handle the variety of needs of children in a particular community served by one or more schools, can be devised to include students of varying levels of training from a variety of different disciplines. Such program-oriented experiences should be coordinated through the primary mental health professional,

but in many cases, depending upon the interpersonal sensitivity
and sophistication of the individual student, substantial responsibility for the program can rest with the student himself.
In many of these programs, supervision must be shared between
the mental health professional and the individual student's de-
partmental affiliation; the former relating to the operation of
the program and the latter assisting in the technical details of
the specific tasks at hand.

ISSUES AROUND SUPERVISION AND TRAINING

In both the program and agency models described above, the
most difficult task is making the initial step of entering the
school, diagnosing the problem, and establishing an agreed-upon
role.   There are undoubtedly a multitude of issues to be faced
in this reward: decisions related to entree through the teachers' organization, through the administration, or the school
board; determining which requests for help are realistic and
which are not; deciding whether you are being "used" or manipu-
lated for this or that faction; determining who can be relied
upon and who cannot; and most of all, establishing an atmosphere
of trust between the consultant and the school personnel.   Because these issues set the tune, so to speak, of the entire consultation relationship, the manner and technique of entree, as
broadly defined, is seen as crucial to the total course of the
experience.   It is clearly the most difficult and challenging
part of both agency- and program-oriented consultation and an
area in which the most training and experience are required.

With this in mind, we have sought to provide each advanced
trainee with at least one experience in which an entree must be
created and implemented.   This procedure can be seen in marked
contrast to more traditional practices where the structure of
the consultation is arranged beforehand by the supervisor, and
the trainee consultant fills the slot already defined and agreed
upon.   Although this older procedure has much to recommend it,
it does not provide experience in the most critical area of the
consultation experience: namely, the entree into the school and
the definition of the consultation role.

In making use of both program- and agency-oriented consultation models, the role of the supervisor is both crucial and
precarious.   Regardless of which trainee fills a given slot and
in what capacity he serves the school, it is most often on the
supervisor's name, contacts, and prestige that the opening becomes available.   It may be a formal written request to the supervisor, a call by the supervisor seeking openings, or a call
by the trainee in the supervisor's program to the particular
school.   In any case, the supervisor's name and institution become directly or indirectly attached to the program.   In any

case, the supervisor's name and institution become directly or
indirectly attached to the program.   In any moderate-size training program, interest from a number of schools is sought for
training purposes, but very frequently service is not delivered.
This is often due to program preferences, trainee interests,
etc.   This can easily place the supervisor and his institution
in a bad light, since at one point the word is out that he is
soliciting openings and at another point he must refuse at least
some schools.   Since schools seem to frequently know which consultant is where in the area, it is easy to see why some individuals feel they were "passed up" for another school.   Although
irrational in many respects, this situation often generates
considerable amounts of hostility which is frequently directed
to the supervisor and his program.

The supervisor can also be the target of considerable hostility even in the schools in which service is already being
delivered.   As stated, the supervisor and his program is in
some way identified with each of his trainee's programs.   It
would stand to reason, then, that if a major altercation arose
between a school and the assigned trainee consultant, the
supervisor and sometimes his separate and independent programs
may come under question.   Communication among schools is surprisingly extensive when it comes to "grape-vine gossip."   When
the word circulates that Supervisor X's trainee badly mishandled
the program, issues of trust and confidence may come to the fore
in many of Supervisor X's own programs.   It has been our experience that a supervisor has a tremendous personal stake in the
outcome of his trainee's programs, above and beyond his expected teaching commitment.

This situation has both positive and negative aspects.   It
has led in most cases to an intense and beneficial supervisor-
trainee relationship in which both parties spend substantial
amounts of time reviewing the development of the program.   The
commitment is positive and is certainly more than simply "going
through the motions."

Its negative characteristics, however, warrant concern.
Because of the almost mandatory commitment by the supervisor,
there can arise some tendency for him to overextend his influence on the trainee.   This can occur not so much as a way to insure a worthwhile experience for the trainee, but to protect
himself, either in terms of his own programs or in terms of his
own need to have the community see him as the primary consultant.
To this extent, supervision of the trainees' consultation experience can lead to many more subjective influences than in most
other activities where supervision is required.   The very fact
that the supervisor has more than a purely educational stake in
the trainees' experience can, to varying degrees, reduce the

supervisor's level of objectivity. In extreme instances, it could truly be a case of the blind leading the blind.

To protect against such possible circumstances, and to insure a worthwhile experience for the trainee, we have sought to frequently add a third or fourth member to the supervisory conference, or to require all trainees to attend regular staff meetings. During such meetings, each program is discussed in detail with colleagues who have indirect knowledge of a variety of community programs. These kinds of procedures have been initiated in an effort to use the extra parties as objective, interested individuals who can help separate and clarify some of the complexities that can arise in areas where both supervisor and trainee have more than a passing interest. There have been several incidents where a few comments by an interested third colleague has brought to light issues that were obscured by a variety of reality and personal factors.

Concurrent with the standard supervisory meetings and staff review conferences, we have also requested that each trainee keep a detailed written record of each and every contact between himself and the school. We have emphasized a need for detailed reporting of the consultations so that as many of the issues relating to role development can be recorded. This practice serves a variety of purposes. First, it forces the trainee to consider, in detail, the actions he took while at the school, the reactions of others who were in his presence, the changes that may be occurring in the way he is perceived, the comfort he feels in being in this school, etc. Such a practice, then, requires the trainee consultant to review the entire experience and consider the kinds of alternatives he may have before him.

The second and equally important role of the written record is to provide a recorded history of a program from start to finish. We have found this kind of document of unlimited value in preparing the next trainee consultant who enters the school. Each new consultant, then, has a written record of the development of each program as well as a description of those approaches that were useful and those that were not within a given school. Surprisingly, we have found very little trainee resistance in this practice. It appears that it becomes very difficult to not see the value of the written history after reading a detailed account of what has occurred the previous year in the school one is about to enter. These documents usually do not end up as case reports but as a series of sequential notes about the development of a program.

UNRESOLVED ISSUES IN SUPERVISION

Along with psychotherapy supervision, there remains a number of complex issues in consultation training that lead one to seek new approaches and teaching techniques. These issues are raised here not in an attempt to present what may be preceived as the unsolvable, but to bring attention to some of the realistic problems that must be kept in awareness during the development of a training program, or indeed, during any kind of individual supervision.

Supervision of the consultation process is by the trainee's report only. Unlike psychotherapy where direct observation, or audio and video tapes are frequently used, the consultation supervisor receives information only through the medium of the trainee's verbal report.[1] If the trainee is insensitive or unaware of an undercurrent or possible manipulation, it is very difficult for the supervisor to point this up and deal with it appropriately. So the supervisor must remain intently aware of possible inconsistencies, unanswered questions, and subtle experiences reported by the trainee; in effect, to conceptualize what might have occurred given his knowledge of the situation. This can often lead to undirected speculation that can add more diffuseness to an already unstructured situation, and the danger of running to the extreme of questioning everything is present. Supervisors must remain aware of the dangers at both ends of the continuum; overspeculation from insufficient data and taking the verbal report at face value only.

One possibility we are beginning to explore, in this regard, is placing two trainees in the same school at the same time. While this procedure can often create some unnecessary confusion, if roles are defined clearly, the two consultants can often provide a useful check and balance system. For example, one trainee may devise a program for teachers around a given issue while the second consultant works with the administration. Since both trainees are in a position to gather large quantities of data concerning the school's functioning, they can use each other for support as well as information sharing. Coordination of functioning is, of course, crucial and great care must be exercised to maintain role definition. This procedure can reduce, however, the possibility of inaccurate observations going unrecognized for it adds an additional observer to the school.

Another area of concern is related to the difficulty in assessing the effectiveness of a trainee in a given role. Al-

---

[1]We have experimented in the use of audio tape recordings of consultant-consultee interactions but have not found their use feasible at the time when they would have been most useful. Although recordings have been obtained after the programs were in operation, we have had little success in taping the crucial, initial stages of the consultation process.

though it is often difficult to determine the outcome of almost any consultation relationship, when the training component
is added the issue can easily become extremely complicated.
Yet we are all required, at one level or another, to render an
assessment of the trainees we supervise. What criteria do we
use to accurately indicate the trainee's behavior in the consultation role? We cannot easily measure change in school functioning as a result of the consultation contact; requests for
additional help from the school do not necessarily indicate productive growth; and lastly, since most of our information comes
from the trainee himself, we have few if any external measures
to rely on. Most of us depend, I would imagine, on a series of
rather unspecifiable factors such as "impression," "opinion,"
or "feeling." The distance between the trainee's actual on-the-
job behavior and the supervisor's impression of that behavior
is far greater in the area of consultation than in most other
domains where supervision is utilized. In cases where undergraduates are involved and official grades must be entered, one
can give all A's or set up a pass-fail system. But we must
constantly be aware of the ways we assess each trainee and the
pitfalls of relying too heavily upon subjective impressions--
especially when many of our own programs are involved.

Although the models discussed above can be useful tools for
aiding in trainee placement, they are not panaceas for the ambiguity of the area. There is always the danger that programs
will be altered in mid-stream, for reality or non-reality
events can intrude on the program's development. Any number of
other issues can cause one to ponder whether the trainee is e-
quipped to handle the new turn of events. Sometimes it is necessary to remove a trainee from a program when issues change and
problems are re-focused. Often, these changes have little to do
with the trainee himself, but the experience provides understandable frustration to both the trainee and the agency or
school. For example, staff changes or budget cuts can force
programs out of existence or substantially change the orientation of a given program. Such realities force the consultant
to alter his goals radically and to re-negotiate a new contract
with the school. He may have to halt his assistance to the a-
gency's program development group and focus on the staff's feelings of anger and resentment around the unexpected turn of e-
vents. If he is an undergraduate or otherwise inexperienced
individual, he may not have the skills necessary to undertake
this second function. In such a situation, the trainee consultant may either have to be replaced or the program at least will
have to be temporarily halted. The supervisor must always be
aware of such possibilities and have some kind of contingency
plan available if the situation warrants. In most cases, school
staff or agency personnel are aware of the possibility of radical program change well in advance of the actual implementation

date and it is the supervisor's responsibility to stay abreast of the situation in order to increase his chances of having an appropriate contingency plan available.

Another major issue has to do with the rather substantial time commitments required for effective training. With enlarging departments, it often seems that everyone is seeking a slice of the trainees' time and frequently, being a new area, consultation programs pick up a remaining hour or two here and there. Often, these hours do not even closely correspond with, for example, the elementary school teachers' meeting time. In effect, then, the supervisor must be a party in rearranging a substantial portion of the trainee's schedule to meet the requirements of a staff meeting in a nearby school. It can frequently be difficult to justify such a move considering the realities of scheduling in a university setting.

The length of a given program is often crucial to the selection of the trainee who will eventually fill the role. Consultation and intervention programs do not often meet the schedules of the university's term or semester system. Sometimes, a full year or more is required in a given program and a legitimate issue arises as to what kind of student can commit that amount of time in a single program. Obviously there are very few, but there are some: special undergraduate students, psychiatric residents, and some graduate students who have identified a particular interest early in their training. In the majority of instances, however, most programs run several months--most likely across academic semesters--and plans can be made to include numbers of students. So, although time factors must be accounted for, they can be made in many seemingly impossible cases where outlined programs can be presented beforehand to the appropriate faculty members.

Throughout the course of this discussion, I have focused on the supervisor's, trainee's, and institution's problems without mentioning the problems of the school in accepting and working with a trainee consultant. The question may be asked, how do school personnel react to an individual in training acting as a consultant in their school? In general, our experience has been quite favorable, for it depends not on trainee vs. "full" consultant issues, but upon the consultant himself--whoever he may be. Although apprehensive at first, many schools accept the trainee openly when they see he is honest as to what he can and cannot do. Such factors as unpretentiousness, not "coming on too strong," respect for school personnel as fellow professionals, and willingness to acknowledge inadequacies and gaps in knowledge place the consultant on the level of a real person, not an individual above and beyond it all who has all the "answers."

The acceptance of a trainee consultant into the school can also be facilitated by arranging the initial contract as a two-way process. For the delivery of service to the school, the school agrees to provide the institution with a training experience for a qualified person. In some cases, the school agrees to fulfill its part of the bargain by doing more than providing such an experience. In a pre-school consultation program, for example, one of our child psychiatry fellows struck up a profitable arrangement. Interested in the behavior of three-year-olds, he agreed to lead a two-hour weekly meeting of parent group leaders if the school would allow him to observe young children in class and to discuss what had occurred with the teachers afterward. This two-way contract bolstered the school's self-esteem to think that it had something to teach a child psychiatrist. It was as if the agreement declared that the consultant had some skills that could benefit the school, and the school had some skills that could benefit the consultant. Such mutual respect led to a very satisfying experience for both parties.

CONCLUSION

Gerald Caplan, in his recent book, makes a point which bares closely on the present discussion.

> ". . . if students are too closely supervised and if they are spoon fed by being presented only with safe and simple artificial training exercises, their learning will be inhibited because of lack of challenge. It is important that they be involved in doing a real job and not in "make-work"; and that they learn, particularly in consultation, to prepare for the unexpected. This means that the practicum should, as much as possible, be a segment of a real-life experience, with a minimum of ivory-tower academic preciousness." (1970, p.339)

In moving our training programs in this direction, we have concurrently developed a multitude of new problems and this chapter has attempted to focus on some of them. The more independence we provide for our trainees, the larger the variety of disciplines we draw from, and the less experience our trainees have, the more we will be faced with the problems of placement level, supervisor subjectivity, trainee evaluation concerns, etc.

Although it has become quite clear that advanced levels of training are required for a variety of consultation programs, there are a substantial number of roles that can be filled by individuals with little experience from diverse disciplinary backgrounds. Acknowledging the difficulties of supervision, role definition, and confidence levels, individuals with little or no mental health or consultation experience can be effectively trained to fill a useful role in the school.

From past experience, these kinds of training opportunities seem to develop not out of plan, but out of opportunity. While sometimes useful, this state of affairs cannot offer us any substantial knowledge and skill in developing techniques and procedures to train the growing numbers of interested students from a variety of backgrounds. We must take a closer look at our training programs in this area and develop experiences for our people not necessarily based on tradition, but centered on meaningfulness for both school and trainee, and related directly to the kinds of skills which need to be developed for effective consultation in a school setting.

REFERENCES

Bindman, A. The clinical psychologist as mental health consultant. In A. Bindman and A. Spiegel (Eds.), *Perspectives in Community Mental Health*. Chicago: Aldine Publishing Company, 1969.

Caplan, G. *The Theory and Practice of Mental Health Consultation*. New York: Basic Books, 1970.

Cohen, L. *Consultation: A Community Mental Health Method*. Atlanta Ga.: Southern Regional Education Board, 1964.

Rhodes, W. Training in community mental health consultation. Paper read in symposium on problems of mental health consultation in the schools. American Psychological Association, Chicago, 1960.

6. ORGANIZING INTERVENTION

A freelance consultant to a school is constrained neither by his job description nor by ever-expanding service demands and obligations. In contrast, consultants operating out of a community mental health center often are faced with making compromise allocations of personal resources to meet as many demands as possible within the catchment area. Dr. Stein discusses the value of "management by objectives," as a way to help a community mental health center develop an effective school intervention program. This approach stresses the importance of clarification of goals, development of policies, and the process of goal-setting. Management by objectives also calls for assessment of already present services.

As desirable as it might seem, it would be inefficient and largely ineffective to allow mental health staffs to work as they choose, when they choose, and where they choose, without regard for comprehensive planning, goal-setting and management. It is not always self-evident that the amount of time spent by health professionals in bureaucratic organizational meetings, structure development, policy setting, planning and the like, is worthwhile or useful. However, Dr. Stein argues that without such planning and organization, many of the best intentions and high aims of mental health professionals will be frustrated. Failure can result either from internal dissesion within the mental health organization or from services unmatched or inaccurately understood community needs.

Readers working in a large organizational setting should consider Dr. Stein's example for its suggestion on applying management principles to development and operation of an effective school intervention program.

A COMMUNITY-SCHOOL INTERVENTION MODEL OF

A COMMUNITY MENTAL HEALTH CENTER

David D. Stein
Yeshiva University

Every comprehensive community mental health center (CMHC) must come to grips with developing a framework for the planning and operation of its services. Under the mandate of the prime CMHC Act of 1963, each Center must possess at least five essential components (Inpatient, Outpatient, Partial Hospitalization, Emergency and Consultation and Education) and has the option of adding any or all of five more components (Diagnostics, Rehabilitation, Precare and Aftercare, Training and Research and Evaluation).

As a result of these stipulations, a CMHC offers a wide variety of services. It deals with numerous staffing problems especially in terms of integrating and coordinating professional and non-professional staff. And, it attempts to develop a means for relating to community residents, groups and agencies at the same time that it must grapple with its own organizational structure and staff functioning.

In the initial conceptualization of the comprehensive CMHC, little consideration was given to feasible models of administrative structure or to appropriate philosophies of management. As a result, most management positions were filled by professionals with little if any experience as managers (Glasscote and Gudeman, 1969). They tended to enact their roles as either benevolent clinicians who allowed their respective staffs to carry out their responsibilities as they saw fit, or as relatively authoritarian chiefs who exploited and perverted the mental health hierarchial structure of psychiatrist on top and non-professional at the bottom. The CMHC as an organization had little sense of direction, of overall goals and objectives, of policies, of community priorities, of long range plans, or of internal linking of various units and services. The basic guidelines from the

CMHC Act afforded minimal support once the "show got on the road."

The Sound View-Throgs Neck CMHC was no exception to this rule and after about four years of operation, it is still plagued by many of these problems. During the last two years, however, the Center has begun a process of administration which attempts to deal with the aformentioned issues and the thrust of this chapter then is directed toward explicating how a relatively rational mechanism of planning and operation is applied to the Center's Community-School Programs (CSP). (The admittedly inelegant title, CSP, was nevertheless decided upon because it encompassed the notion that the community was part of the school system and simultaneously differentiated this service from traditional ones that are based on agreements made between professional agencies and schools proper).

Our CMHC, in 1969, stimulated by its then Associate Director and now Acting Director, moved toward a model of administration based on Drucker's (1954) Management by Objectives (MBO). This philosophy of management has been applied rather successfully to profit making businesses and organizations, and, in addition, has proved successful in the social service field, as for example with the YMCA. This approach basically calls for a systematic assessment, development and working through of organizational goals, objectives and policies, etc. by actually involving all levels of personnel in the process. It is cyclical in nature allowing for the repetition of necessary steps as periodic review is called for. Changing conditions within the organization and without are anticipated and incorporated in the MBO plan.

At about this same time, I took over as the Center's Diredtor of CSP, after spending almost two years as a staff psychologist whose primary responsiblities were around school consulta ion in the Consultation and Education Service. Although the Center has yet to formally and completely follow the MBO procedure, it is moving in that direction by modifying and grafting on certain ideas and concepts from the basic MBO scheme. Even through this discontinuous process, many key staff members have developed the spirit of MBO in their planning. Thus, what follows is an account of how the Center has attempted to develop an intervention model for its CSP. This model includes six steps which follow pretty much in order. One of our aims for the near future is to refine this model and incorporate it with a formal MBO approach.

A GENERAL COMMUNITY DEVELOPMENT FRAME OF REFERENCE

Within the mandate of the federal legislation for community mental health centers to provide adequate patient care, the purpose of the SVTN-CMHC is to aid in the development of the SVTN community's capacity to care for its mentally ill, prevent mental illness, cope with illness-producing tensions and become a stable and vital community. This multi-purpose mandate stresses community development and the role of the community in dealing directly with many of its problems. Therefore, the general framework for CSP took the following form: (quoted from the Center's CSP Policy)

"Center policy for Community-School Programs derives out of the general community development framework for the Center. Emphasis shall be placed on aiding the community-school system to develop capacities to care for both children with problems and organizations which foster unhealthy environments for education and human development. This implies that whenever possible, interventions will be made at a system or sub-system level so that individuals will be aided by the benefit producing effects of healthy systems. For children, however, who are in need of intensive psychiatric care, SVTN-CMHC shall provide the appropriate services or arrange for them to be made available.

Within the mandate of the CMHCs Acts, to provide consultation and education to the community, SVTN-CMHC views the schools, the children, the parents and the community-at-large as part of a basic system. Efforts to intervene through consultation and treatment shall derive from regular ongoing contact with the elements constituting this system. Particular concern is given to developing parents and the organizations which represent them so that they may take a more active role in the educational process of their children."

This framework allowed for a relatively comprehensive approach to community-school problems because it encompassed system level interventions that would presumably lead to the improved mental health of individuals while simultaneously providing direct care at secondary and tertiary prevention levels. It should be noted that this seemingly benevolent resolution of opposing notions for a basic framework came about only after two years of heated debate over the general thrust of the program. Many staff members opted for traditional psychiatric care of children or case-centered consultation with teachers and guidance counselors while others advocated systems-level interventions highlighted by organizational development approaches to principals, other administrators and school department chairmen.

MECHANISMS FOR ASSESSMENT OF COMMUNITY NEEDS AND PROBLEMS

Although the Center had been in operation for two years in 1969, no truly systematic assessment of community needs and problems had been undertaken. Ad hoc task forces had been set up to accumulate data in a variety of mental health areas, but little was done with these data once they were collected. At this time, however, staff agreed that it would be necessary to bring together whatever data were on hand and in addition, to collect further relevent information.

By this time, one of my colleagues with some help from me, had done considerable work in organizing a grass roots community group whose focus was on school-related matters. The need for such a group grew out of a nucleus of 10-15 responsive community residents who felt that serious problems existed primarily in the public schools and that the local School Board was not responsive to their needs and wishes. Through the development of this group, which expanded rapidly to about 30-40 core people, with a peripheral membership of over 100, we were able to discern a multitude of community-school problems from the community residents themselves. Although we had become aware of some of these problems through our school consultation program, only the full dimensions of these concerns became evident when expressed by the members of this group. Clearly, narcotics, dissatisfaction with teaching practices--both academic and interpersonal (i.e.- subtle and overt forms of prejudice toward minority group children), and general school-community relations were the top concerns. In addition, overcrowding, questionable curriculae, and the need for more minority group teachers and indigenous non-professionals to be employed by schools, among others, were popular issues. Thus, this grass roots group played a major role in helping the Center assess community needs and problems.

In addition, we talked informally to many Parent Associations (PA) members, to the local School Board, to school personnel, and to the Board of Education's District office staff. (Incidentally, in this area, almost all parent organizations exclude teachers, as contrasted to the traditional PTA). Our own staff members supplied us with considerable information on the basis of their regular consultation experiences in schools.

Finally, we talked to members of the Center's newly formed Community Advisory Boards whose job it has become to advise us as to which schools and/or PAs we should give the highest priority for intensive services.

With the cooperation of the Center's Urban Planner, we collected data on the percentage of overcrowding in each school, the ethnic breakdown of students by school, the number and kinds of supplemental educational and mental health programs currently operating in schools and the type of clinical coverage provided by the Bureau of Child Guidance whose function is to give mental health services as the official arm of the Board of Education. Representatives from other school-related agencies such as the Bureau of Attendance and the Public Health Nurses gave us data on their case loads and the kind of problems they confronted.

INTERLINKAGE OF FOUR MENTAL HEALTH PROGRAM AREAS: CLINICAL, COMMUNITY ORGANIZATION, COMMUNITY-SCHOOLS, HUMAN SERVICE NETWORK

After all of these data were amassed, a formidable task which took roughly two to four months, we sat down and allocated the problems to the various units and services within the Center. It should be noted the CSPs are offered through one of the Center's three line Divisions, Community Services. So allocation to units and services occured almost entirely within this Division. As further clarification, Community Services consists of six services, three of which are multi-purpose mental health teams each serving a separate geographic area within the Center's total catchment area. Three additional Staff services were created to deal with agencies and concerns that cut across the geographic boundaries: one coordinates all Center activities in and around the primary and secondary schools (Central CSP); another maintains a skill bank and works with various agencies toward the creation of a formal network of human services (Central Human Service Network); and the third deals with community organization issues (Central Community Organization).

One constraint we operated under was that these out-patient services, which offer agency, school and community consultation in addition to direct patient care, were originally formed to service a geographically defined sub-catchment area of the community. Hence, the problems and needs of the entire catchment area were allocated to all relevant units and services even though the actual distribution of problems in the community was more heavily concentrated in certain areas. Had we begun this process when the Center was opened in 1967, we would have better structured our internal organization to reflect the distribution of problems in the community.

Basically, each of the three multi-purpose services covers 5-10 public and parochial schools and each service had 1-5 staff members who spent part or all of their time working in CSP. Consultation to school related agencies was handled jointly by Central CSP and Central HSN. Narcotics problems fell primarily to Central Community Organization. Organization of school oriented community groups was assigned to both Central C.O. and Central CSP. Consultation to individual schools was handled by the staff in each of the three multi-purpose services. Now that our child psychiatric program has expanded, the clinicians treat children individualy or in family therapy. Hospitalization of children is being worked out between the Center on the one hand and the City and State Hospitals within the medical college complex on the other. Funding information and future program development for CSP is handled by myself with heavy in-house consultation from the Center's Research and Development Division. The area of mental retardation is dealt with both by special school system staff and through selected help by the newly formed Rose Kennedy Center and the Pediatric Department in the Einstein complex.

POLICIES

During 1969, the Center worked hard at developing written policies which could be used as guides for the day-to-day operations of our staff as well as for program development. I was responsible for the formulation of these policies and spent many hours discussing issues with staff and community before seeking authorization of written policy. Our current CSP policy has been officially endorsed by both the Center staff and by our Community Advisory Boards and is reviewed periodically for appropriate modifications.

Aside from the basic preamble of the policy statement which calls for a general community-school system approach, a series of procedures was developed to aid in the implementation of this policy. For example, our staff members consult first with PAs to assess the mental health needs of the school and their own PA. If the PA feels it would like us to offer services to the school, we go with their president and/or delegates and negotiate with the school principal and any of his staff as to the exact services to be rendered. A Community School Board (CSB) member is invited to sit in on these negotiations and final agreement is written and signed by five parties; the principal, the CSB member, the District Superintendent, and the PA president. Steps for the implementation of the services and criteria for evaluation are included in the written statements.

If the PA would prefer us to spend all our time doing organizational development work with them (usually we offer 7 hours/week to be divided between a particular school and its PA) we sign a similar written agreement with the PA. In this case, the school system is not involved in the negotiations.

Another example of our policy is that for children who live in our catchment area but go to a school out of the area, we will only treat them in our clinics and will not venture into schools out of our area, although we may spend some time on the phone talking to school personnel. We also have policy to cover the situation when a child goes to a school located in one of our sub-catchment areas but lives in another. In this case, we try to handle the child's problem within the context of a program we have operating **in the school**. If this is not possible, then it is the responsibility of the clinic which covers the child's residence to develop an appropriate treatment plan.

PRIORITIES

This is an area where we have had considerable difficulty. Once the problems have been specified and allocated to units, we have tacitly, rather than overtly, agreed upon priorities. One of the reasons for this short coming is that we are still developing our planning process and have just not yet dealt with this explicitly. In practice, we operate on the premise that for CSP, developing PAs and helping them relate better to school administration is crucial. (Although narcotics problems of youth are a primary concern, the educational establishment has developed means, albeit superficial, for primary prevention programs to which we offer substantial consultation.) We are especially eager to work with PAs that are either fairly well developed and want some consultation on tightening their structure and programs or ones that may be fairly primitive in organization but who sense the importance of getting organized and desire assistance.

Moreover, when working in schools, especially in Junior High Schools, we deal with adolescent boys who are considered pre-delinquent and try to create an experience for them that leads to giving them more power and responsibility over their lives. For example, in one program, we are moving toward getting the boys to play a regular role in the screening of some of their peers whom the principal might wish to suspend. The object is to train the boys to act responsibly so that the principal will continue to utilize them as part of the regular school suspension procedure. Thus, our emphasis is on re-socializing boys by giving them some determination over their

lives rather than exploring psychodynamic bases of maladjust-
ment.

In addition, and whenever possible. we try to train school
personnel to lead counseling/ therapy groups of students, to
better organize a guidance department, and to utilize different patterns of grouping children during lessons.

With the advent of newly elected CSBs, grass roots community interest has waned considerably. Although there is still
a need to air hot educational issues in a community context,
a responsibility currently being abdicated by the school board
and by educational leaders, it is unlikely that the Center will
again spend much time organizing independent community groups
to fill this void. Whatever can be accomplished by working
with PAs will form the basis of our efforts to educate the
prime community, which, incidentally, is poorly represented on
the CSBs in this area.

PROGRAMS

The summary of priorities, then, is developing PAs, training school personnel to perform appropriate mental health
functions, working with adolescent boys, and giving clinical
and narcotics consultation. From these priorities, we have
tried to develop programs which can address these needs.

In the early stages of program development, we try to
raise and answer the following questions as a basis for legiti-
mizing the instigation of programs. Naturally, we are not always able to satisfactorily meet these criteria, but again,
we are moving in that direction.

1. To what ranked priority does this program relate?
2. Examine the adequacy of staff skills and the a-
   vailability of staff time for implementing this
   program.
3. How does this program relate to, interlink with,
   and reinforce other programs being planned or
   in operation?
4. Have all appropriate Center staff persons been
   consulted in the early stages to cnntribute to
   to the development of this program? Have the
   CABs been appropriately consulted?
5. How does this program aid the community in
   developing its capacity to deal with the problem?
   a) train people?
   b) develops leadership capacity?
   c) develops competency and

structural effectiveness of
organizations?
d) commits persons or organizations
to work with the Center?

On the basis of these criteria, then, we can demonstrate
how a particular program, for example the development of a PA,
would be judged. First, after the choice of a PA, based on the
recommendations of our CABs, we could say that a program of
organizational development with such a group relates to one of
our highest priorities. Secondly, the staff assignment to the
PA is made on the basis of having an experienced worker on hand
who has planned to allocate enough time to work on this task.
Thirdly, this program interlinks with other programs in the
following ways: a) the parents learn how to better function
as a PA (i.e. they learn how to structure their groups with an
executive board, committee set-up, agenda planning, program
development such as workshops on curriculum, how to help their
children with homework, etc. in addition to the typical functions of fashion shows and candy and cake sales). These learnings are transmitted to parents from other schools through an
informal network of communication and as a result many parents
are then able to raise issues intelligently at a monthly Dis-
trict-wide meeting of PA presidents and executive board members and at a public school board meetings b) these actions reinforce our efforts to perform organizational development work
with other PA groups as the various aspects of our training
are shared. Also, this program reverberates to school personnel, especially principals, who now begin to see the real concern for involvement of parents in school matters. In this way,
we are more able to include parents in planning meetings with
school staff, in critique sessions of our programs, and in general, anytime we have something important to do in a school.

Fourthly, before we begin an organizational development
program with a PA, we consult in particular with appropriate
community organizers on our staff who may have culled important
information on issues related to that PA. We will also discuss
how our CSP workers' efforts will relate to our community organization workers' community development plans.

Fifthly, in terms of aiding the community to develop its
own capacity to deal with problems, we are **training** community
residents, i.e. the parents, to become responsible and enlightened leaders in their community. We expect these parents to
expand their horizons in terms of their PA's functioning and to
relate this newly gained competency to the pressing educational
issues which confront the schools and children. And finally,
such an intervention does tend to commit persons and organizations to work with our Center, not only in the CSP area, but

as members of our CABs and in other programs and services.

CONCLUSION

This, then, is our basic framework for moving from definitions of the problem to program development and operation. As
I have already mentioned, this framework currently serves as a
guide and is utilized unevenly throughout the Center. I would
guess that beginning CMHCs would profit even more from such
an approach because they could structure their total organization, staffing patterns, and services either following or con-
comitantly with such an approach. Further, the educational establishment itself could profit from a more rational system of
analysis and implementation.

I think it is important to say that any rational attempt to
plan in an organization implies the influence of value systems
in the process. In the last decade, there has been a call for
an "end to ideology" with the assumption that our basic system
is adequate and that only technological tinkering is required
to maximize effeciency. The process as described in this chapter does not fundamentally make that assumption. It is my con-
tention that such a process could lead to programs and services
which could be described at either end of the radical-conserva-
tive continuum. The values and beliefs of the users of such
a framework will perforce influence the outcomes. It should be
apparent at this point what the underlying assumptions are
which guided our staff members through the planning process.

What is important, however, is that some kind of systematic
approach be utilized in the delivery of services. Professionals
cannot "do their own thing" when working in organizations. It
is only when such a systematic approach is utilized that one
can begin to examine the operating premises of the planners.

I might also mention that many components of the Management by Objectives approach were deliberately excluded from
this scheme although they are used in the Center. These components deal with job descriptions, evaluation and supervision
of employees' work performances, various fiscal and budgetary
matters, and program evaluation in terms of objectives reached.
This latter issue is certainly of crucial importance and is
really the next step in our framework. It is currently somewhat underdeveloped because it is just this year that we have
really stabilized our community-school programs. Nonetheless,
most of these services are being seriously evaluated this year
and the outcome, based on consumer ratings as well as our own
objective and subjective analyses, will form the basis for next
year's plans.

REFERENCES

Drucker, Peter F. *The Practice of Management*. New York: Harper & Row, 1954.

Glasscote, Raymond M., & Gudeman, Jon E. *The Staff of the Mental Health Center*. Washington, D. C.: The Joint Information Service of the American Psychiatric Association and the National Association for Mental Health, 1969.

Editor's note: The author wishes to express his appreciation to his colleagues, Carl Harm and Erlene Collins, both of whom along with Dr. Stein developed the basic conceptualization of this intervention model and to Sutherland Miller, whose overall leadership in matters of administration gave impetus to his thinking in this area.

SECTION III

SCHOOL INTERVENTION PROGRAMS:

EXAMPLES, ISSUES AND PROBLEMS

7. ANALYSIS OF STUDENT DISSENT

Ecology is used to mean different things by different authors. In the case of Drs. Carroll, Bell, Brecher, and Minor, the term ecological refers to an understanding that the school environment is a complex one and that input on any level will have an impact on any other level. Therefore, intervention in school mental health could take place at the level of teachers, the children themselves, parents and administrators, and all of these parts will affect the others. Evaluation of the impact of the intervention can be understood in terms of its impact on all other elements of the system. These authors acted as indirect system modifiers, concentrating on the kindergarten through second grades in a private inner city school system.

This chapter is written from the perspective of program coordinators who are themselves not the direct service agents. Some of the suggestions and points raised are unique to that relationship. Among the points mentioned: 1) interveners should make the commitment at the highest level for a period of time sufficient for the program to be successful; 2) before successful intervention can take place, a long-term personal commitment nnd trust must be developed on the part of the consultant; 3) the consultant needs to learn the system before he leaps in with his knowledge and advise, and he needs to define a clear role for himself and to determine the kind of roles his staff will take; 4) the staff assigned should match unqiue aspects of the job; 5) consultant teams should be supported by the coordinating staff and provided with backup training when necessary. The coordinators of the program should be prepared to enter into the school and help the staff consultants before trouble reaches these coordinators.

This chapter describes several innovative approaches which can be used with teachers, children and parents in ways to affect the ecological system within the school by promoting personal development both among the teachers and pupils.

Like many workers in school intervention, these authors see development of adequate assessment vehicles as a primary problem.

AN ECOLOGICAL ANALYSIS OF AND PRESCRIPTION FOR

STUDENT DISSENT

Jerome F. X. Carroll
Albert A. Bell
Marshall W. Minor
Harold Brecher
Counseling Services Project
Philadelphia, Pennsylvania

The initial response of most societies to social disturbances is to assume that something is wrong with the perpetra-
tors of the disturbance, rather than the system within which the
"trouble" arises. In other words, the assumption usually is
made that the dissenters are "sick" and the system is healthy.

This line of thought requires that something be done to the
dissenting individual. He may, for example, be counseled, ad-
monished, suspended, dismissed, admitted to a mental hospital,
sentenced, banished, or eliminated. Which course of "corrective
action" will be taken will depend on such factors as: a) what
particular social norm has been violated, b) the manner in which
the norm was violated, c) the prevailing circumstances or situation at the time the violation occurred, and, d) the perceived
degree of threat engendered by the act in the minds of the "norm
bearers" who have the power to evoke sanctions.

There is mounting evidence, however, that many social ana-
lysts are beginning to view social unrest from a different perspective. Instead of adopting the more narrow, intrapsychic
model of behavior disturbance--one which assumes something is
amiss within the dissenting individual's psyche--the emphasis
has shifted to an ecological model of mental heatth, with special emphasis upon prevention (Schiff and Kellam, 1967; Auerswald, 1968; Shaw and Rector, 1968; Cowen, 1969; Griffin and
Reinherz, 1969; and Rhodes, 1969).

The ecological model views social unrest as being sympto-
matic of a network of underlying, interacting "systems" which,
in a variety of ways, impede the individual's efforts to achieve

self actualization. Remediation, therefore, is directed primarily toward the malfunctioning systems, rather than the individual adversely affected by these systems.

If we apply the ecological model to the phenomenon of student dissent, the educational system becomes the "client" whose pathological condition must be examined, diagnosed, and treated. Its structure and organization, as well as the functioning of its various subsystems, and their interaction, would need to be carefully and critically studied. So too would its philosophy, goals, policies, practices, curricula, standards, personnel, and other essential elements. A number of critics have already enumerated and discussed many of the more salient problems of our educational institutions, including: Holt (1964, 1967 and 1970), Goodman (1964), Friedenberg (1965), Coleman, et al. (1966) Conant (1967), Farber (1967), Kohl (1967), Borton (1969), and Gross and Gross (1970).

In a broader sense, however, the entire matrix of interacting systems--of which the educational system is but one part-- also has to be carefully scrutinized. In other words, the society in which the educational system is embedded would also have to undergo a vigorous and objective critical analysis. Here too a significant number of men and women, representing a diversity of experience, education, training, and interests have already recorded their critical analyses of the American scene, including Fromm (1955), Packard (1960), Mumford (1961), Carson (1962), King (1963), Friedan (1963), Clark (1964), Malcolm X (1965), Nader (1965), Cox (1966), Kennedy (1967), Cleaver (1968), Goodman (1968), Kerner (1968), Wlaker (1968), Melman (1968), and Pett (1970).

Therapeutic interventions, then, would take the form of "systems remediation." Furthermore, if lasting improvement is to be attained, it is essential that the therapeutic intervention or reform not be localized, but rather generalized throughout the entire matrix of interacting systems. This is because social systems have a strong tendency to regress to their previous state whenever treatment/reform is constricted to an isolated segment of the total system (Fromm, 1955).

The ecological approach, in the case of student dissent, would necessitate the involvement of a number of diverse disciplines, since no one discipline possesses sufficient knowledge and methodologies to accomplish the task alone. Psychology, on the other hand, can and should be in the forefront of any multidisciplined undertaking of this nature. This preeminence follows from psychology's historical concern with behavioral processes such as learning, growth and development, adjustment, and other related psychosocial phenomena.

Having suggested that the educational system is "sick," let us first turn our attention to the basic purpose of any institution. Institutions evolve as a result of society's efforts to provide for socially sanctioned means of gratifying its members' needs. Gardner (1968), however, has noted that, with the passage of time, institutions tend to "rigidify" and "decay." When this occurs, he maintains that institutions tend to ". . . smother individuality, imprison the spirit, thwart the creative impulse, diminish individual adaptability, and limit the possibility of freedom."

He further states that as ". . . the institutions grow increasingly resistant to criticism, the critics grow increasingly hostile, and the stage is then set for violent collision between angry critics and sluggish institutions."

A corollary of Gardner's "rigidity and decay" principle might be that when the sluggish or alienated institution seeks to suppress of oppress the dissenting element of the population it theoretically serves, rebellion will surely follow. Thomas Hayden, one of the "Chicago 7," stated this in somewhat simpler terms when he remarked to Judge Hoffman, "Don't you see that there is an inescapable relationship between oppression and rebellion?" (Lukas, 1970).

Although rebellion may sometimes be the only means of achieving social reforms (Douglas, 1970), other less desirable outcomes are also possible. As Myrdal (Diamond, 1969) has stated, "Riots lead to repression, violence to counterviolence. At the end, there is nothing left but the police state (p. 73)."

Gardner (1968) feels that society can avoid violent revolution through planned, continuous, innovative reform of its institutions. We must ask, therefore, whether our educational institutions are in tune with the needs of the students. We might also seek to determine how flexible these same institutions are and the extent to which they are able and willing to innovatively adapt their existing programs and policies to the changing conditions that characterize our times.

The fact that student dissatisfaction and dissent is a generalized phenomenon, extending from the elementary schools (Argent, 1969; and Sexton, 1970), through the high schools (Divoky, 1969; Montgomery County Student Alliance, 1969; Janssen, 1970; High-school power, 1970), up to and including the colleges and universities (Carroll, 1969; Diamond, 1969; and Hadden, 1969), strongly suggests that our educational institutions are not adequately meeting the needs of the student. Perhaps one of our most important tasks then is to determine what are the relevant needs of the students which are being frustrated by the schools?

Holt (1970) argues that education should prepare an individual to live a good life. The definition of what constitutes a "good life," however, is one of the major points of disagreement between student dissenters and the administrators and faculty of their schools. The basis for this disagreement, I maintain, is one of the principle causes of student dissent, whether violent or nonviolent.

One need only examine the criteria by which academic potential and achievement are presently assessed by the schools to appreciate the nature of this difference. The schools, in the main, advocate and apply criteria which pertain to a relatively impersonal, dehumanized version of a "good life," one defined almost exclusively in terms of science and technology. Primary importance is thus attached to the rapid acquisition of greater and greater amounts of highly specific scientific and/or technical knowledge, as well as the means of processing and utilizing such knowledge. Relatively little emphasis, by contrast, is devoted to what Borton (1969) has called "psychological, affective, humanistic, personological, eupsychian, or synoetic education."

Diamond (1969) traces this emphasis to World War II, when "academics went to war," that is, they began to get involved in lucrative war related research. This event triggered what proved to be an uninterrupted influx of literally millions of dollars into the schools from the government, the military, industry, and big business. Although these funds in many ways helped improve our system of education, they were not without their negative aspects too.

Educational standards, curricula, teaching techniques, faculty hiring and promotion, and many other aspects of the educational system began to be more and more shaped by the contractors and grant dispensers' definition of the "good life." A depersonalized, bureaucratic, mechanistic, scientific-technological, materialistic, mass production - mass consumption model of the "good life" thus emerged, and it was toward this end that the schools began to mold their students.

Many dissenting students, on the other hand, challenge what they believe to be the lopsided scientific-technological emphasis of the schools and grow increasingly suspect of and alienated from its underlying economic philosophy and practices. Instead, they press for greater emphasis upon existential and humanistic concerns.

From the dissenters' perspective, a "good education" is one which would:

. . . facilitate the student's search for meaning, purpose and significance in his life
. . . maximize the student's personal freedom to
decide for himself how he should think and behave
. . . aid the student in his struggle to discover and know who and what he is
. . . permit, encourage, and assist the student
to know and express his authentic or "real self"
. . . enable the student to actualize his human
potentials (Fromm, 1968, particularly emphasizes man's
capacity to love, to use his reason, to create and
enjoy beauty, and to share his humanity with all fellow men)
. . . encourage and assist the student to gain a
significant degree of control over his own destiny,
especially his own educational experience
. . . enable the student to evolve a personally
affirmed philosophy of life with its attendant moral
and ethical value systems
. . . cooperate and assist the student to know,
engage and become personally involved and concerned
with the common destiny he shares with his fellow
man
. . . facilitate the student's efforts to discover, to experience, and to give full expression
to his unique, individual nature

Given that a "philosophical/value gap" separates most of
the student dissenters from the majority of school administrators and faculty, let us consider some of the reasons why this
present generation of student activists have been so vigorous,
intense, and effective in their protests. I believe the following qualities distinguish the individual who is able to function
as an effective social change agent. I also believe many student dissenters evidence these qualities.

1. The change agent must be well aware of various
defects, deficiencies, inequalities, injustices, weaknesses, etc. of the system he wishes to change.
2. The change agent must have personally experienced some of the pain and frustration which the "sick"
system creates.
3. The change agent must strongly believe in the
possibility of changing the system; he must also be
very confident that he can personally do much to effect
the desired changes in the system.
4. The change agent must have a deep commitment
to the goal of effecting change, as well as a rich resource of energy to invest in the process of bringing
about the desired changes.

5. The change agent must be relatively free of entanglements with the system he seeks to change, that is, he must not be too deeply "in hock" to the system; the more the change agent needs what the system is presently offering, the less able he will be to effect significant changes within that system.

6. The change agent must have a high degree of tolerance for pain, frustration, ridicule, social ostracism, and other forms of punishment.

7. The change agent must have at least one confidant who will, at a minimum, listen with interest, in an empathic, non-judgmental, accepting manner to the private thoughts, feelings, and aspirations of the change agent.

8. Finally, the change agent must evidence a high degree of logic and patience in planning and implementing his strategies for effecting social change.

Briefly applying these qualities to student dissenters, we see that the majority seem to be well aware of much of the pathology which pervades contemporary educational systems. This condition of heightened awareness derives, to a large extent, from the rapid and significant development of our communications media, especially TV (McLuhan and Fiore, 1967). They most certainly have felt the pain and frustration generated by the diseased system.

Although dissenters vary considerably with respect to their belief that the system can or should be changed, i.e. saved, by their untiring efforts to effect change, one would have to infer some degree of self-confidence in their undertakings.

Commitment is always a difficult quality to assess, but here again, our judgment should be guided by observable behavior. On this basis, we would have to infer a degree of commitment which, at a minimum, exceeds that evidenced by the vast "silent majority" of whom some governmental figures speak so admiringly. Since energy and youth are generally synonymous, I feel this issue can be quickly dispensed with.

Regarding the matter of entanglements, we see that student dissenters seem particularly "free" when we compare them to their school administrators and faculty. In addition, student dissenters seem to be saying quite clearly that they are deriving relatively little value from their educational experiences.

Youth's tolerance for pain and frustration has been fairly well documented. Perhaps this is one of the major reasons they are made to fight their country's wars. Since it is mostly the adult "establishment" which expresses its disapproval, and not their peers, the dissenters are usually not subject to an intolerable degree of social ostracism. Furthermore, since student dissent is a social phenomenon, the dissenter usually has access to a sympathetic, empathetic ear.

Regarding the last quality of logic and patience, we see that here too the majority of dissenters have chosen to work within the existing system to effect evolutionary reforms, rather than violent revolution. The evidence to date, that is, indicates that the majority of dissenters have shown an admirable degree of patience and logic in planning and executing their diverse strategies to achieve their ends.

What can be done then to avoid the "violent collision between angry critics and sluggish institutions" predicted by Gardner (1968) and to achieve the crucially urgent nonviolent reform of our educational institutions? I would recommend the following:

1. The ecological model, rather than the intrapsychic model, should guide our analysis and remediation. Our primary concern, in other words, should be directed toward understanding, diagnosing, and treating a disturbing system, as opposed to a disturbed individual.
2. School administrators and faculty must provide readily accessible, easy-to-use channels for direct communications between themselves and the dissenting students. In addition, a genuine openness and receptivity to the dissenters' concerns must be shown by school authorities if the institutions they represent wish to effect nonviolent reform and be relevant to the needs and aspirations of the students they serve.
3. School authorities should expend special effort to accurately discern and understand the philosophies, needs, goals, and values of the dissenters. These factors should then be articulated to the structure and function of the existing educational system.
4. Compromises, in terms of educational goals, policies, and practices must then be struck between the schools' present heavy emphasis upon the scientific-technologically oriented definition of the "good life" and the newly emergent student dissenter counterpoint which emphasizes the existential needs of man and humanism.

In deciding what compromises should be made and how they would be implemented, students--especially dissenters--must have a significant voice in the decision-making process. Deliberations on these compromises, furthermore, should be conducted in "open" sessions so that all interested and concerned parties will have the opportunity of witnessing and participating in the process. When and if decisions are reached by the deliberating body, they should be subject to ratification by the entire academic community, including some representation of parents and citizens living in the environs surrounding the institution.

5. Finally, special provisions should be made periodically to assess the effectiveness of the entire educational system--including the most recently formulated reforms. This reassessment process should also include representatives from every group affected by the educational process, including graduates.

The proposed reassessment process should, furthermore, be the basis for additional innovative system reforms. In this manner, a continuous cycle of evaluation, reform, and re-evaluation can be achieved, thereby increasing the likely effectiveness and relevance of education at all levels.

The ultimate empirical test of the success or failure of the process I have outlined above--assuming this society does not further deteriorate into Myrdal's police state--could be determined by carefully noting the frequency, intensity, and scope of future violent forms of student dissent. Violent protest, I believe, nearly always reflects a decaying, rigid, alienated institutional malaise.

By the same token, these same parameters could be applied to nonviolent student dissent. In this case, however, they can be interpreted as healthy signs of a relevant institution in the process of renewal and growth.

REFERENCES

Argent, R. D. Pupil unrest begins in the first grade. *School and Community*, 1969, 56 (3), 19, 89-91.

Auerswald, E. H. Interdisciplinary versus ecological approach. *Family Process*, 1968, 7, 202-215.

Borton, T. Reach, touch and teach. *Saturday Review*, 1969, 52 (3), 56-58, 69-70.

Carroll, J. F. X. Understanding student rebellion. *Adolescence*, 1969, 4, 163-180.

Carson, R. *Silent spring.* Boston: Houghton Mifflin, 1962.

Clark, K. B. *Dark Ghetto.* New York: Harper & Row, 1964.

Cleaver, E. *Soul on ice.* New York: McGraw-Hill, 1968.

Coleman, J. S., Cambell, E. O., Hobson, C. J., McParland, J., Mood, A. M., Weinfeld, F. D., & York, R. L. *Equality of educational opportunity.* Washington, D. C.: U.S. Dept. of H.E.W., Office of Education, 1966.

Conant, J. B. *The comprehensive high school: A second report to interested citizens.* New York: McGraw-Hill, 1967.

Cox, H. *The secular city: Secularization and urbanization in theological perspective.* New York: Macmillan, 1966.

Diamond, E. Class of '69: The violent years. *Newsweek*, 1969, 73 (25), 68-73.

Divoky, D. (Ed.). *No place to send a kid.* New York: Avon Books, 1969.

Douglass, W. O. *Points of rebellion.* New York: Random House, 1970.

Farber, G. The student as nigger. *California Aggie*, May 31, 1967, 69 (117), 3.

Friedan, B. *The feminine mystique.* New York: W. W. Norton, 1963.

Friedenberg, E. Z. *Coming of age in America: Growth and acquiescence.* New York: Random House, 1965.

Fromm, E. *The sane society.* New York: Holt, Rinehart, & Winston, 1955.

Fromm, E. *The revolution of hope.* New York: Harper & Row, 1968.

Gardner, J. W. Continuous renewal: Best route to orderly social change? *The Philadelphia Inquirer,* December 15, 1968, Section 7, 1.

Goodman, P. *Compulsory mis-education.* New York: Horizon Press, 1964.

Goodman, P. The empty society. In R. Perrucci & M. Pilisuk (Eds.). *The triple revolution: Social problems in depth.* Boston: Little Brown & Co., 1968.

Griffin, C. L., & Reinherz, H. Z. Prevention of the "failure symdrome" in the primary grades: Implications for intervention. *American Journal of Public Health,* 1969, 59, 2029-2034.

Gross, R., & Gross, B. (Eds.). *Radical school reform.* New York: Simon & Schuster, 1970.

Hadden, J. K. The private generation. *Psychology Today,* 1969, 3 (5), 32-35, 68-69.

High-school power. *Newsweek,* 1970, 75 (10), 63.

Holt, J. *How children fail.* New York: Pitman, 1964.

Holt, J. *How children learn.* New York: Pitman, 1967.

Holt, J. Why we need new schooling. *Look,* 1970, 34 (1), 52.

Janssen, P. (Ed.) What's wrong with the high schools? *Newsweek,* 1970, 75 (7), 65-69.

Kennedy, R. F. *To seek a newer world.* New York: Doubleday, 1967.

Kerner, O. (Chm.) *Report of the national advisory commission on civil disorders.* New York: E. P. Dutton, 1968.

King, M. L. *Letter from Birmingham jail*. *The Christian Century*, 1963, 80, 767-773.

Kohl, H. R. *36 children*. New York: New American Library, 1967.

Kozol, J. *Death at an early age*. Boston: Houghton Mifflin, 1967.

Lukas, J. A. 5 in Chicago trial get 5-year terms and $5,000 fines. *The New York Times*, February 21, 1970, 119 (40,936), 1, 50.

Malcolm X. *Malcolm X speaks*. New York: Grove Press, 1965.

McLuhan, M., & Fiore, Q. *The medium is the massage*. New York: Random House, 1967.

Melman, S. American needs and limits on resources: The priorities problem. In R. Perrucci & M. Pilisuk (Eds.) *The triple revolution: Social problems in depth*. Boston: Little Brown, & Co., 1968.

Montgomery County Student Alliance. A student voice. In Ronald Gross & Beatrice Gross (Eds.). *Radical school reform*, New York: Simon & Schuster, 1969, Ch. 10, 147-160.

Mumford, L. *The city in history: Its origin, its transformations, and its prospects*. London: Secker-Warburg, 1961.

Nader, R. *Unsafe at any speed: The designed-in dangers of the American automobile*. New York: Grossman, 1965.

Packard, V. *The waste makers*. New York: McKay, 1960.

Pett, S. Whatever happened to the quality of life? --American survey. *The Philadelphia Inquirer*, February 15, 1970, Section 7, 1, 3.

Rhodes, W. The disturbing child: A problem of ecological management. In P. S. Graubard (Ed.) *Children against schools*. Chicago: Follett Education, 1969.

Sexton, P. How the American boy is feminized. *Psychology Today*, 1970, 3 (8), 23-29, 66-67.

Shaw, M. C., & Rector, W. H. *Modification of the school environment through intervention with significant adults*. Chico, Calif.: Western Regional Center of the Interprofessional Research Commission on Pupil Personnel Services,

1968.

Walker, D. (Dir.) *Rights in conflict.*   New York: E. P. Dutton, 1968.

8. TEACHER-CENTERED CONSULTATION

Dr. Broskowski teaches at a university, trains graduate students, and practices teacher-centered consultation. Following a brief discussion of problems of models, Dr. Broskowski provides detailed concrete examples of programs that serve the functions of helping to train his students, provide service to the school system, and in most cases, provide the opportunity for evaluative research. The consequence of the programs appear in terms of greater awareness of the interdependence of teachers, pupils, administrators and community, more openness and less perceived threat on the part of the professional staff, and the development of continuing change and innovation as an ongoing desirable part of the teaching role.

Using the concept of boundary spanners, much like that of gatekeepers, Dr. Broskowski illustrates how important it is to bridge the gap between various subsystems within the organization and outside the organization. In this particular case, the loss of one boundary spanner brought nearly cataclismic results to the school and to Dr. Broskowski's involvement.

Within a systems theory, this chapter provides an example of process consultation, providing mutually derived diagnosis and determination of issues and mutually derived solutions to the problems. Readers will note that the most substantial impact on disruptive or emotionally disturbed children in the high school resulted from contingency management. Concern over discipline and maintenance of the school as a stable environment is seen as a central mental health need.

The completeness of this presentation serves as a model for a school intervention program.

TEACHER-CENTERED CONSULTATION

IN AN INNER-CITY JUNIOR HIGH SCHOOL

Anthony Broskowski
Harvard University

Schools, like psychology, is something most lay persons feel free to talk about by virtue of having had first hand experiences as students. Psychologists may be prone to compounding this error by trying to apply principles of psychology within a school system without first developing some models of schools as organizations and some models of consultation tailored to fit such systems. Too often we may follow our most familiar strategy, the doctor-patient model, in trying "to help the school" (patient) and experience frustration when our attempts are resisted or fail.

The purposes of this chapter are a) to present a model of the school as an organization, b) to present a model of consultation suited to such an organization, and c) to describe a program of consultation to an inner-city junior high school that was based on these two models.

SCHOOLS AS OPEN SYSTEMS

Our model of schools is one based on open-systems theory (Bertalanffy, 1968; Katz and Kahn, 1966; Miller, 1955; Parsons, 1951). This model views the school as a complex organization with permeable boundaries, residing within a larger environment that exerts pressures on the boundaries, and with which it must interact. As an open system, the school receives inputs across its boundaries, operates on these inputs within the boundaries, and transfers outputs back into the environment. The inputs include such physical factors as money, personnel, materials, and pupils, as well as such abstract entities as community values and goals. Within the boundaries there exists a hierarchy of status and authority, governing rules and normative systems, and differentiation of roles based on various task functions. The outputs include the obvious commodity called graduates and the less obvious factors called ideas, values, attitudes, and skills.

The model becomes increasingly complex when it focuses on the internal operations of the system and how these operations are influenced by, and influence in turn, the external environment. The goals of the organization are in part determined by the environment which has control of the necessary resources for the organization's survival. These goals, in turn, are often multiple, vague, and conflictual with one another. For example, not only is the school supposed to teach facts to children, it is also supposed to socialize them to fit the prevailing norms of the community and to help promote their physical and emotional health. Given the ambiguity and frequently conflictual nature of these goals, the system must develop an elaborate method of operation so as to insure continual support from the environment.

Another important aspect of open systems is the necessity to monitor the environment for information regarding the output and to feed this information back into the organization at various points in order to make any necessary internal corrections in the production of the output. This feedback functions to keep the system in a stable equilibrium with its environment. To maintain equilibrium the feedback should be **negative** in the sense that it should operate to subtract from the internal processes that are producing errors or deviations in the output. Positive feedback, in systems terms, is that feedback which **amplifies** deviance, leading to a spiraling increase of error and more error. The squealing feedback one hears from a loudspeaker system, when the microphone is too sensitive to its own speaker output, is an example of positive feedback. In relation to school systems, feedback can come in terms of long range outputs, (e.g. graduates of a four year program) or on a daily basis, (e.g. reports from parents about child's behavior). Although feedback is very important to keep a system in stable equilibrium, some systems tend to close up their own boundaries and make the boundaries less permeable so as to protect the system from what are viewed as threatening outside forces or negative information. Consequently, much useful feedback is also shut off and the system cannot easily and rapidly correct internal processes in relation to changing environmental needs for different outputs. This phenomena is not unlikely what clinicians observe in patients who are described as repressive or no longer open to new experiences. The short range effect is a sense of security in a threatening environment. The long range effect is a dysfunctional system that has difficulty surviving in a changing environment.

Schools in particular are wrought with problems of maintaining sufficient boundary permeability. Persons who work within the system feel the school has a very "thin skin" (Miles, 1967) and feel easily subjected to demands, criticisms and controls by outsiders, from politicians through parents, (not to mention university consultants). Outsiders, conversely, feel the schools have impermeable boundaries and are no longer subject to local control, a traditional American value in relation to public schools. Parents in the inner-city feel particularly hesitant or powerless to enter into the system, literally or figuratively.

Another feature of all systems is the interdependency of subsystems within the boundaries. For the total system to operate effectively, each subsystem must be operating effectively and breakdowns in any one of the subsystems will produce reactions in other subsystems, although these reactions, like ripples in a pond, may occur at different times and places, and with varying intensities. The interdependency of subsystems (e.g. teachers) within a school is very real but often unrecognized by the participants, who see themselves as independent agents with a common goal and overlapping classes, a situation quite different from mutual interdependence.

A final feature worth mentioning about schools as open systems is the functioning of boundary spanners. These are persons within the system whose functions include spanning the boundary between the internal subsystems and the environment. The principal, as manager of the system, will serve this role, but so will all the faculty to the extent they relate to the parents of their pupils. Boundary spanners are important carriers of feedback but their effectiveness within the organization is often compromised by others within the organization who lose trust in the boundary spanner and often see them as lacking ultimate loyalty to the organization and its values. Boundary spanners may even be viewed suspiciously as breaches of secret information to other systems in the environment. To those familiar with schools in inner-cities, the situation will sound like the attitudes of some teachers toward their principal, not a helpful protector, but a person to fear and mistrust.

For a more complete account of schools as open systems, showing how the myriad problems of schools are **systematically** related, one should read Matthew B. Miles' (1967) classic article, "Some properties of schools as social systems."

PROCESS CONSULTATION

Our model of consultation derives from the literature and techniques of change theory and organizational development (Argyris, 1962, 1965; Bennis, Benne, and Chin, 1961, 1969; Lippit, Watson, and Westley, 1958; Schein and Bennis, 1965) and is best exemplified by Schein's (1969) concept of "process consultation."

Schein points out that the most prevalent model of consultation could be called the "purchase model." In this case, a buyer (manager or organization) purchases the expert services or information of a consultant to fill an already identified need of the buyer. The success of the consultation will depend on whether the buyer has correctly identified the need, can correctly communicate this need to the consultant, has correctly assessed the ability and expertise of the consultant, and whether he has "thought through the consequences of having the consultant gather information, and/or the consequences of implementing changes which may be recommended by the consultant (Schein, 1967, p. 5)." These four preconditions are frequently lacking and can be expected to be lacking particularly in schools. In schools consultants may be called in to serve latent functions, such as giving the impression to outsiders that the school is working on important problems.

Another feature of the purchase model is that upon completion of the sale and the exit of the consultant, the organization is usually status quo in terms of lacking certain resources which required hiring the consultant in the first place. That is, the consultant applies his particular expertise to the organizational problem but does not teach the organization how to solve or fulfill a similar need by itself in the future.

In contrast, process consultation involves the organization and the consultant in joint diagnosis of the organizational problems, with particular focus on the processes within the organization that need improvement.

Quite another model of consultation resembles the doctor-patient model whereby a consultant is called in by top management to give a diagnosis of the difficulties in a subsystem and is also expected to prescribe a helpful remedy. This is generally done with the patient-organization remaining relatively passive while being examined. In contrast, process consultation calls for the entire organization to be active not only in its own diagnosis but also in generating its own remedy. Process consultation overcomes two great difficulties of the doctor-patient model when applied to organizational consultation. One, it overcomes the usual resistance on the part of subsystems to yield the information needed for an accurate diagnosis. Two, it reduces the terminal inability of the system to understand, or its unwillingness to implement, the consultant's recommendations. Process consultation, by actively involving the organization throughout the problem-solving process, tries to increase the organization's own diagnostic and problem-solving skills, thereby leaving it with more than it had when the consultant entered the system.

Finally, it should be noted that the process consultant need not be an expert in solving the unique problems that are eventually uncovered. Rather, he needs to be an expert in involving people in self-diagnosis and in teaching general problem-solving skills and strategies. In short, he needs to be an expert in developing a helping relationship (Schein, 1967). This final point is important in relation to schools for it legitimizes, in part, the entry of noneducators into a formal system of education and in turn offers moral support to consultants trained in traditional clinical psychology (graduate students or faculty) when they find themselves in the midst of foreign territory, better known as an inner-city school building.

The program described below illustrates to some extent the utility of these two models in carrying out consultation with a school system. Not all facets of the program relate to the two models. In fact, the content of the final activities used by teachers is more easily related to traditional principles of psychology. The models are best related to the processes by which these activities were arrived at and were most useful in helping the consultants interpret events and direct their behavior in the absence of complete information.

THE CONSULTATION PROGRAM

In the summer of 1969 the principal of a racially mixed junior high school approached the author requesting assistance in counseling for the "many emotionally disturbed children" in his school. The principal's plan was to have graduate students in clinical psychology do the counseling on the school premises under the supervision of the author, a clinical psychologist and faculty member of a graduate training program. For many reasons I immediately rejected the idea in my own mind but began to explore with the principal some of the other problems he faced in the school. This mutual diagnostic process involved the principal and gradually led both of us to see the necessity for primary preventive activities as opposed to the treatment of already existing problems.

The principal came to this school after riots following the death of Dr. Martin Luther King in 1968 had closed it down. He and about eighty percent of the faculty were white. Approximately forty-five percent of the students were black. The old principal had resigned under community pressure and about fifty percent of the old faculty left with him. The current faculty, therefore, consisted of many teachers new to the school and most of these were young persons who had just received their degrees in 1967 or 1968.

Upon arriving at the school the new principal organized a

Parents Advisory Committee and a Students Advisory Committee. Both committees were given some real power over decisions directly affecting their own constituencies. He also instituted many other small changes which had the immediate effect of reducing tensions within the system as well as reducing environment pressures on the system's boundaries. By the spring of 1969 the school had settled down and the principal was attempting to improve the educational and socialization functions.

Our mutual diagnostic efforts led to the tentative plan for graduate students to enter the system as consultants to teachers around issues and concerns at the level of the classroom. No direct services to individual pupils nor consultation around individual pupils would be provided. Only teachers who requested consultation would be seen, with the limitation that the number not exceed the number of available graduate students, unless several teachers made a request as a small group. This strategy grew out of our awareness that the number and magnitude of problems exceeded our resources and that the currently felt needs of the teachers were the most reasonable areas to try change. Furthermore, consistent with process consultation, the teachers needed to be involved if changes were to be implemented by the teachers.

Arrangements were also made to provide "incremental credits" to volunteering teachers. These incremental credits are given by the School Board and can be applied toward required educational advancement and eventual pay raises. While this arrangement provided status and sanction to the program, incremental credit proved to be far less an incentive for teacher participation than did the intrinsic possibility of improving classroom effectiveness. The opportunities for professional and social interactions with their own colleagues also stimulated teacher participation. By and large it was the new and younger teachers that volunteered for the program. Of a faculty of 40 teachers, 22 initially volunteered and 16 persisted in activities with consultants throughout the program.

The first contact between the graduate students in the psychology program and personnel from the school occurred in September, 1969, with a meeting of the principal, the author and fourteen graduate students from the Psychology Department. At this meeting the principal gave a brief history of his school during the time he had been there. He reviewed many of the crises that had occurred and steps that he had implemented to bring about an immediate reduction in tensions. The graduate students asked questions and learned more about his view of the school and his goals for involvement. The meeting ended with the understanding that the graduate students would come out to the school and for several weeks simply become familiar with the teachers, the students, and the environment of the school. They would not give advice nor provide any answers to problems that the teachers might raise.

These first several weeks were planned as a period of entry and trust-building between ourselves and all the personnel in the school building. Early in the second week of school the author and the graduate students were invited to the school faculty meeting and at this time we presented to all the teachers our proposal to assist them with ideas or projects that were teacher-initiated. We did not ask for volunteers or commitment at this time. We told them we would be around the school each day (2 or 3 graduate students were on school premises each day) and available for questions or ideas. We stressed our acceptance of their difficulties, the confidentiality of all contacts, and our role as teacher-orient consultants, not as "spies" for the principal or the university. Trust came slowly. As expected, our saying so did not immediately make it so in the minds of the teachers. Our subsequent interactions with them, however, overcame a great deal of mistrust and evaluation anxiety. I stress the gradualness of this process because our acceptance and understanding of their difficulties only became genuine as we gradually immersed ourselves in the day to day school operations and did, in fact, begin to see the school environment with the eyes of an "insider." The fact that we initially crossed the boundary at the invitation of the boundary spanning principal did not help to endear us to those teachers who already felt threatened by evaluation.

In moving about the school the consultants remained sensitive to the issue of boundaries and the sanctions needed to cross such boundaries. Permission from the teacher, for example, was always requested before a consultant entered a classroom for observation. We judiciously avoided giving advice for problems that teachers might raise, particularly those that focused on individual pupils. At the risk of initially appearing as useless consultants, we tried to head-off passive requests for direct help by reminding the teachers that after five to six weeks we would work actively with those teachers who had indicated an active interest in pursuing some project of personal interest. This answer was generally accepted.

Resistance to our efforts was also present and took many subtle forms. Most prevalent were subtle jokes about head shrinkers and psychoanalysis. We generally responded to these with a serious reaffirmation of our role. By virtue of the voluntary nature of teacher involvement, it was easiest for resistance to take the form of withdrawal. Because we were not trying to suggest specific changes, there was no call for too much resistance.

During this time the consultants met together as a class and compared field notes. Many similar observations were noted and we began to get a better idea of the school as a complex social organization. The most crucial and pressing problem to emerge from these meetings was the teachers' overriding concern for order and control in the classroom. This concern expressed itself in many forms and behind almost every teacher's expressed interest was the question; "How can I keep my students settled down and behaving properly so I can teach rather than discipline all the time?" Secondary concerns revolved around improving teaching behavior and selection of classroom activities to promote widespread interest and learning. Most persons in the school were concerned primarily with personal safety and secondly with the reputation of the school in the community. Teachers were also concerned with their reputation in the eyes of the principal and their peers. The concern for community reputation, however, was not one of excellence in education so much as one of the school being safe and orderly. One's peer reputation as a teacher appeared to rest more upon the academic achievement of one's pupils. Furthermore, there was little awareness of teacher and administration interdependence, and in its place a sense of distrust and competition among teachers who were not personal friends. It was difficult under these conditions for teachers to engage in self diagnosis for the source of problems and they were more prone to see the source of problems residing in the pupils, administration, or environment.

In approximately the fifth week of the school term, the teachers who volunteered for the project met with the graduate students for an all-day workshop at the Clinical Psychology Center of the University of Pittsburgh. The workshop focused on small group exercises and simulated classroom experiences designed to improve the teachers' communication and problem solving skills. Secondarily, the workshop served the purpose of building esprit de corps among the teachers and graduate students and generating some new ideas for classroom interventions. The workshop ended with a general meeting during which teachers began to specify their concerns and interests and the graduate students began to pair up with teachers according to the interests of the teachers.

Beginning in the sixth week of school, specific projects were initiated. These projects consisted of one to four participating teachers and one to three graduate students working with them as a team. Throughout the semester, the graduate students continued to attend the author's seminar on techniques of planned change, consultation, and group process and were supervised by the author in their work at the school. The author's primary field task was to coordinate the separate projects and to make available necessary resources through the principal's office or the Department of Psychology. He also supported the principal through some anxious decisions and served to interpret the teachers' projects to the principal and other concerned parties.

These first six weeks were the most anxiety-provoking for both the consultants and persons within the school system. Our orientation of process consultation, however, led us to expect anxiety due to a lack of initial directions and certainty. Furthermore, our view of the school as a complex open system discouraged us from making early interventions which might eventually lead to problems in other parts of the system. We saw all the components as interdependent and part of our process consultation task was to make the persons within the system aware of such interdependence. For example, while it is obvious in industry that production, market, and sales are mutually interdependent, as are employees on an assembly line, the normative belief in the school system was that each teacher functioned separately and apart from her colleagues, and that good or poor performance by any component in the system had no direct bearing on any other component. While this tends to be partially true, we hoped to demonstrate that good teaching at 9 a.m. made it easier for someone else at 10 a.m., and that good communication among teachers in the lounge made a difference in teacher morale, which in turn influenced administration, which in turn helps to protect teachers from forces outside the boundaries, and so forth. In brief, we needed at least six weeks to grasp the systematic complexities and internal norms that governed the system. Although anxious, we were able to delay rushing in with our own pat solutions. Our patience and oneness paid off when it came time for the teachers to propose their own projects, growing out of their personal interests and specific classroom difficulties. We now had motivation to change, coupled with responsibility and initiative for directing such change.

The following projects grew out of our mutual interactions. In reviewing them, a lot of the details and excitement is lost but the reviews serve the purpose of demonstrating the scope of change that can take place under these circumstances. Whether or not each individual project had validity for improving education is, at this point, less important than the question of whether or not outside consultants can help persons inside of a system undergo self-diagnosis and self-directed change.

Skills in Small Group Techniques

In this project, two graduate students met weekly for at least one hour with four home economic teachers who were interested in using small group exercises designed to increase the students' interpersonal sensitivity and group cohesiveness. The graduate students drew from over 100 exercises used by small group practitioners and tailored these to fit the teachers' needs and current curriculum issues. The exercises were first taught to the teachers by explanation, demonstration, and their own active participation. After a teacher mastered an exercise, she then used it in her classrooms. The exercise would be introduced into the classroom in order to generate data which would then be discussed by the students and the teacher. For example, following an exercise in which two persons take turns leading one another blindfolded, the teacher would lead a group discussion of the importance of trust and how it feels to be dependent on another person. This would naturally be extended to a discussion of how sharing and trust apply to the classroom tasks of cooking or sewing.

Two of the teachers on this project were particularly excited by these methods and continued to use experiential exercises, while the other two stopped using them after several weeks. These circumstances allowed for some project evaluation to be conducted by comparing the two sets of teachers in terms of their students' reactions to a 12 item questionnaire which was designed and administered for the first time before the two teachers decided to stop using the exercises. The 12 items were written to get at feelings of being accepted, ability to work with others, being understood and appreciated as an individual, and willingness to give and accept help. The questionnaire was administered the second time at the end of the first semester. All responses were anonymous. Three of the teachers administered the items to their 7th, 8th, and 9th grade classes. The fourth teacher gave it only to her 7th and 8th grade classes. Statistical analysis of before and after changes in group means indicated a significant increase in score for the two 9th grade classes whose teachers had continued to use the exercises ($t=5.48$, $p < .005$), and a significant decrease in the 9th grade classes where the exercises were discontinued ($t=4.78$, $p < .005$). There were no significant changes in any of the 7th or 8th grade classes. These results also agree with the subjective impressions of the teachers who felt the exercises had the most impact on the older students.

Behavior Modification

This project was designed to teach and clarify the essential principles of behavior modification and their use in the regular classroom. Four teachers participated in this project and at times one of the vice-principals also sat in on the meetings. Two graduate students were involved as consultants. One of the teachers had previously taken an in-service training course on behavior modification during the summer at the Board of Education. This course was intended to give each teacher the information they would need to teach other teachers at their respective schools about behavior modification. A programmed text covering these principles of learning and contingency classroom management had been developed by psychologists at the school board. Unfortunately, without on-line support, teachers from this in-service course had not been able to implement changes in their respective schools. Also, concepts merely talked about in the college classroom were not easily applied in the inner-city classroom by an inexperienced teacher.

The meetings between the teachers and graduate students focused on providing additional clarification and anecdotal sharing of information regarding the use of these techniques in their classes. There was some initial resentment and resistance among the teachers towards the two graduate students which took the form of challenges and skeptical comments regarding the potential of this technique, particularly in classes with a large number of acting-out adolescents. Gradually, however, the teachers began to focus their attention on their own behavior and the use of their reinforcements in the classroom and became less concerned with the threat of evaluation by the graduate students. One teacher began to reinforce students by giving them small classroom responsibilities such as handing out paper and pencils. Another teacher decided that in the future he would see what peer groups formed in the classroom so that as the term progressed he could use peer group membership as a reinforcement for orderly behavior or working on lesson plans. Gradually the teachers began to think of small changes they could implement and became increasingly impressed by how these principles could bring about a change in the classroom behavior of students.

This project continued into the second semester and included the involvement of undergraduate student volunteers from a course taught by one of the graduate students. The undergraduates worked in pairs as observers and recorders of baseline behaviors. The consultants and teachers would then work out a program of intervention using reinforcement techniques, to extinguish negative behaviors and reinforce positive behaviors. After five to six weeks the undergraduates would reenter the classroom and record the new baselines of the same behaviors. The results of this project were very favorable and have been described in more detail by Hadley and Wener (1970).

Videotape Project

The aim of this project was to make the teachers more aware of their teaching styles and the effect that these styles have upon their classes. The primary vehicle for this learning was the use of videorecordings of the teacher in the class. Originally, the project had been planned so that the several teachers who would be videotaped or tape recorded would meet as a group to discuss the tapes and the types of teaching styles represented in each of the tapes. This did not prove to be feasible, however, because of the initial resistance that the teachers had in being compared with one another. They appeared to be extremely threatened by having other teachers see what they were doing in their classroom lest they appear to be inadequate in the eyes of their colleagues. The graduate students understood that these feelings existed and modified the project so as to provide individual feedback to each teacher regarding the tapes that were made in his or her class. This proved to be quite effective. The teachers began to see the manner in which they related to the children in their class. One teacher, while watching the videotape of one of her classes, exclaimed: "I thought I smiled at least once in a while," indicating her surprise at how gloomy she appeared to the children. Part of each videotaping also included shots of the pupils and their behavior in class. On several occasions, these tapes were played back on TV for the students to observe. There seemed to be a direct benefit through this technique becuuse subsequently many students would comment about the degree of disorder and disruption they observed. One teacher in this project was also involved in learning behavior modification techniques in the above project. Putting these two together proved extremely fruitful. The videotape project led eventually to a more complete proposal for the research and development of this technique, which, if funded, will serve as one consultant's Ph.D. dissertation.

Classroom Motivation in Special Reading Problems

This project centered around the remedial reading class. The first stage was a lengthy meeting between the teacher and two consultants. During this stage the consultants obtained information about the physical facilities, reading materials, procedure and content of the classroom sessions, and other topics pertinent to this particular teaching situation. At this time, the consultants first made suggestions for innovations and these were discussed. This initial phase was helpful to the extent that the teacher reported that she now had a clearer idea of how to work with the children and the goals she was trying to accomplish. She felt she was able to use this first phase consultation successfully because the consultants were not part of the formal school system and held no real authority to evaluate her.

During the second phase, the consultants visited the classroom and observed the teacher and the children. They tried to

speak with the children about what they liked and disliked about
the class and what kinds of things they liked to read. Little
useful information was reported to be gained through this procedure.

In the third phase, the consultants implemented several
ideas in the classroom. One aim, at this point, was getting
new reading material to be used by the students, which would
be more related to their personal experiences. The consultants
brought in Black Heritage Series comic books, obtained from the
Coca-Cola Company. The consultants also guided the teacher in
setting up a reinforcement point system for a particular problem
class. The activities valued more by the teacher were worth
more points. These points could then be cashed in to do activities that the students wanted, such as going outside, talking
to one another, or watching television.

In the final phase, the consultants followed up and evaluated their efforts. The reinforcement system ran very smoothly and worked extremely well. The students expressed enthusiasm about this technique and they would begin each period with
planning how many points they were going to make and what they
were going to do with them. The class became more orderly and
the students seemed to work much harder. The teacher was so
pleased that she started this system in another class.

Systems Approach in a Single Classroom

This project began at the initiation of a single teacher
who wished to clarify the complexities surrounding "the fixed
learning attitudes" of her students. The consultants began by
observing the teacher and students as they normally function in
her various classes. It soon became obvious that the students
were reacting against the teacher's maintenance of a tight and
rigidly formal method of instruction. Although her preparation
was excellent, for various reasons the students would act disruptive or inattentive. The aim of the consultants centered
around the understanding of what was happening between the students and teacher in one particular classroom. First, a model
was drawn up based on sociometric analysis of seating arrangements and inter-student communication patterns. It seemed that
there were several different subgroups of students; a few who
were always motivated and attentive, some who never entered into
the classroom activities and appeared completely withdrawn from
the classroom process, while a large minority seemed to be able
to swing either way. In other words, this latter group could
be distracted and participate in a disturbance or they could be
attentive and productive. The students who belong to this latter group tended to form a cohesive subgroup within the class-

room and it was this group that the consultants tried to modify. By systematically collecting behavioral data, consultants worked with the teacher in identifying various trends and trouble spots in her classroom system. The events that they measured included such things as the number of students who were out of their seats, the number arguing, the number of outbursts, or the number of private conversations. They also recorded the number of times the teacher attempted to induce order in the classroom by saying "settle down." After plotting these two different frequencies on various charts, the consultants observed the following patterns: 1) disruptions generally occurred during the late middle part of the classroom period; 2) the frequency of teacher reprimands showed a high correspondence with the onset of disruption; 3) the greatest variation in measures of disruption were generated by the "swing group" 4) when asked to subjectively plot the amount of classroom disorder over time, the teacher indicated awareness of these trends but had little insight as to what was creating them or what she could do to change them.

After several joint discussions, the consultants and the teacher concluded that the initial interest of students was often washed out by the teacher's rigid need to stick to a lesson plan. For example, she might say "we have to write now so we can't talk about that issue." Also, "extreme" opinions generated in a class discussion were frequently ignored even though they were highly relevant. This led to the "extremists" mounting a campaign against the class order and having an influence on the middle-of-the-road group to go their way in creating disruption. Also, the instructional materials were not highly varied and boredom became a crucial factor leading to disruptions towards the end of the period.

To implement change the consultants met several times with the teacher to develop alternate approaches. Increasing student involvement through such devices as student committee meetings, group competition, and other innovative techniques proved to have influence on the middle-of-the-road students, which in turn influenced the entire class. The teacher paradoxically reported having a greater sense of personal control in determining the classroom atmosphere, and feeling less victimized by the proclivities of a few individual students. She also began to recognize the importance of maintaining the interest of the swing group which tends to set the atmosphere for the class. Most importantly, she began to see how fruitless it was to simply admonish a student without appropriately reinforcing the correct behaviors. In general, it became clear that the class itself, like the school, operated in systematic fashion, and interventions in one subsystem could have an effect on other subsystems.

Psychodrama Project

This project was an attempt to combine techniques from such areas as creative dramatics, psychodrama, and small group techniques to use in the teaching of drama in the junior high school classroom. One consultant worked with an English teacher and began a very gradual process of teaching these techniques moving from simple exercises (e.g., nonverbal dyads) to more complicated ones such as sociodrama. A wide variety of such techniques were attempted with varying degrees of success. The teacher found simple non-verbal techniques to be of the greatest use in the classroom setting. More complicated techniques were seen as distracting the students from the central focus of the class. Essentially, the project seems to have opened new areas of source material for the teacher, although it is difficult to evaluate any specific impact at this time.

Discussion Groups for Interracial Problems

This project involved the setting up of a small group to discuss techniques and ways of handling racial problems as they arose in the classroom. The instructor and one graduate student met with a counselor and six to seven teachers to talk about racial problems that had occurred in the school and discussed different ways in which they could be handled. Most of the discussion initially focused on abstractions about racism and prejudice but the teachers gradually came to deal more specifically with situations that are actually happening in the school. The project also involved the introduction of some reading material to increase the teachers' understanding of the Black student as he in turn is becoming aware of his heritage and racial history. This project continued into the second semester but eventually ended when participants felt they had accomplished their initial goal.

Environmental Engineering

This project arose out of a teacher's interest in the effects of seating arrangement on classroom atmosphere. This teacher and her consultant experimented with different seating and lighting arrangements and the use of bulletin boards controlled by student committees. It was generally concluded that environmental cues could be useful supplements to verbal rules and norms for developing classroom order. Also, by allowing the students to have partial control over some aspects of their environment, they appear to take more interest in its maintenance and their own conduct in the classroom.

These eight projects were carried out over a period of three months and several continued for another three months. At this time the principal was appointed as the assistant school superintendent of another geographical area of the city and a new principal took his place. The new principal was not open to our involvement in the school and began to change many aspects of the school rules. In general he was less permissive and more controlling of the teachers' options. Very quickly the school atmosphere began to deteriorate; over sixteen faculty members requested a transfer to a new school in the following year and there were three false fire alarms and two small riots within two months. All of this data is secondary to the main focus of the chapter but is presented for the sake of historical completeness and to demonstrate the importance of top level commitment in any change program. Leaving aside for the moment the fact that the total program eventually collapsed because of a change in principals, what can be said for its benefit and how are these outcomes related to our models of open systems and process consultation?

One, the program led to a greater awareness of the interdependence of the teachers, vice-principals, principal, pupils and other subsystems. In particular, the teachers began to see the principal as a potential source of support and valuable information. His role of a boundary spanner was far less threatening. The teachers in the project became, as expected, more cohesive. Initially, many of the teachers had expressed resentment about being abandoned in a hopeless situation and cut off from any sources of help that did not have strings attached or were not loaded with evaluation. Furthermore, they felt that previously most advice was generally condescending and usually critical rather than positive, particularly when it came from traditional sources such as supervisory personnel or visiting teachers. A few teachers who had initially planned to terminate their teaching career and seek new employment had decided to give it another try.

Two, the program helped to open the system to useful inputs from the environment. Not only were we accepted but eventually the teachers allowed greater inputs from the pupils. I believe the teachers felt the school's skin to be less unbearably thin and felt enough security to allow feedback to circulate within the system.

Three, the program introduced some specific innovations into the school and more importantly, began to stimulate a normative philosophy of planned change, experimentation, and risk-taking. Their willingness to risk change was related, in turn, to their feelings of less environmental pressures to maintain the status quo. The feeling of less environmental pressure to maintain the status quo was also related to their new perception of the principal and the fact that they were more open to more

complete and accurate environmental feedback asking for change.
They were also showed greater trust in their own abilities to
initiate and implement innovations. The projects grew out of
small group diagnostic and planning efforts so that the outcomes
of the projects were not seen as the consultants' "expert" solutions for teacher problems.

On our side of the ledger the program had several beneficial outcomes. It made us more aware of the problems confronting a school principal and teachers, particularly in a racially-
mixed school dealing with pupils in that critical period of adolescence. The program allowed us to try out some models and to
test our skills on the firing line. To this extent the graduate
students must be praised for their perserverance, creativity,
and ability to develop helping relationships with some terribly
beleaguered teachers. The fact that we left our offices and
spent our time in the teachers' own territory was a factor helping our acceptance.

We also learned some useful information about problems in
the larger community surrounding the school. Problems of hous-
ing, ethnic and racial tensions, unemployment, crime, drugs,
and a dozen other issues, were expressed in various ways within
the school. To this extent the program was one relating to more
general community psychology.

Finally, the projects convinced the faculty and students that
that field research could be combined in a meaningful way with
applied consultation. Our major regret is that we did not set
up extensive methods to evaluate the overall program. The tim-
ing and urgency did not allow for slow and considered research
planning. Our sudden exodus precluded gradual evaluation.
Given more time and opportunities, however, a more rigorous evaluation would certainly be called for.

Process consultation and open systems theory may not be the
optimal models to use for school consultation programs. A com-
parison and evaluation of several models is certainly needed.
These two models did, however, provide a starting point and a
base of security for some relatively inexperienced graduate students and their equally anxious faculty member. The existential
reality and confusing phenomena we call schools and education
could probably be explained by many different models; we happened to find these two most compatible with our own previous training.

There were, of course, some failures and shortcomings of
the specific program and the models we used. We did not reach
all of the teachers since we rested strongly on motivation and
teacher interest. Obviously any comprehensive program that ex-

pects comprehensive results will eventually have to include all the teachers within the established boundaries. We relied on a very favorable consultant/consultee ratio. Any realistic program will have to develop ways to get maximal change effort with minimal consultant time and energy. We did not persist and follow through when a change in principals was brought about. A serious program would provide continual support and continuity. With some greater effort on the part of the faculty, some acceptance and continuity might have been established. Graduate student resources, however, were being demanded elsewhere, and the situation deteriorated so rapidly that our own motivation to persist was quickly eroded. To overcome this serious problem, any consultation program should be developed with invitations and sanctions at a level higher than the principal, allowing for better continuity, given a stable source of consultant resources.

It is impossible to describe all the actions and outcomes connected with this program, but at least one stable principle stands out: in gaining entry, in maintaining sanctions, and in planning change, do not stray from the primary internal resources of the organization, the people who make the system operate. The internal operations of any system must ultimately be consistent with the values and needs of the persons within the system and consultation cannot operate in the long run against this powerful force. Assuming an open system will make adaptive changes to survive, the consultant can best operate as a mechanism for feedback and a creative source of alternative techniques and strategies from which the system can make its own choices.

REFERENCES

Argyris, C. *Interpersonal competence and organizational effectiveness.* Homewood, Illinois: Richard D. Irwin, Inc., 1962.

Argyris, C. *Organization and innovation.* Homewood, Illinois: Richard D. Irwin, Inc., 1965.

Bennis, W. G., Benne, K. D., and Chin, R. (Eds.). *The planning of change,* (1st Ed.), New York: Holt, Rinehart, and Winston, 1961.

Bennis, W. G., Benne, K. D., and Chin, R. (Eds.). *The planning of change,* (2nd Ed.), New York: Holt, Rinehart, and Winston, 1969.

Bertalanffy, Ludwig von, *General systems theory.* New York: George Braziller, Inc., 1968.

Hadley, T. and Wener, A. "Utilization of undergraduates for classroom behavior modification." Unpublished manuscript, University of Pittsburgh, 1970.

Katz, D. and Kahn, R. L. *The social psychology of organizations.* New York: John Wiley and Sons, 1966.

Lippitt, R., Watson, J., and Westley, B. *The dynamics of planned change.* New York: Harcourt, Brace, and World, Inc., 1958.

Miles, M. Some properties of schools as social systems, in Watson G. *Change in school systems.* Washington, D. C.: National Training Laboratories, 1967.

Miller, J. G. Toward a general theory for the behavioral sciences. *American Psychologist,* 1955, 10, pp. 513-553.

Parsons, T. *The social system.* Glencoe, Illinois: Free Press, 1951.

Schein, E. H. *Process consultation: Its role in organization development.* Reading, Mass.: Addison-Wesley Co., 1969.

Schein, E. H. and Bennis, W. G. *Personal and organizational change through group methods.* New York: John Wiley and Sons, Inc., 1965.

9. BEHAVIOR MODIFICATION TRAINING

Dr. Chandler works in a mental health agency which has, as one of its functions, a school liaison and training program. He speaks in this chapter of the school as a complex social system which needs to be understood before a consultant can work effectively. Particularly he emphasizes that the system must maintain itself to survive, and any consultant interested in that system must help that social system support itself. He reminds the reader that schools are not hospitals, pupils are not mental patients and psychological consultants need to alter their behavior and perspectives to match the demands. There are three major roles potentially useful to the consultant joining the system: 1) identify with the school by stressing educational interests and background; 2) develop a guest-host relationship in which the consultant is the well-mannered guest operating in the host's home; 3) act as confidant with private relationships between faculty and consultant.

Each of these three methods has its advantages and disadvantages which are discussed briefly by Dr. Chandler. He outlines four principles which he says are shown to be helpful in becoming an effective consultant for a school system. The consultant should: 1) accept referrals in the vernacular; 2) recognize and understand the implicit process or model used by the teacher in making the referral; 3) remember that the school defines the terms of the consultant's intervention; 4) when compromised, make clear the minimum requirements for a continuing relationship.

This program is narrower in scope and more specific in goal than those suggested in the chapters by Langmeyer et al., or Bower. However, it is more typical of individual consultants as they seek to develop a working relationship with a school system. The points raised here seem to be relevant to anyone trying to consult with a school system.

PROVIDING TRAINING IN BEHAVIOR MODIFICATION

TECHNIQUES FOR SCHOOL PERSONNEL

Gail E. Chandler
Hamden Mental Health Service

As roles in community mental health continue to broaden, the professional hesitates to conjecture where he might find himself plying his trade or what indeed his trade might be. Psychologists have "traditionally" acted as consultants to schools. Lately, however, consultation has been broadened to include formal training for school personnel, notably training in behavior modification techniques for teachers (Hall, 1968; Becker, 1967). In addition, those with credentials in fields other than psychology, especially social workers, have found themselves performing the same teacher training functions.

For some time, the author has been presenting in-service training seminars for teachers and other school personnel to acquaint them with principles of behavior modification and to provide them with an opportunity to begin using operant techniques in a planful way themselves. This chapter is written to communicate the author's experience to others. An initial section will pertain to the school as a social system, since understandings derived from this kind of analysis have been helpful both in overcoming problems of "entry" and in maintaining an effective consultant-like relationship throughout the program. The subsequent section will relate more specifically to the management of behavior modification training programs in schools.

THE SCHOOL AS A SOCIAL SYSTEM

Mental health services function as a social system. That is, professionals concerned with mental health share somewhat similar value and belief systems, express aims that are comparable, relate to each other in terms of a common identification and tend to see and relate to professional roles in mental health with some agreement. Workers in the same mental health facility will agree even more closely as to values, aims and appropriate roles. Indeed, where such agreement is not in evidence, the facility functions poorly, morale is poor, and services inadequate. The facility will then attempt to "slough off" members or factions whose values, aims and role enactments have become too dissonant with respect to the social system as a whole. Furthermore, and here is the point, social systems must take care for their own efficient functioning. They operate within the context of a larger community network of interdependent systems, each subserving by appropriate role enactment, the values and goals of the larger system. For one subsystem to blunder in its performance is to risk replacement by an ambitious understudy--a newly developing subsystem or an expanding older one.

What is true, then for mental health is equally true for education, and those social systems principles that validate the maintenance of a mental health facility or service are the same as those that validate the maintenance of a school system. The point cannot be made too strongly. All too often the mental health worker who finds himself outside of his special preserve will come to grief for having failed to recognize the values, aims and prescribed roles of a system that is different from his own or, recognizing these, has judged them in terms of his own system alone and not in terms of the larger system under which both are subsumed.

Schools, then, are not mental hospitals and teachers are not psychiatric aides. Schools exist for a variety of legitimate (or legitimized) reasons: to transmit knowledge, to develop skills, to inculcate values, even to contain youthful subgroups seen as potentially destructive in the community. Roles within an educational system relate to these aims. Thus, school administrators must be concerned with the appearance their school makes in its community, teachers must bear allegiance to their own institutions, implementing positive and negative sanctions in accordance with prescrived values, and indeed, contracting with students and utilizing incentives within a framework only partly of the teacher's own making. To expect otherwise, to wonder that those within an educational system do not believe and act as those within a mental health system is naive. More than that, it can be destructive. If the mental health worker succeeds in "converting" the school representative, the resultant role dissonance for him may impede, not help, performance. More likely, the mental health worker will succeed only in reinforcing an impression that psychologists, social workers and the like are indeed a threat.

The problem, then, is how to relate to a system different from one's own in such a way as to facilitate appropriate functioning within that system when, as a matter of fact, one's base system, merely by being different, can represent a potential threat. The problem is, of course, generic to all modalities of social service (or any social interaction, for that matter) and typified formally in the individual counseling relationship, especially where based upon phenomenological considerations (Rogers, 1970).

Essentially, two approaches to resolution are possible, one emphasizing identification with the role of educator, the other disdaining such identification. If, in fact, the mental health worker has functioned as a teacher or administrator within a school system, he can allude to this experience, hoping that an empathetic bond will be established. Such an approach has been found quite useful. The mental health worker is able to exhibit first-hand knowledge of and respect for the boundaries within which change is licit. He proceeds to press, in one way or another, for such change. It should be pointed out, however, that this attempt to gain acceptance, to overcome the "entry" problem, may not always succeed. Implicit in the statement that one has in the past functioned in a certain role is the fact that one no longer does. The mental health worker, then, could be condidered one who had been privy to school functioning (and school "Secrets") and is now in a position to employ such knowledge in the service of a **competing** system. The mental health worker, in other words, could be viewed as a turncoat, to be defended against at all costs.

If, now, the worker has no school credentials, or chooses not to disclose them, he must present himself unambiguously as representing values and performing in roles which are to some extent foreign (and potentially inimical) to schools. His role, then, and the complementary role for the school, becomes clear. He is "guest" and the school is "host." Under such conditions it becomes clear that the host must, while behaving with courtesy, retain for himself such functions as the determination of priorities, utilization of his resources, allocation of time, etc. In addition, the host maintains an appropriate social distance (cf., e.g., Goffman, 1959), protecting his guest from the "family secrets" which would embarrass the guest (i.e., by presenting material which could be dealt with only in violation of the agreed-upon roles). The guest is, reciprocally, not expected to divulge in detail the basis for his status, whatever that may be, within his own system. The distance so established makes communication possible by reducing potential (mutual) threat. In such a way, much can be accomplished in terms of limited systems modification.

For more radical systems change, a more intimate rela-

tionship is required, one in which risk (again, mutually experienced) is greater. The appropriate role would then become
"confidant," a role marked by privileged communication based
upon trust. Such a role cannot be demanded. It is awarded,
with time, and after careful testing.

The principles enunciated above suggest certain specific
ways for the mental health consultant to relate to schools:

1) Referrals should be accepted in the terms
(and, so far as possible, the exact language)
they are presented in. The complaint, "Johnny is
a loud-mouth and a pest" could be translated by
the mental health worker into, "Johnny is reinforced for inappropriate verbalizations and inappropriate social interactions according to a
schedule which is maintaining such verbalizations
and interactions with high frequency."
Though useful as an academic exercise for the
worker, from a social systems perspective, it is
important to demonstrate to the educator that
communication will be in the terms of the educational institution. Especially where the worker
is concerned with maintenance of the child in
school in preference to drawing him into a system of direct mental health services, the worker
will refrain from language which could suggest
that the child's behavior is so deviant as to be
inexplicable without reference to a special lexi-
con. On the other hand, the experienced worker
will avoid creating the impression that the school
is somehow deficient for not being able to remed-
iate the problem without "outside" assistance.

2) Ordinarily the school representative will
have a hypothesis on the basis of which he is attempting to explain his problem. The hypothesis can be, "You can't teach kids like this."
"I don't understand why he does it (and could
handle the situation if I did)," "We need to
learn ways of dealing with children like this,"
or another. Just as appropriate inter-system
role relating suggests acceptance of the problem
in the terms of the referring person, it also
suggests acceptance (at least tentatively) of
his explanatory hypothesis. Since, as Freud
suggested, most behaviors are over-determined
(explicable to some degree on the basis of a
variety of "causes"), the worker should not feel

that his professional integrity is being too greatly compromised. However, mental health sophistication need not be attributed to the educator. For example, where "understanding" is presented as a solution by the educator, it should not be assumed that what is meant is insight into intrapsychic dynamics. "Understanding" can be accepted in terms of appreciation of the influence of immediate consequences.

3) In general, the educator's determination of where, when and for how long the mental health worker will be permitted to function must be accepted. Again, the principle is that the educator is more familiar with the requirements, and the ability to withstand stress, under his system than someone belonging to another system. By demonstrating respect for these determinations, the mental health worker shows a willingness to interact in a way that both permits continued communication and provides safeguards against inappropriate inter-systems incursions. The worker may hope that in time a more intimate (more potentially growth-inducing) relationship can be achieved.

4) A final suggestion relates to a fundamental prerogative of the "guest"--his right to specify his own requirements within the relationship agreed upon. This prerogative, moreover, represents a responsibility as well, if an honest relationship is to be maintained. Thus, if the terms in which the problem is presented ("I can't work with such stupid (retarded) kids"), the proposed hypothesis ("His whole family is rotten (and he will be too)") or the limitations in interaction ("I just have 10 minutes this week") represent intolerable restrictions, the mental health worker needs to make this position clear. Most of the time, however, some compromise can be reached through which the school representative can maintain himself safely within his system (as he should) and the mental health worker can expect to achieve a limited goal.

PRESENTING BEHAVIOR MODIFICATION TRAINING

TO SCHOOL PERSONNEL

The preceding has dealt with general principles of inter-

systems consultation, with some examples drawn from school consultation. This section will relate more specifically to the
author's experience in conducting seminars in behavior modification for teachers and school administrators. A detailed
description of the format for such seminars can be found elsewhere (Chandler,1969). Suffice it to say here that the seminars
have met typically for eight two-to three-hour sessions once or
twice a week. In the teacher groups, both experienced and inexperienced teachers have participated, together with the school
principals and superintendent. In the administrator groups,
principals, assistants to the superintendent and the superintendent have met together. No group has consisted of more than 25
members. Activities for the seminars have consisted of readings, some lectures, discussions, viewing of films and experience in behavioral observation and recording,implementation of
a simple behavior modification intervention (typically differential social reinforcement), and evaluation. Evaluation has
been in terms of the effectiveness of the specific intervention
and also in terms of the extent to which the seminar succeeded
in attaining broader pre-specified goals.

Insofar as possible, those same behavior modification principles by which teachers are to change certain behaviors are
employed by the seminar leader in his attempt to change certain
behaviors of the teachers. Specifically, the leader's objectives for the seminar are specified in writing at the first
meeting, and participants are asked to develop similar individualized objectives for themselves. The importance of framing
these objectives in behavioral terms is stressed. The relationship between meaningful quantitative evaluation and clear behavioral objectives is likewise emphasized. And, as in all
good teaching, the leader attempts to reinforce successive
approximations on the part of seminar participants, to ignore
a number of dissonant comments and to identify and develop participants as "models" with respect to a procedure, technique,
or what have you. From time to time, when such teaching via
behavior modification techniques has been employed, the attention of the group is called to this fact. That is, the leader's
own behavior is analyzed from a behavioral point of view. For
example, the leader will inquire as to the effect on group
members of his differential reinforcement and will report on
the consequences with respect to his own behavior of differential reinforcement on the part of the group. The principle
here is that learning will be enhanced when techniques are
identified and labeled and when awareness is encouraged.

Let us turn now to some specific tactics:

The importance of relating within the school context has

been discussed above. Here it should be emphasized that school people will present the leader with specific problems they are currently experiencing and their expectation will be that specific "advice" will be provided. That is, the school person will be testing the consultants ability to maintain appropriate inter-system distance while at the same time communicating effectively. In many situations, the situation will be complex and the network of reinforcement contingencies will be difficult to untangle. A temptation is to view the presentation of such situations as a devious move to discredit the leader and to respond in such a way as to avoid the issue. The author's experience is that, in the majority of cases, the problem is presented simply because it represents a vexing situation. An evasive response will be more likely to discredit the leader than a response which, while recognizing the complexity of the problem, suggests one or more alternatives which might provide at least temporary respite. Frequently, this is all the questioner expects.

Another consideration in relating to teachers is that the role prescribed for classroom teachers has been a lonely one, at least before the advent of team teaching. Most teachers spend almost all of their work day either literally alone (preparing lessons, correcting papers, etc.) or in the company of only children. Teachers, then, frequently appreciate opportunities to discuss their activities with understanding adults. Talking in the seminar, then, should be encouraged. Justification might simply be on grounds of promoting the teachers' mental health by providing an opportunity for ventilation. It should be borne in mind, moreover, that learning is always an interactional process (c.f., e.g., Postman & Weingartner, 1969) and that relevant teacher talking (or perhaps even talk whose relevance is not immediately clear) is generally preferable to intensive note-taking. (The emission of a response is a prerequisite to reinforcement.) Moreover, it sometimes happens that one teacher is better able to relate to another's problems than someone who is not a teacher. Of course it is always possible, once this strong reinforcer (opportunity to talk) has been identified, to present the reinforcer contingent upon desirable teacher behaviors (successful completion of an assignment, for instance).

When the leader himself talks, our experience is that his topics should be as directly relevant as possible. Studies involving rats and pigeons may, for one reason or another, fascinate a psychologist. It would be a mistake to assume that they would also hold a group of school people spell bound. Similarly, applications of operant procedures in clinical settings or in situations involving grossly deviant behavior may have a certain dramatic impact, but most school personnel would not see that these applications had bearing on their own classroom situations. Any advantage in attending to such studies, then, might come from their establishing the leader as coming from a different setting. Once established, of course, the point does not need to be continually pressed.

A final word needs to be said about sanctioning within the social system of a school or school district. The principal, for a school, or superintendent, for a district, normally exercises considerable control with respect to his building or district. To attempt to conduct any mental health program within his province without prior endorsement (or at least acquiescense) could entail substantial risk. Conversely, if the sanctioning person can be brought to a condition of some enthusiasm for a program, its chances of success are greatly improved. Many of the behaviors of teachers can be changed in the course of a well-planned seminar. To be maintained once the seminar is over, requires a reinforcement schedule that is built into the school system itself.

REFERENCES

Becker, W. C., Madsen, C. H., Arnold, C. R., and Thomas, D. R. The contingent use of teacher attention and praise in reducing classroom behavior problems. *The Journal of Special Education,* 1967, 1, pp. 287-307.

Chandler, G. E., Removing barriers: a description of overcoming an "entry" problem and providing indirectly for improved mental health services for school age children. Mimeo, 1969.

Goffman, E., *The presentation of self in everyday life.* Garden City, New York: Doubleday and Company, 1959.

Hall, V. R., Panyon, M., Rabon, D., and Broden, M., Instructing beginning teachers in reinforcement procedures which improve classroom control. *Journal of Applied Behavior Analysis,* 1968, 1, 315-322.

Kroth, R. L., Whelan, R. J., and Stables, J. M., Teacher application of behavior principles in home and classroom environments. *Focus on Exceptional Children,* 1970, 1, pp. 1-10.

Postman, N. and Weingartner, *Teaching as a subversive activity.* New York: Delacorte Press, 1969.

Rogers, C., *On becoming a person.* New York: Houghton Mifflin, 1970.

10. PRIMARY GRADE INTERVENTION

This chapter represents a brief tract in support of a broadened concept of the teacher's role. Dr. Barocas sees that teachers can be and need to be social engineers and that their training as diagnosticians and referral agents is anti-good mental health. The classroom, particularly in the early years, is a "pivotal setting" which represents the greatest and most direct potential for intervening positively on behalf of the child. The solution proposed by Dr. Barocas is that of a sophisticated contingency management program.

Dr. Barocas' indicates that he sees the most effective intervention taking place prior to kindergarten but beginning with pregnant mothers. That is primary prevention!

INTERVENTION IN THE PRIMARY GRADES AS A MENTAL HEALTH STRATEGY

Ralph Barocas
University of Rochester

The introduction of innovation in any social system is not a task to be undertaken by the easily discouraged. Most social institutions, the schools included, move slowly. In this manner, the institution conserves itself and protects its integrity. Administrators are careful in the introduction of new programs, often pursue safe, low-risk alternatives and may even resist evaluations likely to produce a fair test of the program because of the political realities of program failures (Campbell 1969). Unimaginative administration notwithstanding, we are all convinced of the need for innovations that would instrument maximally supportive environments for educational and personal development.

The expansion and alteration of the schools' role in the provision of health services beyond the fundamentals of reading, writing and the doing of sums is well known. The school nurse, dental clinics, innoculation programs, and health education are now accepted components of the school experience. Similarly, the school has also been responsive to the more amorphous symptoms of "mental illness." Thus, psychologists and social workers are observed in the organizational schema of the school system. Although often found to be working in cloakrooms, these mental health professional are a line budget item each year, with the assurance that any attempt to delete this item would be met with great resistance. It is the adequacy of these systems of delivering mental health services to the school child that required continued evaluation and question.

Albee (1959; 1963; 1967) has repeatedly cautioned that the vast projected needs for mental health services so far outstrip our manpower resources, that we will be impotent in the face of it. Our current standards and expectations are such that unless enthusiastic and active intervention is undertaken, the overall quality of mental health care available to Americans will deteriorate. Futhermore, qualitative differences in service will continue to be accentuated on the basis of income.

In addition to expanded training of professionals, which will not approximate the need, two other avenues have been pursued. Nonprofessionals have been employed in a variety of settings with professionals as consultants and trainers. Thus, college students as companions (Holzberg, 1963), sophisticated housewives (Rioch, 1967), bachelor-degree level persons, (Sanders, Smith, and Weinmen, 1967), inner-city youth (Klein, 1967), and retired people (Cowen, Leibowitz & Lebowitz, 1968), are all examples of attempts to exploit previously unused pools of manpower.

The emphasis on the early identification and primary prevention of emotional disorders has been the second line of effort. The belief subscribed to here, is that the earlier the behavioral problem is detected, the greater the likelihood of quick, economical and effective intervention. Although early detection is an extremely desirable course to pursue, its effectiveness is diminished somewhat by our current state of knowledge. That is, many disturbances are susceptible to treatment early, but are difficult to identify. Later, more easily identified treatment alternatives may be limited. Stated differently, the earlier a disorder is detected, the more likely the treatment will be successful. But, the nearer to the initiation of the disorder, the more difficult it is to observe.

Essentially, the conception of early detection transfers the focus to problems in children and particularly, children in the school setting. Still treatment oriented, these procedures characteristically provide attention, professional or otherwise, to the child upon identification as a "problem." These are basically reactive procedures, and although often aggressive and ambitious, are not preventive. A more profitable alternative to "after-the-fact" treatment programs, thus far only minimally exploited, is to design environments, both physical and interpersonal, that promote health.

It is utopian to expect that every citizen can be provided with a uniformly high level of interpersonal skills that will permit the achievment of a rewarding and satisfying life. But, certainly, some social roles are more critical for the development of these abilities in children than others. A plausible criterion for the importance of a particular role to the development of competence is the amount of time spent with the child. Consequently, the primary school teacher might be more important in the development of healthy emotional attitudes and behavior than the school bus-driver who, in his turn, may be more important than the supermarket cashier.

The teacher, particularly in the primary grades, where there is minimal room-change, is uniquely placed. He is in a position to make repeated observations of a child's behavior; he delivers praise and punishments which are the vehicles of shaping the child's education and personal growth; and not to be overlooked, may monitor the consequences of his efforts on the child's behavior. Given the centrality of the teacher's role in the development of effective and productive social behavior in the child, the teacher's skills as a social engineer becomes critical.

Teachers generally complete some psychology courses to meet certification requirements. Typically, these courses provide information about "mental mechanisms," "psychological needs," and "the helping professions." With the exception of special education programs, the teacher receives no direct training in, a practicum sense, for the development of skills applied to adjustment processes. A common outcome of these training procedures is that teachers are trained to **interpret** and **diagnose** the child's behavior, particularly in response to their own failure in "handling" the child. The focus then, is not on the actual disruptive, or isolative, behavior of the child, and continued coping with these behaviors in the classroom. Instead, the teacher is encouraged to develop psychodynamic explanations, e.g., what needs are being satisfied by these behaviors?

In a facetious, but incisive way, Haley (1969) proposed a set of procedures to ensure failure in psychotherapeutic treatment. These include: resisting the acceptance of overt behavior as the problem, because it is merely a symptom; avoidance of operational language as it applies to intervention procedures; and emphasis on a single treatment modality for all patients. Preparatory training for teachers, and as Haley indicates, for many mental health workers, conforms to this model of failure.

Although the teacher's professional status is never compromised, he is taught parameters of his competency as it applies to the child's problems. The teacher, despite the latitude of what constitutes a classroom problem, is instructed to refer the child to the mental health professional. The child is then caught up in a potentially unfortunate series of bureaucratic procedures designed to bring more and more narrowly specialized competencies into play in more and more different physical environments than the one in which the behavioral dysfunction is identified.

The teacher, either at his wit's end or feeling that he is

unable to provide the indicated care, refers the child to another professional, such as the school psychologist. The psychologist, not unlike most others providing service to the public, is characteristically over-worked. He has a back-log of
referrals that require attention; he must make a new set of referrals; and simultaneously, he must arrange feedback opportunities for parents and teachers. Often, he is supportive and
reassuring to both teachers and parents, but does not articu-
late a specific treatment for the child. If the child's behavior persists despite the teacher's renewed and enlightened efforts to be both firm, reassuring, kind and tolerant of the
child, a decision is made. This decision is one that acknow-
ledges that the child is so **sick**, that the individualized treatment in non-school setting is required. It might be in the
form of referral to a child guidance clinic, or if the child
is **really sick**, the more controlled and intensively therapeutic environment of residential care is indicated.

These procedures also permit the teacher and mental health
worker to experience satisfaction for having obtained "the
kind of treatment the child needed." This description is neither uncommon or exaggerated. But the point that often escapes
us is that the teacher is already influencing the child's
growth. Rather than limiting the teacher's scope of competence
explicit statement of how the teacher's activities effect the
growth of child is required. An irony exists here, for while
people in the schools often speak of education in terms of the
"whole child," efforts are constantly directed toward limit-
setting of the teacher's activities when mental health is mentioned. Worse yet, it is often the teacher himself who engages
in the limit-setting and may be most vocal in resisting the expansion of his responsibilities to the child.

Rejection of pediatricians, psychiatrists, psychologists,
speech therapists, social workers and all other health workers
is not implied here. Instead, the central position that teachers, particularly in the formative years of the primary grades,
hold in respect to the child's personal growth is emphasized.
Secondly, because of the centrality, and the fact that his efforts **do** effect growth, the consequences of his interpersonal
behavior on the child's repertory should be made explicit--
thereby **expanding** his competency and skills in working with
the "whole child." The teacher is already a mental health
worker, whether he likes it or not. Up until recently, he has
been aware of this role in the sense of diagnostician often
acting as the primary source to the school mental health worker.
Although his teaching efforts may have therapeutic and preventive consequences, these are typically adventitious. Similarly
there may be circumstances where the teacher's unintentional

efforts diminish the child's effectiveness.

In the same manner that we are all mental health workers
because our behavior has consequences for others, it is profitable to cause teachers to be more aware of the consequences
of their behavior. Not all children can be maintained in the
classroom, but it is contended here that many more may be
worked within the general classroom setting than presently are.
Children are not animals, but laboratory experiences with animals have an important message for us. When an experiment with
an animal fails in that the desired behavior is not obtained,
it is the rare experimenter who explains that outcome by stating the animal is **stupid** or **crazy**. Rather the good experimen-
tor looks to his procedures; to his own efforts that have contributed to the unanticipated and unwanted outcome. Similarly
it would seem that many, although not all, problems encountered
in the classroom may be controlled by the teacher by examination of his responses to the child's behavior. Much data has
been accumulated that supports the view that behavior persists
only when the consequences are rewarding to the child. Because the teacher's behavior is an important response consequence to the child, the teacher, by becoming aware of the relationship between his behavior and the child's, has an important therapeutic tool at his disposal in the classroom context.

A second advantage to treating the child in the classroom
is that is where the problems are occurring. Again, there is
much work to suggest that behavior is the product of the interaction between a person's history of experience and the situ-
ational consequences. Insofar as these current and more immediate behavioral contingencies determine ongoing behavior,
then, the altered management of these contingencies in the
classroom should yield changes in behavior. Thus, working with
the child in the context where the problems occur is to be preferred to situations where different contingencies are influencing behavior. Treatment in a different setting (e.g., a
Mental Health Center; or even the use of teacher-aides) then
may have value for changing the child's behavior in the direction of a more productive life, but it would appear to be less
direct than the teacher's efforts in the classroom.

Traditional psychotherapeutic procedures minimize the importance of consequence and current contingencies in their
roles of behavior maintenance. This is not to suggest that
able psychotherapists are not aware of the current contingencies in the psychotherapy situation. Yet, the implicit model
here is one that views therapy as a created opportunity for
cognitive change. In turn, these changes generalize to, and
mediate, overt behavioral change in "non-therapy hour" environ-

ments. There, these "new" behaviors are maintained by the rewards and satisfactions they obtain for the person. Densiti-
zation, implosive therapy, and the role-play procedures all
attempt to recreate the environmental contingencies that cause
discomfort for the patient. They are successful treatment procedures to the extent that the "imaginings" approximate the
non-therapy situation.

Generalization is the vital question in considerations of
efficacy of all psychological treatment procedures, and of
course, is of consequence here. The issue of the trans-situa-
tional nature of problem behaviors aside, would teacher induced
behavior change covary with change in the home? In work directly addressed to this question, Wahler (1970) evaluated the
consequences of a successful home modification program, administered by parent(s), on changes in occurrence of similar behaviors in the school setting. His data indicates a failure
to generalize, and prompted him to suggest that efforts be ex-
pended on the identification of pivotal settings which will
yield maximal generalization.

For the young child, i.e. K-3, whose modility is essentially limited to the school and home settings, concerted efforts by teacher and agents in the home should be maximally
effective in producing behavior change.

The mental health worker's role must be modified as well.
Where previously, much time was occupied with testing and referral, with very little time spent in treatment, now treatment is redefined to entail **training** and continued consultation
of parents and teachers. This newly constituted mental health
team of teacher, parents, and school mental health worker will
seek to modify the child's existing environment by altering
the response contingencies in the life contexts of the child.
Those procedures are pursued with a minimum of discontinuity
unlike that caused by more conventional therapeutic intervention. These latter experiences not only remove the child from
the behavior settings where problems occur, but one can only
speculate as to the consequences of designating a child to appear at a special building where special people do special
things with him.

Two general points remain to be made. The first is related to the implementation of programs in the public schools;
the latter is a closing comment on the development of a true
prevention program.

It has been our discomforting experience, and apparently
it is not an isolated instance, to have encountered resistance

in the schools to agreed upon programs. Working in the schools is something not unlike working in a prison. In the prison where the key word is rehabilitation, psychotherapeutic procedures are not viewed as a genuine rehabilitative technique, and therefore, may be assigned a priority below that of getting the crop in. Similarly, the schools hesitance, sometimes viewed as passive-aggression, is observed in latenesses, missed appointments, or changed priorities. Programmatic progress is impeded by this reluctance, and the word **sabotage** is occasionally heard describing the behavior of an administrator, teacher or mental health worker. Psychodynamic explanations offered for the schools reluctance for full participation, typically entail defensiveness. Teachers, administrators and school mental health workers are **threatened** by the expertise of the consultants, or they **resent** the intrusion on their perceived competence. Yet, if we are to apply our own behavioral counsel to ourselves, these explanations would be set aside. Instead, we would acknowledge the failure on our part to develop an adequate reward procedure for shaping the schools personnel's response to the program.

Efforts should be directed toward the development of reward systems which transcend the benign chicanery of selling the program which includes the assurance to teachers that they will not be exposed to severe criticism, and simultaneously, exploits the competiveness that exists among school administrators, by indicating that this innovative program provides an uncommon lustre to his pupil-services offerings.

In closing, it is fitting to acknowledge that the promises of social engineering and primary intervention are still unkept. The applications only briefly outlined above are treatment oriented and are summaries of needs and proposals for working with children and parents **after** a problem has been identified. But these same procedures, that is, immediacy of consequence and explicit contingencies are also valuable in the development of prosocial behaviors. The encouragement of questioning, of self-expression and of competence in general, is shaped by parental, teacher and, of course, other children's presentations of praise, punishments and tangible "things." There are no compelling reasons not to engage in positive applications. For example, the construction of classroom contingencies designed to foster divergent thinking in the young pre-school child. Materials such as microscopes and typewriters could be phased into a K-3 curriculum. These materials whose access would be contingent upon the completion of low probability preference tasks, would create opportunities for the child to satisfy both intellectual and manipulative "curiosity" simultaneously. These positive kinds of outcomes will contribute to more resourceful behavioral repertories. Simply, the more the child knows about the world, and the more able he is to extract rewards from his environment, the greater the likelihood of a healthy and productive life.

Finally, although current contingencies have been stressed the effects of history are not to be minimized; behavior is always the outcome of the two and must always be linked to what has preceeded. Thus, the probability of problems in the school is partially determined by earlier interpersonal transactions; and consequently, true prevention should be undertaken prior to the child's entry into the public school. Presently we are in the midst of developing a program that would place non-professional behavioral consultants into pre-natal care clinics. The target population is to be mothers carrying the first child. It is our hope that these mothers will be more amenable to our program, if only because they do not have to overcome previous child-rearing practices. Presently non-operational, the program is being directed towards environmental enrichment as well as child management procedures with goals of maximizing satisfaction for the whole family.

REFERENCES

Albee, G. W. *Mental health manpower trends.* New York: Basic Books, 1959.

Albee, G. W. American psychology in the sixties. *American Psychologist,* 1963, 18, pp. 90-95.

Albee, G. W. The relation of conceptual models to manpower needs. In E. L. Cowen, E. A. Gardiner, and M. Zax (Eds.) *Emergent approaches to mental health problems.* New York: Appleton-Century-Crofts, 1967.

Campbell, D. T. Reforms as experiments. *American Psychologist,* 1969, 24, pp. 409-429.

Cowen, E. L., Leibowitz, G., & Leibowitz, Ellen. Utilization of retired people as mental health aides with children. *American Journal of Orthopsychiatry,* 1968, 38, pp. 900-909.

Haley, J. The art of being a failure as a therapist. *American Journal of Orthopsychiatry,* 1969, 39, pp. 691-695.

Holzberg, J. D. The companion program; Implementing the manpower recommendations of the Joint Commission on Mental Illness and Health. *American Psychologist,* 1963, 18, pp. 224-226.

Klein, W. L. The training of human service aides. In E. L. Cowen, E. A. Gardiner, and M. Zax (Eds.). *Emergent approaches to mental health problems.* New York: Appleton-Century-Crofts, 1967.

Rioch, M. J. Pilot projects in training mental health counselors. In E. L. Cowen, E. A. Gardiner, and M. Zax (Eds.). *Emergent approaches to mental health problems.* New York: Appleton-Century-Crofts, 1967.

Sanders, R., Smith, R., & Weinman, B. *Chronic psychoses and recovery: an experiment in socio-environmental therapy.* San Francisco: Jossey-Bass, 1967.

Wahler, R. G.   Setting generality: some specific and general effects of child behavior therapy. *Journal of Applied Behavior Analysis*, 1969, 2, pp. 239-246.

11. HELPING TEACHERS

This selection is noteworthy for three reasons: 1) it reflects the influence of Michigan's Jim Kelly, with its emphasis on an ecological approach to the understanding of schools; 2) it represents a exposition of the development, over a long period of time, of a consultation program; and 3) it illustrates the roles that can be taken by a "helping teacher" as an important mental health adjunct.

Dr. Kelly is well known for showing that a school can be usefully understood in terms of an ecological system and that, therefore, different interventions will have substantially different results. A consultation process needs to consider the differential impact of that process dependent upon the nature of the individual ecological niche. Further work needs to be done to identify the defining signs which would enable a prospective consultant to evaluate his school environment.

Readers may be interested in the continuing development of the consultation relationship and how following minimal successes in early stages, consultation strategy can be modified to accomodate the more acurately viewed needs of that school system.

The suggestions for the use of a "helping teacher" are novel and stimulating. This chapter presents several suggestions for the use of an adjunct mental health person in a variety of roles designed to facilitate positive mental health, handling of difficult, emergency situations, including such things as "the cross-age helping program," "noontime adoptions," "shared learnings," and " hobby period." The perspective school interventionists may want to consider each of these suggestions as potentially appropriate to their own settings.

A SCHOOL THAT GREW

Richard E. Becker
Washtenaw County Mental Health Center
Ann Arbor, Michigan

Linda Harris
Thurston School
Willow Run, Michigan

Preface

This chapter is the account of an elementary school that grew from a fairly rigid, controlled, tradition-bound institution into a more relaxed and innovative school in which the mental health functioning of the child at school and in the community became a primary concern. The emotional atmosphere in the building also changed and improved as children and the staff began to explore new ways of working among themselves and within the community.

It depicts the development of a mental health consultant program carried on by a community agency at very low cost to the public and the desciption of one of these programs carried out by one mental health consultant in an elementary school. It further shows the vision of a dedicated school principal who was willing to support the development of a comprehensive and unorthodox program for improving the mental health functioning of children in his school. It demonstrates how very effective a helping teacher can be in carrying out crisis intervention treatment, assisting teachers, and coordinating mental health services to children in the building. The chapter ter will also attempt to show how a whole teaching staff, once it has the support of its administration and a guiding mental health structure, can use its own resources in maximum ways without having to refer numerous children to treatment agencies while still having to deal with these children on a day to day basis without help during a long wait for services.

The Development of a Mental Health Intervention Program

In the fall of 1967, a Mental Health Consultation Program was established in the Willow Run School District in Ypsilanti, Michigan, by agreement between the school district and the Washtenaw County Mental Health Center. The consultants were psychologists, social work practitioners from the community, psychiatric residents, and PhD. level clinical psychology students in training at the University of Michigan. The program was administered and carefully cultivated by Dr. James G. Kelly of the University of Michigan Department of Psychology. Weekly group meetings between the consultants and Dr. Kelly were held in order to coordinate the program, share consultation experiences and to have the consultants respond to the school and community need. The consultants usually spent about four to six hours per week involved in various aspects of the program and there were ten of them, costing the public approximately $15,000 per year altogether.

The School Mental Health Consultant Program was designed by the Washtenaw County Mental Health Center as a preventive mental health program. It was offered to the Willow Run School System because of the latter's high incidence of behavior problems and mental health difficulties with children and the Center's recognition of the area's need for help.

Willow Run is a unique area because the only factor that establishes it as a community is its schools. The school district crosses over two townships which govern the area. There is only one shopping center, no public transportation and no police department. Protection services are provided by the county sheriff's department.

With a population of 60% white and 40% black, Willow Run has been the scene of chronic racial conflicts during recent years. Further, the population consists of lower socio-economic and upward mobile lower middle income families. The people in the area seem to work largely in the service industries or in the automobile industry. The population is largely southern in origin, both black and white. The origin of this population base stems from WWII when a work force was drawn from the South to work in the bomber plants. The automobile or automobile related industry now dominates the area as the primary employer.

Thurston serves approximately 400 children and is almost totally a white school, there being only a few black children. This was not a segregated school. Each of the elementary school areas was determined by a court order. Whether some other

subtle type of real estate segregation has gone on is open to
question. One result of this kind of sociological and racial
composition is that children from this school had more difficulties when they were thrust into a very racially mixed
junior high school setting. The junior high and senior high
schools have had chronic difficulties with acting out, delinquency and racial disturbances. Thurston School is typical
of other elementary schools in the district in having a very
large number of children from one parent homes, broken homes,
homes with a step-parent and children who make their homes with
relatives.

The result of some of the factors described above is a
highly strained school situation. There is a constant air of
tension or turmoil which leads to high turnover of teaching
staff, lowered quality of educational programs and widespread
dissatisfaction on the part of parents and students.

In the spring of 1968, a mental health consultant was a-
ssigned by the Mental Health Center to Thurston Elementary
School. The purpose of establishing a mental health consultation in the setting was to effect change through the use of
child centered clinical skills, an awareness of social systems
and ways of helping a social system make use of its strengths,
and to develop a comprehensive, on-going school program geared
to meet the needs of children, the school, and the community.

The success of a Mental Health Consultation Program depends on administrative sanction. This was certainly the experience of the consultant at Thurston School.

Initially, the principal and several teachers were skeptical of haphazard intervention and wanted a statement of
length of commitment the consultant proposed to make to the
school. He committed himself outright to at least a two-year
system. The principal, Mr. Harold Elston, was very clear in
his desire to do several things within his school: to improve
the mental health of children; to improve the mental health
atmosphere within the building; and to build a mental health
program that would involve the teachers more directly in problem solving with children and ultimately to involve parents
more completely in the school.

These were generalized goals and it was up to the consultant and the principal to evolve a structure and manner in
which to carry them out. The consultant and the principal
evaluated the power structure in the building which consisted
of a strong, fairly rigid, verbal, conservative group of teachers whose generalized response to problem children was, "you

can't do anything for him, after all, look at the family he
comes from," "send him to the child guidance clinic," "refer
him to the school social worker." There were one and a half
social workers for the whole district at that time. The liberal wing of the staff group was smaller and inhibited by the
power of the long term staff, with the exception of one teacher who was outspoken, extremely hard working and very willing
to get involved in new ideas. As it happened, the conservative group was composed of upper elementary grade teachers
and the lower elementary teachers formed a more liberal faction.

In setting up the initial program, the principal and the
consultant decided to have the teacher define their own needs.
In introducing the consultant to the teaching staff, the principal emphasized the fact that the consultant would be there
to help develop a mental health program within the building
and to help them deal more effectively with their children.
Whereas the teachers might have expected to be able to turn
over "problem children" to the consultant for some kind of
treatment, this program was deliberately set up to use the
consultant's clinical skills to help the teachers help their
own children. The principal pointed out in the beginning that
the consultant could see very few children individually.

For that first program, in the spring of 1968, the teachers asked to have a seminar on behavior problems of children.
In scheduled meetings, the consultant discussed problem symptoms with the teachers and was able to make general recommendations. However, the consultant also tried to be around at
lunch time at least once a week and after school several times
a week. His intention was to gain acceptance informally into
the social system. This also made him available for individual case consultaiton, which soon became obvious as the primary
teacher need.

Response to the initial program was lukewarm. The teachers felt that they were interested in hearing only about upper
or lower elementary children. They were not viewing their
school as an overall community in which everyone at times can
contribute help to others.

The school year ended, but the consultant and principal
maintained a few contacts during the summer. The fall of 1968,
brought the consultant to offer the principal a different kind
of program geared to fit the needs of individual teachers,
but also to accomodate interest groups within the school. Concurrently at this time, the principal and the consultant made
substantial moves to support the liberal wing of the staff,

this is being done by the principal in hiring more innovative
staff and by the consultant helping to legitimize the role of
the leader of the liberal group. With their support, she was
able to take the initiative in developing   more diversified
programs.

The type of program set up between 1968-69, involved
splitting the staff into an upper elementary and a lower elementary group, a division typical of elementary school structuring. It was set up this way partially to deal with the
criticism of the previous year's program, but primarily to fit
the political reality of the social system. The aim here was
eventually to be able to program the two groups together, but
for the meantime to start where we were. The consultant set
up a small mental health committee consisting of the leader
teacher of the lower elementary group and the leader of the
upper elementary group, the principal and the consultant. The
two teachers were to act as the coordinators to all referrals
made by teachers in their group. A formal referral was constructed. When a teacher wanted a child screened with the
consultant, she filled out the form and gave it to the coordinator teacher in her group. The Mental Health and Human
Relations Committee met on Friday noon to go over the referrals,
and a screening meeting was held each Tuesday in order to discuss the case in depth and to arrive at a generalized school
treatment plan. At this time, the school system liquidated all
psychological and school social work services due to financi-
al problems. Initiating this program became somewhat easier
as a result because the consultant was able to convince the
teachers that they needed to develop resources from within
their own school building in order to resolve problems with
children.

During the course of that school year, 26 formal referrals
of children were made to the consultant, and general treatment
plans were arrived at with all of them. At a screening, the
coordinating teacher took responsibility to get all teachers
presently relating to the child to the meeting to make a contribution toward planning to help him function better. During
the course of the year, a total of four children were referred
to the child guidance clinics for individual treatment. The
screening meetings were well attended, averaging four to five
teachers a meeting after school hours.

The primary result evolved from the year's experience was
the creation of a school-wide atmosphere of concern for the
mental health of children and the building of a beginning
through the Mental Health and Human Relations Committee and
the mental health screening settings that could actively work

toward resolution of children's emotional problems.

With the coming of the 1969-70 school year, discussions had been carried out during the summer between the mental health consultant, the principal and the leader of the lower elementary school teachers as to how we would further develop the program. The response of the teachers to the Mental Health Consultant Program from the previous year was very favorable. A number of teachers expressed an interest in taking a more active part. As a result, the Mental Health and Human Relations Committee was expanded to a membership of six, including four teachers from the lower elementary group and two from the upper elementary teacher group. A helping teacher was added later. The principal and mental health consultant served as ex-officio members of the group attending sporadically and on a supportive basis only. The purpose of this development was to have the Mental Health Committee become the teachers' own program, not dominated by administration or the outside influence of the mental health consultant.

At this time a very welcome addition was made to the Thurston School staff, a helping teacher. Because the Willow Run School district had not had psychological services the previous year, in 1969-70, it hired two school social workers for two schools and instituted a Helping Teacher Program, assigning one helping teacher to each of the other elementary school buildings.

Though this program had been planned the previous year, the helping teachers did not actually get their building assignments approved until the first day of school. Consequently, the Mental Health Service Program set up by the principal, consultant and Mental Health Committee chairman had to be quickly adapted to include the helping teacher. Roles were reviewed and the helping teacher took over the role of providing direct services to teachers with problem children and became the coordinator and expeditor of basic school treatment plans coming out of the Mental Health Screening Committee meetings. The chairman of the Mental Health Committee acted as stimulator to encourage all teachers to take discussion about problems with pupils to the helping teacher. The helping teacher and committee then would determine what cases would be discussed in depth at the Mental Health Screening meetings.

The Role of the Mental Health Consultant

The mental health consultant at Thurston School spent four to six hours a week working variously with the principal, the helping teacher, the chairman of the Mental Health Committee,

and with individual teachers. He worked with the principal on
district school administrative problems, development of school
programming, staff problems, and development of a Mental Health
Program in the school. His consultation with the helping
teacher most often concerned the problems of particular children. He also discussed with her the role of the helping
teacher in relation to other staff members and worked with her
to develop a comprehensive program for specific teacher intervention with problem children. He also discussed the helping
teacher's program to expose children in the school to methods
of resolution of human relations problems.

The consultant worked supportively with the Mental Health
Committee to encourage the development of a positive mental
health atmosphere among the staff and the children in the
school. The committee acted as a forum to develop mechanisms
to create a more active, vital teacher group, dedicated to
understanding and dealing with children and their problems in
positive ways.

The consultant also met with individual teachers at their
request to discuss progress of children. These discussions
often took place informally during coffee breaks or lunch
hours, though a teacher could request a more formal appointment if she wished.

At the end of the school year, the mental health consultation was evaluated by the school in this way:

The school mental health consultant has been
extremely helpful in a variety of ways. For three
years, he has helped the staff understand and deal
with children, understand and relate to one another
better, and develop school programs. He has met
regularly and individually with the principal, the
helping teacher, and the chairman of the Mental
Health Committee, as well as meeting occasionally
with the committee as a group and serving as a
valuable resource every Tuesday after school for a
screening meeting of particular children.

He has been able to remain therapeutically objective as well as being warm and understanding when
meeting with individuals and groups. In the screening meetings he invariably comes up with several
very specific, viable suggestions to help the staff
work with a youngster or his parents, and he always
provides keen insight into the problem. He has
been able to fulfill his role in a non-threatening

manner, something which is not easy for a consultant to accomplish. He is well liked and highly re-
spected by the staff.

Throughout the school year, he has had significant contact with at least fifteen out of seventeen classroom teachers during either a Mental
Health Committee meeting or a screening, as well as
talking with the staff informally in the lounge or
at staff parties.

His advice has been sought in regard to approximately forty children.

Individual case consultation formed the keystone of the
mental health consultant's role at Thurston School. The effectiveness of this type of consultation depends on the consultant's experience in carrying out treatment with children, his
awareness of community services, a good knowledge of child development and a respect for the individuals with whom he is consulting. In discussing the emotional problems of children with
teachers, a consultant must do a great deal of listening to
the behavioral and developmental information conveyed by the
teacher. He must listen also to the teachers' frustration
and hear the good things they are doing to handle the problems
in order to recognize and support them. The consultant frequent-
quently has asked teachers what they thought a child was seeking in his behavior, and was pleased to find a very high degree
of awareness and sensitivity on the part of teachers. When he
makes suggestions, the consultant must be sensitive, supportive
and aware that he, himself, is more accustomed to dealing with
children singly than in groups.

The consultant has an obligation to remind a teachers'
group that a child's behavior has meaning and is motivated by
some factor, whether emotional or organic in nature. His role
is to conceptualize a child's problematic behavior in such a
way as to enable the group to see certain areas of need in the
child and to formulate some concrete ways of responding to
these needs. Interpretations must be made in a meaningful way.
Information and impressions needed to be derived from teachers
are: What does the child do; why does she think he does it; are
there developmental factors to be considered, or are there
sociological or psychological factors of a pathological nature
involved. The teachers' attitudes and feelings about the child
must be solicited and an attempt made to evaluate how much of
what a child does is normal behavior and how much is unusual.
If a child's behavior is interpreted as attention getting, are
there ways in which teachers can plan to give him favorable
attention in acceptable ways? If a child is too inhibited but

shows much repressed anger, safe ways for expression of this
feeling should be found within the confines of the school program.

In working with a group of teachers, the consultant draws
information from each person who has had contact with the child
or his family or who is familiar with some areas of his performance. The type of program which we developed set up a basic
school treatment plan with various members of the child's teaching team taking various responsibilities. For his part, the
consultant was prepared to offer specific recommendations, so-
licit other suggestions from the group and planned to review
the work attempted after two or three months.

So far, the program appears to be successful as measured
by the varying degrees of improvement shown by individual children and by teacher enthusiasm for the program.

The mental health consultant was most involved in the de-
velopment of two Mental Health Programs at Thurston; the Mental
Health and Human Relations Committee and the Mental Health
Screening Committee meetings.

Mental Health and Human Relations Committee. Last year,
the scope of the committee had broadened. It was composed of
seven members: a kindergarten teacher (chairman), two second
grade teachers, a third grade teacher, a fifth grade teacher,
a sixth grade teacher, and helping teacher, with the principal
and consultant acting as ex-officio members. The committee
met regularly each week at lunch for forty-five minutes to discuss children who were having problems and to arrange for the
weekly screening with the consultant.

The committee did many other things, such as having a
Thanksgiving breakfast for the staff in order to attempt to
lift morale, and it also gave a Christmas party.

The committee also suggested and completed a medical tag-
ging system for the children's cumulative records as well as
giving each teacher a complete list of children in the school
who had significant medical problems that might arise during
school hours such as: diabetes, heart problems, epilepsy, severe
asthma attacks, etc. The committee also accepted responsibility
for inviting speakers from the child guidance clinic and family
service agency to talk with the whole staff about their agency's
services.

The committee further served as an initial sounding board
for new programs suggested by the principal or helping teacher.

They discussed and evaluated the Cross Age Helping Program, the Mental Health Consultation Program, the Hobby Program and Shared Learning. They also discussed and recommended a series of guidance books to the staff.

The committee accepted responsibility for setting up assemblies to be put on by various classes which would encourage a greater feeling of school unity. This desire for unity extended to the school district level when members of the committee volunteered to assist in the district orientation program for new teachers for the next year.

The school mental health consultant met at least bi-monthly with the chairman of the committee at lunch hour. He also met with various committee members of this committee at the weekly screening meetings.

Mental Health Screening Committee Meetings. Each Tuesday at 3:00, the mental health consultant, principal, helping teacher and relevant staff meet to discuss a child whose problems have to be of concern to the child's classroom teacher. This year, the procedure for choosing a child for screening was as follows: If a teacher was concerned about a child in her class, she talked with the helping teacher and/or principal. If understanding and solutions could not be achieved at this level, then the helping teacher asked at the Mental Health Committee if this child could be discussed at the Tuesday screening. Members of the committee then added any information they had about the situation, and decided what school personnel should be asked to attend the screening. No child was screened unless it was desired by his classroom teacher, and unless his present classroom teachers could attend.

The child's current teachers, last year's teachers and speech teacher were asked to attend along with the principal, helping teacher, and mental health consultant. Any other interested staff member was also welcome.

The teacher and helping teacher were expected to familiarize themselves with the child's record prior to the meeting, and to be able to give specific anecdotal information to explain the problem. The helping teacher provided results of a recent handmade sentence completion projective survey on the child. The helping teacher provided the mental health consultant with basic information on the child a few days in advance of the screening, although occasionally this was neglected.

In most cases, the screenings were reviewed; suggestions that had worked were discussed and new suggestions were searched for when the previous ones had failed.

The screening committee meetings have been very helpful
for a number of reasons:

-a teacher's tension concerning a child is usually
lessened in the process, and discussing the child's
problem helps her to clarify the situation in her
own mind.
-it encourages teachers to share their ideas about
children.
-a skilled, objective consultant not trained in the
discipline of education can offer suggestions.
-since the principal is present as well as all the
child's teachers, there is a consistency in the future handling of the child.
-the teacher feels supported.
-achievement of a better understanding of the interaction between the child and his teacher and the child
and his peers.
-very practical suggestions are made, and have at
least been tried in all the cases screened this year.

A total of forty children were screened during the course
of the year with varying degrees of improvement noted with the
majority of them.

The school made no agency referrals until it was felt by
the Mental Health Screening Committee that all school resources
available to the child had been exhausted. Six referrals were
made to agencies: three of which involved chronic marital
problems of parents and three in which the children were seen
for invividual treatment at the child guidance clinic.

The Role of the Helping Teacher

Dr. William Morse of the University of Michigan developed
the Helping Teacher Program as an attempt to move away from
segregated special education classrooms. Though it is a relatively new program, there are already many helping teachers in
schools of Southeastern Michigan. To qualify for a Helping
Teacher Program, a school system does not need to meet standards based on socio-economic factors, size or incidence or
behavioral problems. The school system pays approximately
twenty per cent of the helping teachers' salaries, with the
rest coming from state and county special education funds. To
receive reimbursement, helping teachers must have a degree in
special education in the area of emotionally disturbed children.

Though all of these programs are similarly funded, there are many variations in their actual functioning based on the desires of individual school systems. For example, in Willow Run there are no self-contained classrooms for children with emotional problems. Ann Arbor, however, has helping teachers in each building and a few self-contained classrooms.

Most helping teachers make a concerted effort to avoid a "special education" label. The helping teacher is responsible directly to her building principal rather than to a special education director, and she is not itinerant.   Each program evolves in response to the abilities and desires of the principal, staff, children, community, and helping teacher. Therefore, the program is necessarily different in every school.

Thurston's Helping Teacher Program is designed to help school personnel mobilize school resources in an attempt to meet children's emotional needs. These resources include the principal, classooom teachers, special service teachers, lunch supervisors, janitors and the school secretary, as well as parents and other children. A fundamental concept of the program is that children are not "bad," but that their behavior is a signal. The child's behavior is integrally connected with the child's "life space."

The work of the helping teacher at Thurston School can be divided into two areas which necessarily overlap:

1. Planning with school personnel for individual children thought by their classroom teachers to be having either temporary or chronic emotional problems.
2. Developing preventive mental health programs for the total school.

It is important to note that the program is not one of academic remediation and great care has been taken to see that it does not develop into this kind of "dumping ground."

Planning for Individual Children. When a teacher feels a child in her class is having problems, she can informally discuss this with the helping teacher, who in turn observes the child. She also discusses the referral with the principal and gathers school background and family data. The next step varies. Sometimes the classroom teacher is willing to try to work out the problem with the child, and in this case, the helping teacher takes the rest of the class to free her to do so. Upon request, the helping teacher helps the teacher by suggesting interview techniques. The information gathering and problem solving interview frequently includes the helping teacher, classroom teacher, and child. It is of utmost im-

portance that the classroom teacher be involved in the problem
solving process. Occasionally, the helping teacher sets up a
series of interviews or observations of the child to learn
more. Almost all of the children referred are discussed with
the Mental Health Committee and the mental health consultant
informally. Most of the children with chronic problems are
discussed at the Mental Health Screening meetings which take
place weekly after school. Teachers previously involved with
the child, principal, helping teacher, and mental health consultant work together at screenings to develop specific recommentations for dealing with the child within the school setting. A follow-up session takes place at a later date to review the progress of the child under the team's recommendations.

The helping teacher meets regularly with only a few children. The purpose of the program is to help the classroom
teacher help the child and to help the child adjust to the situation he is in, not to take him out of his environment and
create an artificial situation. It does little good for most
children to form a close attatchment to a helping teacher. Too
often, in such a situation, there is little positive behavioral
carry-over to the classroom, and the helping teacher becomes
an obstacle between teacher and child. Also, the individual
attention given by a helping teacher can serve as positive
reinforcement for negative behavior.

A few seriously withdrawn children are seen regularly by
the helping teacher on a one-to-one basis over a long term.
The helping teacher works with those children individually
until she feels they can benefit from a small group situation.
She then adds peers to form a small group to work together on
a project or athletic activity. When the withdrawn child feels
more comfortable in this group, the helping teacher assists
the teacher in working out a program for the child which does
not include coming regularly to the helping teacher.

Constant communication between classroom teachers and
helping teacher is vital. If communication breaks down, the
efforts of the helping teacher may be worthless, or even destructive.

In her work with different children, the helping teacher
may use many different techniques. These include: individual behavioral modification charts, friendship groupings supervised by the helping teacher, interviews with the parents and
the classroom teacher, suggestions for specific management
techniques for use in the classroom, working with the teacher
to help her understand the child and the interaction between

them, role playing with the child, the Cross Age helping program (described later) teaching the child specific methods for handling emotions, i.e. verbalization, art, pounding clay, throwing darts, etc., giving the child responsibilities within the school, i.e. care of a classroom pet, etc.

One important technique is to find out each day how the child is doing in the classroom and to inform the child whenever developments are positive, i.e. "Mrs. Jones tells me your math paper shows improvement."

Many of the children are seen by the helping teacher because of acute problems, such as a family disagreement, illness in the family, being new in the school, serious arguements with peers, etc. In these cases the helping teacher often serves as a listener on a one-time basis. Usually this is sufficient.

During the 1969-70 school year, the helping teacher worked in the aforementioned ways with approximately 60 children thought to be having chronic or temporary emotional problems. Six children were referred to community agencies. These few cases were referred because of complex family problems which could not be handled adequately through the school.

The helping teacher's role at Thurston has been a very demanding one which required a great deal of intelligence, sensitivity and emotional investment. In coming to Thurston, the helping teacher had the maturity and awareness to evaluate the state of the Mental Health Program and to fit herself into it appropriately. She was quick to identify the more liberal elements of the staff and to align herself with them and support them. She quickly became involved in efforts to offer specific help with particular children. She also moved to determine broader needs of the children in the school, namely: need for consistent academic tutoring, some exposure to a multi racial society in which they live, the needs of noon time children, the need for the building to adopt some sense of school identity, the need of the teachers in the school to identify with the school district, the need for teachers to have relief in the regular classroom in order to handle some crises themselves and the provision of mental health amd human relations texts and film strips for the teachers to use with the children in the classroom. She was extremely effective in implementing these goals and the result is a communally organized school setting rather than a fragmented organization.

The helping teacher role is not one that can be prescribed. It cannot be pre-determined and must respond to the specific abilities, interests and needs of the children, staff, and community. The success of the Thurston experience resides in the hard working and creative efforts of a total school team.

Preventive Mental Health Programs for Groups of Children

The helping teacher assisted the other staff members in initiating and carrying out several preventive mental health programs.

Cross Age Helping Programs. This program was developed by Lippitt of the University of Michigan, Institute of Social Research, set up with the intent to have children help one another both academically and socially. An older child and a younger child work together about 20 minutes a day three days a week during school hours. The "younger" is chosen by his classroom teacher as a child who could benefit from enrichment, remediation or a stable relationship with an older child. The "older" is chosen by his classroom teacher as a child who is doing well academically and would be a good helper, or a child who is doing poorly and would improve his motivation and self-image if he could help a "younger " Another consideration is the child who is having behavioral problems who would benefit from having to work with a younger child who has many of the same problems.

One day a week the "older" meets with his "younger's" classroom teacher to get ideas regarding what the "younger" needs help with that week. Once a week the "older" has a seminar in which he discusses and role-plays such issues as understanding the behavior of others, helping "youngers," reasons for academic difficulties, etc. Last year, the helping teacher conducted two seminars a week and a classroom teacher was relieved of her classroom duties (by the helping teacher) to conduct two seminars a week, each seminar being composed of ten "olders."

The program significantly increased the feeling of school unity and team participation by staff and students together, as well as raised the motivation and self-image of "olders" and provided "youngers" with intensive individual attention. A follow-up evaluation with children, teachers and parents seemed to confirm the fact that the children involved improved both academically and socially.

Noon-time "Adoptions." This was a program attempted last winter to try and solve the problems caused by numerous children staying at school during the noon hour which resulted in crowded conditions. Since there was only one lunchroom mother for every three classrooms, it was difficult for the children to get enough help in organizing themselves to become involved in constructive, relaxing activities. It was decided that each upper grade would "adopt" a lower grade and be responsible for the classroom during the noon hour, and the two classes could organize their own program. The program was not particularly successful, largely due to faulty communication between the teachers in the paired classes. It may be tried again this year but in a more structured manner if the teachers decide to support such a plan.

Shared Learning. Thurston is one of the few schools in Willow Run with a very small percentage of Negro children. Last year, out of 400 children only four were black. The children are extremely prejudiced. Besides perpetuating ignorance, and creating problems for the children, the prejudive they feel creates significant problems for them when they enter junior high school which has a high percnetage of Negro children.

Shared learning is an attempt to help the children learn how to deal more realistically and effectively in a multi-racial society. It also proposes to develop some sense of early identity for the children in relation to the Willow Run School system, thus making the transition from an elementary school to the junior high less traumatic.

This year Thurston hopes to embark on a Shared Learning Program with an integrated elementary school located in Willow Run. This project will be modeled after the Shared Learning Project in Wayne County, Michigan. Interested teachers will participate, and classrooms from each school will be paired. The groups may share the following activities: field trips, parties, joint sings, pen pals, embark on similar units of study, share their learning by means of panel discussions, produce a play, work together on a Friday afternoon hobby time similar to the current one at Thurston except the classes could meet at each other's schools on alternate weeks. The focus is not on racial issues but rather upon the sharing of activities, interests and relationships.

Hobby Period. Several teachers felt that the school did not offer enough for fifth and sixth graders, particularly the boys. A few of the upper grade teachers and the helping teacher met to discuss this problem and decided to ask the students by means of a questionnaire if they would be interested in forming an after school club and in what areas. The response was overwhleming, and the principal agreed to have the clubs during the school time--from 1:45 to 2:45 on Friday afternoon.

There were several objectives for the clubs:

-that the children would be able to interact in smaller

groups which cut across regular friendship and grade
level groups.
-that the children have an opportunity to acquire
new hobby skills which they could enlarge upon outside of school.
-that children who could not find satisfaction
through academic achievement might be able to gain
respect of their peers in other academic areas.
-that school personnel could interact with children
in a less authoritarian and less traditional way.
-that school personnel could get to know more children and vice-versa.

All fifth and sixth grade children were asked to list their
first three preferences for activities. Wherever possible,
the children were given their first choice. All activities
on the list were those the children had originally indicated as
high priority activities. The children were put in groups of
about 13 each. They remained in this group for their activity
for about six Fridays. The teachers also chose the club which
best matched their interest and ability. The activities included: woodwork, cooking (boys and girls), sewing, model
building, knitting, embroidery, checkers and chess, cake decor-
ating, folkdancing, etc. Club leaders included fifth and sixth
grade teachers, school secretary, speech teacher, principal,
helping teacher, mothers, etc. In several instances a lower
elementary teacher was interested in working with the program
so a fifth or sixth grade teacher took her class to free her.
It also enabled the teachers to work with a different age group
of children and a further breakdown of distinction between upper
and lower elementary grades.

After the first session, the children were again asked
their preferences by means of questionnaire for a second session. The teachers were also able to change clubs.

Toward the end of this second session, the teachers lost
some of the interest and enthusiasm for the clubs that they had
had previously. This was probably due to a couple of things--
it was nearly time for spring vacation and some ground rules
needed to be set.

The helpful teacher sent a questionnaire to all the children involved in the clubs asking them if they enjoyed the clubs,
if they wanted them continued, what changes should be made, etc.
Apparently, the children felt their ideas would be seriously
considered, because they filled out the questionnaire carefully.
Each questionnaire the children received they progressively
filled out more carefully, indicating increased trust in the
staff to listen to their ideas and increased involve-

ment in the decision making process. According to their responses, the clubs had been very successful and enjoyable, however, they indicated the need for certain rules. At a later teachers' meeting called to discuss the clubs, the teachers called for the same rules that the children had already requested.

A third session of clubs was held after spring break. The same procedure was followed, however, all these were to be held out of doors and would include fourth graders. They would culminate in a field day just before the end of school. These clubs included softball, volleyball, kickball, track events, 4-square, jumprope activities, tetherball, baton-twirling, frisbee, badminton, scoopball and tug-of-war. The children tried a different activity each of four Fridays.

The clubs will be held this year, after Christmas. The time period will probably be expanded to include all of Friday afternoons.

Mental Health and Human Relations Curriculum Materials.
The helping teacher provided curriculum materials on mental health and human relations for the staff to use in their classrooms.

A series of guidance texts, called *Dimensions in Personality* was presented to the Mental Health and Human Relations Committee for consideration. The committee requested the administration to incorporate this series into the fourth, fifth and sixth grade curriculum. These are being used very successfully this year.

Several programs dealing with mental health issues have been ordered by the helping teacher for use in the classroom next year. These include a workbook and guide for each grade level entitled "Developing Understanding of Ourselves and Others," a set of filmstrip and record on the life of Dr. Martin Luther King, a group discussion manual on "Planned Group Guidance," a set of eight filmstrips, four records, and a teacher's guide entitled "Learning to Live Together," and a filmstrip, record and guide for early elementary grades called "Getting to Know Me." While these are currently being used a staff meeting is planned at which time members of the Mental Health and Human Relations Committee will demonstrate the materials. Other materials consulted were Fink's *Interaction Analysis* and Maple's *Classroom Teaching Materials*.

The helping teacher attempts to share many materials with the classroom teachers, i.e. perceptual materials, puppets, children's books and articles dealing with classroom management techniques, role playing methods, and emotional problems of children.

Summary

The program during the 1969-70 school year was highly successful and we believe that through this positive atmosphere promoted by the Mental Health Committee and Helping Teacher Program many other positive school-wide and community-wide programs were initiated. In the following pages, the various programs developed will be described, all of which involved members of the Mental Health Committee.

Initiated by a new awareness of positive mental health and a new group spirit derived from teachers working effectively together, a new positive atmosphere began to pervade the whole school. This, of course, was beneficial to all of the children in the school.

What we have described is a Mental Health Program developed over a three year period in one elementary school. It is offered not as an absolute model for others to adopt in circumstances which may require quite a different structure, but as a demonstration of what teachers, themselves, can accomplish if they have the support of mental health professionals, be they doctors, psychologists, social workers, or special education teachers in facilitating the classroom teacher's professional competency, knowledge and awareness of the emotional problems of children. And this often is our undoing in trying to work with children with emotional problems in the schools. The classroom teacher may have a disturbed or acting out child in her class from 6 to 7 hours a day among 18 to 40 other children. The usual individual psychoanalytically oriented case consultation is not sufficient to help teachers deal effectively with children in a group. A chance for ventilation of feelings, an opportuntiy to review her own attempts to deal with the child, and help in mobilizing resources and knowledge about the child, his family and his problems come closer to meeting the needs of the teacher in attempting to meet the needs of the child.

The insights provided by clinical skills are still very much needed, but they must be translated into specific basic school treatment plans in order to be of much use in the school setting. These plans can be arrived at and followed with review and accountability built into the program. This sets up further intervention possibilities on behalf of the child at a future date.

Mental health professionals are needed in the schools, but they can be most useful if they can deal with teachers on the basis of respect, recognizing the teacher's unique need for help. Teachers and other school personnel correspondingly are in a unique position to help children with problems if they have the support of mental health professionals.

12. ORGANIZATIONAL TRAINING

Drs. Langmeyer, Lansky and Reddy have taken an organizational training approach to dealing with the school system. Their
focus is on the professional training and organizational development of the school system rather than on either a particular
intervention designed to help children or an interface approach,
as suggested by Dr. Bower, or even a specific training program
in skills for teachers illustrated by Dr. Chandler. Instead Drs.
Langmeyer *et al.* are talking about how to make the system function more effectively from top to bottom. Their strategy is to
improve the functioning of all the subsystems as well as the interpersonal functioning of individuals. Improved mental health
is a byproduct rather than a goal. The example provided in this
chapter illustrates the several stages of intervention from the
top administrators and chiefs to the teaching and professional
staff. Each of the interventions serves a slightly different
purpose unified by concepts of organizational change and development.

The authors stress several points of organization which apply no matter how the training and consultation services are put
together. These principles include: 1) trainers should be visible, accessible and open to input from all members with whom
they come into contact; 2) the trainers should try to work with
all members of any target group rather than with selected individuals; 3) the participants in the target group should participate in goal setting and feedback processes; 4) feedback as a
general principle should allow continued monitoring and successful completion of a project; 5) training should be focused at
concerns that are defined by the target group rather than by the
trainers themselves; and finally, 6) communications skills are
central to any organizational development task and hence much
time should be spent on development of specific personal communications skills.

The major measure of success of this program has been in
terms of personal satisfaction and support by the school personnel involved in it. The authors deferently note that research
today does not show unequivocally that organizational development
leads to improved organizational or interpersonal functioning.

Before we can be certain about impact of this kind of strategy, more needs to be known. The authors, however, have accepted the challenge of several layers of a bureaucratic system which have deflected or destroyed many lesser assaults.

ORGANIZATIONAL TRAINING IN SUB-SYSTEMS

OF A MIDWEST SCHOOL DISTRICT

Daniel Langmeyer
Len M. Lansky
W. Brendan Reddy
University of Cincinnati

History and Theory

There are several ways to help school systems provide
more effective service to their clients. One approach, the one
we take at the Community Psychology Institute (CPI) at the University of Cincinnati, is to work with schools as organizations.
The thrust is to permit school organizations to learn to use
their most potent resource more effectively-the individuals who
work in the schools.

Our approach, which has been labeled "organizational skill
training," focuses on two related issues: the improvement of
the **organizational functioning of subsystems** and the improvement of **interpersonal functioning of individuals.**

Organizational skill training has developed from the early
work on human relations in industry. It began with the discovery of the Hawthorne effect (Roesthlisberger and Dickson, 1939).
which was an increase of productivity among groups of workers
singled out for changes in their physical work environments.
The increased productivity was a function of their feeling
special and increasing their cohesiveness and commitment to the
work group rather than the changes in their physical environment. Early work at the Center for Group Dynamics at the Massachusetts Institute of Technology and then the University of
Michigan added data and impetus to the need to acknowledge the
effects of social processes on organizational functioning
(Lippit and White, 1958; Cartwright and Zander, 1960). A significant technological advance occurred with the development of
the T-group and the advent of laboratory training (Bradford,et
al., 1964). The emphasis on the stranger T-group assumed that

organizational functioning could be improved by increasing the individual competence of organizational members. Although the evidence seems to point to the power of the T-group to affect change within individuals, there is less transfer to the individual's organization (Campbell and Dunnette, 1968; Lansky, et al., 1969). In other words, the T-group by itself has proved to be relatively ineffective in producing an increase in organizational effectiveness.

Several recent trends are evident in the application of the laboratory method and T-group to organizations that try to overcome some of the deficiencies of the stranger laboratory. One major trend is the "family," "cousin," and "interface" laboratories which are done within an organization (see examples in Bennis, Benne and Chin, 1969). A second trend uses non T-group based programs to reach specific goals. Confrontation designs (Beckhard, 1969), union-management laboratories (Blake, mouton and Sloma, 1969), task-directed learning (Fosmire, Diller and Smith, 1968; Fosmire and Keutzer, 1968; Runkel, 1969), pastoral training (Crosby and Schmuck, 1969) are a sample of the strategies being developed. A third trend is to embed skill training, T-groups, and workshops in a program which includes follow-up work in the organization (Davis, 1969; Friedlander, 1968).

Recent work by Program 30 at the Center for the Advanced Study of Educational Administration (CASEA) at the University of Oregon has incorporated many of these trends. CASEA's organizational training emphasizes communication skills, shared norms and expectations about behavior, open influence, decision-making processes, systematic problem search, and problem-solving. The CASEA group and others have also been developing theoretical models (Schmuck, Runkel and Langmeyer, 1969; Schmuck, Runkel and Langmeyer, 1971; Schmuck and Miles, 1971) and technology (Langmeyer, Schmuck and Runkel, 1969; Schmuck and Runkel, 1968; Schmuck and Miles, 1971; Schmuck, Runkel, Derr, Martell, and Saturen, in press) for working in schools. The theory is derived from systems theory (Buckley, 1967) and social psychology (Katz and Kahn, 1966). The model views schools as adaptive, goal-directed, complex systems which, as a rule, do not make full use of their resources for inner growth and for meeting external challenges. Thus, schools, like other complex organizations, do not plan changes in their structures and their functions; rather they tend to react. The ideal system, in Buckley's (1971) words, is "morphogenesis." Others have labelled it "self-renewal" (Gardner, 1963), "organization health" (Bennis, 1966) or flexible problem-solving (Schmuck, Runkel and Langmeyer, 1969). The technology is an amalgam of human relations and organizational skill training from varied sources.

Another important component of our organizational training is the attempt to integrate group training in communication and problem-solving with normal business of the school. In this way, participants can learn and practice new skills and develop new norms for working together with maximal support and opportunity for transferring the new learning to their jobs. This strategy also provides almost immediate feedback regarding the utility of new behaviors for the day-to-day operations of the schools.

The expected outcomes are suggested by terms such as "flexible problem-solving," and "self-renewal": a school system motivated to monitor its own functioning and the changing environment, capable of assessing areas where change is suggested and flexible enough to modify its organizational form and functioning to meet its need effectively.

A Program of Organizational Training

Overview. The following is an illustration of a program focused on the organizational functioning of the administration of a school system and two schools within the system carried out by the CPI. The program was conducted over a period of one and a half years.

The program has had four phases differentiated by population and by purpose. Phase I (A and B) involved most of the top administration of the school district. The purpose of Phase I had been to improve the communication and decision-making of that group. Phase II involved the administration of two schools (principals, team leaders, department heads) and some central office staff who worked with those schools. The purpose of Phase II was to diagnose the readiness of the schools to engage in further organizational work, to demonstrate the approach which the CPI takes in its work, and to motivate the schools to become involved in organizational skill training. Phase III and IV involved the professional staff of the elementary school and the Junior High School in a series of workshops aimed at improving their organizational functioning.

In all phases our goal has been to establish a collaborative consultation with the client system, to improve communication skills, to develop more openness and receptivity between members of the client system and to facilitate the client system's work on its expressed problems. Our work has been greatly facilitated by the initiator and internal contact person, an assistant superintendent for curriculum, who has himself been to several sensitivity training groups and who understands the nature, goals and methods of our work. The support and skill of this key administrator has been invaluable.

Points of Intervention

Phase I (A). With the support of the Superintendent and
the In-Service Coordinator, the Assistant Superintendent met
with the Director and a Professional Member of the Human Relations Institute, University of Cincinnati, to explore the ad-
visability of a workshop for members of the school system. This
preliminary discussion surfaced the need to have a basic communication and commitment workshop which would include the elementary and secondary school principals as well as the Superintendent and Central Office Staff. It was agreed that all participants would be interviewed before the workshop. The interviews which were diagnostic in nature permitted the identification of issues, agendas, factions and coalitions. On the
basis of the data collected during the interviews, two major
goals seemed appropriate for the workshops, viz., the development of functional communication patterns and the introduction of change strategies and their management.

These goals seemed particularly important because at the
time of our initial entry, a number of changes had already
been introduced into the school system and more were being planned. We felt that in the workshop, opportunity should be made
available for participants to practice diagnostic and planning
skills around problem-solving and in the introduction of
change. This was accomplished via temporary task forces which
tackled some current problems they were faced with.

In order to attain these goals, participants initially
spent considerable time in their own identity groups (e.g., Central Office, Elementary Principals, etc.) becoming better acquainted and sharing school-related experiences, positive and
negative. Mixed role groups were then formed permitting differences and similarities between occupants of different positions to be examined. Finally, teams were formed based upon
similarity and relatedness of problems. The objectives of these
teams were to have informal sessions with the Superintendent
and Central Office staff, explore the resources of individual
Central Office staff as related to specific problems, support
each other, and mobilize their own power to initiate change.
Specific techniques were taught, such as the force field analysis, to help the teams become more effective.

The reactions to the workshop were favorable. While some
skepticism remained as to whether the gains in communication
would continue, and some fear was expressed that moderate openness would result in retaliation, many of the misconceptions,

fantasies, and hidden agendas were dealt with openly and realistically. The task groups were quite successful and a series
of recommentdations were enumerated concerning Central Office
staff and Principals' relationships and decision-making interactions. Recommendation was also made for another workshop
and the availability of such training for individual schools
within the system.

Phase II. As a result of the recommendations and success
of the Phase I workshop the Assistant Superintendent and representatives of two system schools met with the staff of the
CPI to discuss extending organizational training. The general
feeling among those present at the initial meeting was that
organizational training in the schools could help them become
more proactive with regard to problems rather than reactive
(crisis oriented). Since both schools were using a team-teach-
ing method, representatives, viz. team leaders, administrators,
and Central Office staff working directly with the schools, were
asked to participate in an initial workshop.

Preliminary to this workshop, considerable diagnostic data
was accrued through pre-workshop questionnaires and visits to
the two schools. A stipulation of the contract, as is our policy, was a commitment to share a summary of data with participants.

The goals of the workshop were fourfold: 1) to learn about
one another and the functioning of the school organization,
both necessary for future planning; 2) to introduce participants to communication and problem-solving skills; 3) to practice skills in shared situations; and 4) to begin to diagnose
internal problem-solving processes and needs.

Workshop activities were varied and included practice in
paraphrasing, perception checks and other communication skills.
A problem-solving sequence was introduced and provided another
vehicle for practicing the above skills within the context of
a "real" situation. Considerable time was spent on presenting
MacGregor's (1961) "Theory X" and "Theory Y" and discussing the
theory's implications for the management of the schools.

The workshop had differential impacts on the two schools.
The participants from the elementary school had a particularly
positive experience at the workshop and very quickly decided to
go ahead with additional work with the entire school faculty.
On the other hand, in the Junior High School, there emerged
strong conflict between the administration and the department
heads. The administration was reluctant to administer the
school in any way other than by highly centralized control,

ambiguity of responsibility, and a theory X cosmology with regard to the professional staff. The department heads had strong reactions to being treated, in their perception, as children. Another way of viewing the impact of the workshop was that the elementary school principal was not threatened by the vision of collaboration with his staff to the extent that the Junior High School principal was. The Junior High School principal left the workshop with a great deal of apprehension about insituting an organizational training program in his school.

Phase III. As a direct result of the elementary school principal's favorable experience in Phase I and his selected staff's experience in Phase II, he requested that the CPI explore further intervention strategies in his school. A questionnaire was administered to the entire professional staff and the data compiled. A number of issues were generated around interpersonal openness; role definitions, especially the team leader's role; all help-giving being down or parallel rather than two-way; and a lack of team-work or team decision-making.

It was determined that an initial three-day workshop would be held to deal with global issues and interpersonal relations. It was hoped that concrete action steps for specific problems could be initiated following considerable experience and didactic input. The major emphasis of the first workshop was skill practice and work on the decision-making and interpersonal relationships within teams.

A two-day follow-up workshop was scheduled two weeks after the initial workshop in order to determine how the problem-solving had progressed and to permit the consultation team to observe the teaching teams while they actually taught and planned. This workshop provided an opportunity to deal with the work of the teams in vivo. As a result, the consultation team was able to point to some outstanding resources within the school that had previously gone unnoticed. The workshop also provided an opportunity to demonstrate a model for self-renewal. A good deal of progress was made during this workshop on defining the team leaders' role and the options opened to the teams for their method of working together. In all, it was an exciting series of workshops.

Phase I (B). A recommendation made after Phase I had been that the group composed of the Superintendent, Central Office, secondary and elementary school principals meet again for additional training. The group convened a year later again at a state park where they would be away from their work load and interruptions.

The primary focus of this workshop was for the participants to deal with stereotypes, assumptions and fantasies developed upon minimal data in a moderately closed system. Participants attempted to look at the stereotypes that their specific group had toward the other and what they felt were stereotypes toward themselves.

On the second evening a school board member who was very supportive of retreats and workshops was present. He informed the participants that the Board was strongly behind this concept and that they wanted him to convey these sentiments to the principals and the Central Office staff. The Board member also clarified some misconceptions and rumors about the School Board that had been plagueing the participants.

Phase IV. As indicated previously, during Phase II, the principal of the Junior High School and his staff had considerable difficulty dealing with the issues surfaced during the Phase II workshop. A recommendation from the Assistant Superintendent that they have further training and consultation was turned down by key personnel in the Junior High School. They preferred to take a "wait and see" position. The CPI staff agreed not to push these clients into further work when the client maintained he was not ready. However, as the year progressed and Phase III took place followed by Phase I (B), coupled by slow but continued movement and integration of learnings from Phase II the principal, with support from key administrators and faculty, requested consultation from the CPI.

Data from Phase II and our diagnostic questionnaire made clear several issues: 1) a controlling, "Theory X," administration, 2) minimal participation of the faculty in decision making, 3) an assistant principal whose title was "curriculum helper" but who functioned as disciplinarian and head janitor, 4) staff conflicts over school philosophy, 5) lack of experience and skills in team teaching, 6) misuse and underuse of resource teachers and counselors.

Consistent with the issues raised, the intervention was a workshop designed with three major components: 1) the production of descriptions of the school as it would be if it were operating optimally, 2) an analysis of others' roles that help and hinder one's role performance, and 3) negotiating between roles for performance that maximize one's own role performance.

At the end of the workshop, participants were asked to share their outcomes and to discuss commitments for the future. There was much optimism. What was particularly helpful was a

supportive statement by the principal as to his positive commitments to the process begun during the workshop; a statement
which indicated his willingness for change and his receptivity
to the feedback that he had personally been given.

The work with the Junior High School was continued by an
administrative intern in the district and a former graduate student from the CPI who had worked in the program and had a position at a university close to the district. Their consultation
continued to emphasize problem-solving and organizational self-
renewal. An evaluation of the entire consultation is contained
in a dissertation by the intern (Poole, 1971). The evaluation
suggested that problems had indeed been surfaced and that individual staff members felt more confident and comfortable with
the communication skills introduced during the program. Evidence existed that several of the departments had improved
their meetings and the amount of sharing of information and
feelings. Participants reported many of the experiences of
the workshops to be personally valuable. However, participants
did not report significant organizational changes for the school
as a whole. They reported a good deal of disappointment that
problems had not been eradicated during the course of the workshops and that they still had issues to work through.

Strategies and Decisions

The system concepts of boundaries, sub-systems, components; goal directedness; openness and adaptability; and the
variety pool, along with the social psychological concepts of
norms and roles, communication, behavioral styles, climates,
and morale should guide organizational training interventions.

We think that the following goals for organizational training grow out of our theory. These serve as objectives as we
intervene in school systems to improve their organizational
functioning:

1. Increase understanding of how people in different
   parts of the school affect one another.
2. Develop clear communication networks up and down
   and laterally.
3. Increase understanding of the various educational goals in different parts of the school.
4. Develop new ways of solving problems through
   creative use of new roles in groups.
5. Develop new ways of assessing progress toward
   educational goals in the school.
6. Involve more people at all levels in decision-
   making.
7. Develop procedures for searching out innovative

practices both within and outside the school.

Despite the different training designs described earlier, our work with any particular target group has emphasized problem-solving or communication skills, or both, and has involved the following components and strategies:

1. Visibility of the training staff. One of the most important sources of learning available to the target group is the training staff's behavior. It is visible as they work through some of the problems encountered: how the trainers handle the suspiciousness and distance during initial contacts with the target group, how the diagnostic interviews are conducted, how the data from these interviews are fed back to the target group, and how the trainers deal with intense emotional situations. For the trainers not to be open to feedback,to be defensive or hostile, would be a serious deficit. The trainers should model the kind of individual and team behavior that we want to develop in the target group.

2. System Strategy. As much as possible we work with all the components of a bounded system: all the teachers on a team or in a school: all the principals. The system strategy also suggests that we work with those systems in a district that have important contact with the target group. Without including a large portion of the target system and trying to build support through other systems close to the target system's boundaries the chances of the training maintianing itself is very slim.

3. Commitment through the involvement of the target system in planning. We try to involve the target group in setting goals and plans for its own growth. We see our role as consultants as offering our resources to the target group and helping them in a collaborative mode. This is one of the most difficult components of our intervention strategy because of fantasies about our "magic" and because of the difficulty of collaborating with a "representative" group of members of the target group. Initial decisions about who should negotiate with the consultants are usually made on bases other than representation and communication effectiveness. Still, with all of the difficulties, we try to build commitment and feedback mechanisms through the

inclusion of the target group in its own diagnosis and planning.

4. Feedback and System Stability. A major emphasis of our training is on generating and utilizing feedback about the state of the system. The feedback can, theoretically, help stabilize the system and, conversely, point to parts of the functioning of the system that could be changed to increase overall effectiveness.

5. Training is Focused on Expressed Concerns of the Target Group. Organizational training can be carried on with almost any content. We try to generate content from the target group for two reasons: a) this typically increases interest and commitment in the training and; b) it also is the first step in any problem-solving sequence. It is not unusual for a target group to report that the workshop was,the first time, organizational issues, almost everyone acknowledged were pressing problems in the school, were talked about by the total staff.

6. Emphasis on Communication Skills. To the extent that most of the organizational functions within the target group are "carried" through interpersonal interactions, we feel that a first step is to improve the communicative process.

These strategies are summarized in the following sequence of the typical training program with a target group.

1. Initial contact with members of the school district (so far, our contacts have been initiated by members of the school district).

2. Commitment from the school district and from us of specified amounts of time and energy; setting up the contract; establishing our role as consultant, change-agent, and trainer; clarifying the status of the trainer as consultant to the entire school district rather than to one segment such as the administrators.

3. Data-gathering concerning educational goals and concerns--diagnosis.

4. Feedback of data to the target group.

5. Setting goals for organizational training with the target group.

6. Carrying out a training program over an extended time period.

7. Data-gathering concerning effects of the training.

Concluding Remarks

Argyris (1969) described a consistent pettern of interpersonal behavior observed in 163 meetings of groups in various organizations. He describes partern A in the following
way: "We found in the 'typical word' (Pattern A) a tendency
toward minimal expression of feelings, minimal openness to
feelings and minimal risk taking with ideas or feelings. The
most frequently observed norms were concern for ideas (not
feelings) and conformity (ideas). The norm of mistrust also
tended to be high (but had to be inferred from other data than
the observational scheme since individuals did not tend to
show their mistrust openly).

"The consequences of Pattern A behavior were relatively
ineffective interpersonal relationships and ineffective problem-solving of task issues that were important and loaded with
feelings. When solutions were achieved, they did not tend to
be lasting ones. The problems therefore seemed to recur continually. Finally, members seemed to be blind to the negative
impact that they tended to have on others (partially because
it violated the norms to give such feedback); they were accurately aware of the impact others have upon them, but careful
not to communicate this impact openly or directly (p.898-899)."
Organizationally, Pattern A reflects a state if low health and
relatively ineffective problem-solving.

The evidence is very strong that individuals can learn
and behave in interpersonally effective ways within the isolated settings where these skills are developed (Argyris, 1969;
Gibb, 1971). But that it is extremely difficult to translate
the atypical interpersonal world of Pattern B (Argyris, 1969),
that characterizes these settings into existing Pattern A organizations (Campbell and Dunnette, 1968, Argyris, 1969). The
evidence is also clear that although the task of transforming
an organization into one that fosters self-renewal and Pattern
B behavior is difficult, it is not impossible. Since the
amount of re-learning and re-socialization that is required to
be successful is considerable, the amount of commitment that
a school system would have to make to the effort is also considerable. This commitment has not been evident in most of
our work. One of the serious problems of implementing an organizational change program in schools is that school systems
seem to be unwilling to take the time perspective of the change
agent and so expect far more from the early consultation than
is reasonable (Sarason, 1971). But the future is likely to
be brighter with more teachers and administrators becoming
exposed to the values and technology of organizational change
and with the improved theory and technology being developed by
practicners and professionals. For the sake of our children

and the generations to come, let us hope and work.

REFERENCES

Argyris, C. The incompleteness of social psychological theory: examples from small group, cognitive consistency, and attribution theory. *American Psychologist*, 1969, 24, pp. 893-908.

Beckhard, R. The confrontation meeting, In Bennis, Benne, and Chin (Eds.) *The Planning of Change*, (2nd edition), New York: Holt, Rinehart and Winston, 1969, pp. 478-485.

Bennis, W. G., Benne, K. D., and Chin, R. (Eds.). *The Planning of Change*, (2nd edition). New York: Holt, Rinehart, and Winston, 1969.

Bennis, W. G., *Changing Organizations*, New York: McGraw Hill, 1966.

Blake, R. B., Mouton, J. S., and Sloma, R. L. The union-management intergroup laboratory: strategy for resolving intergroup conflict, In Bennis, Benne, and Chin (eds.) *The Planning of Change*, (2nd edition), New York: Holt, Rinehart and Winston, 1969, pp. 176-191.

Bradford, L. P., Gibb, J. R., and Benne, K. D. (Eds.). *T-group theory and laboratory method*. New York: Wiley, 1964.

Buckley, W. *Sociology and modern systems theory*. Englewood Cliffs, New Jersey: Prentice Hall, 1967.

Campbell, J. P. and Dunnette, M. D. Effectiveness of T-group experiences in managerial training and development. *Psychological Bulletin*, 1968, 70, pp. 73-104.

Cartwright, D. and Zander, A. *Group dynamics* (2nd edition). Evanston, Illinois: Row, Peterson and Co., 1960.

Coch, L. and French, J. R. P. Overcoming resistance to change. In Maccoby, E. E., Newcomb, T. M., and Hartley, E. L. (Eds.). *Readings in social psychology* (3rd edition), 1958, pp. 233-250.

Crosby, R. and Schmuck, R. Transfer of laboratory training. *Human Relations Training News,* 1969, 113, pp. 3-5.

Davis, S. A. An organic problem-solving method of organizational change, In Bennis, Benne, and Chin (eds.) *The Planning of Change,* (2nd edition). New York: Holt, Rinehart and Winston, 1969, pp. 357-370.

Fosmire, F., Diller, R., and Smith, M. D. Social psychology as a laboratory course. paper presented at the meeting of the Western Psychological Association, San Diego, March, 1968.

Fosmire, F. and Keutzer, C. Task-directed learning: a systems analysis approach to marital therapy, Unpublished manuscript, University of Oregon, Eugene, Oregon, 1968.

Friedlander, F. A comparative study of consulting processes and group development. *Journal of Applied Behavioral Science,* 1968, 4, pp. 377-399.

Gardner, J. *Self-renewal: The Individual and the Innovative Society.* New York: Harper & Row, 1963.

Gibb, J. R. The effects of Human Relations Training. In Bergin and Garfield (eds.). *Handbook of Psychotherapy and Behavior Change,* New York: Wiley, 1971, pp. 839-861.

Katz, D. and Kahn, R. L. *The Social Psychology of Organizations.* New York: Wiley, 1966.

Keutzer, C., Fosmire, F., Diller, R., and Smith, M. D. Laboratory training in a new social system: Evaluation of a two-week program for high school personnel. Eugene, Oregon, University of Oregon, June 18, 1969, 52 pp. (mimeo).

Langmeyer, D., Schmuck, R. A., and Runkel, P. J. Technology for organizational training in schools. *Sociological Inquiry,* 1971, 41, #2, pp. 193-205.

Lansky, L., Runkel, P. J., Croft, J., and MacGregor, C. The effects of human relations training on diagnostic skills and planning for change. Eugene, Oregon: CASEA, University of Oregon, 50 pp. (mimeo).

Lippitt, R. and White, R. K. An experimental study of leadership and group life. In Maccoby, E. E., Newcomb, T. M., and Hartley, E. L. (eds.). *Social Psychology,* (3rd edition), 1958, pp. 496-510.

McGregor, D. M. *The Human Side of Enterprise,* New York: McGraw Hill, 1961.

Poole, E. A. A study of the effects of an organizational problem-solving intervention strategy on the development of self-renewing characteristics of a school faculty, Unpublished Dissertation, School of Education, Indiana University, 1971.

Roethlisberger, F. J. and Dickson, W. J. *Management and the Worker.* Cambridge: Harvard University Press, 1939.

Runkel, P. J. The campus as a laboratory, In Runkel, Harrison, and Runkel, *The Changing College Classroom,* San Francisco: Jossey-Bass, Inc., 1969, pp. 134-155.

Sarason, S. B. *The Culture of the School and the Problem of Change,* Boston: Allyn and Bacon, 1971.

Schmuck, R. and Runkel, P. *A Preliminary Manual for Organizational Training in Schools.* Eugene, Oregon: CASEA, University of Oregon, 1968.

Schmuck, R. A., Runkel, P. J., and Langmeyer, D. Improving organizational problem-solving in a school faculty. *Journal of Applied Behavioral Science,* 1969, 5, pp. 455-482.

Schmuck, R., Runkel, P., and Langmeyer, D. Theory to guide organizational training in schools, *Sociological Inquiry,* 1971, 41, #2, pp. 183-191.

Schmuck, R., and Miles, M. B. *Organization Development in Schools,* Palo Alto: National Press, 1971.

Schmuck, R., Runkel, P., Derr, B., Martell, R., and Saturen, S. *Handbook for Organizational Training in Schools,* Palo Alto: National Press, In Press.

13. DESEGREGATION INTERVENTION

Dr. MacLennan's experience in a school desegregation crisis provides a useful illustration of a social action strategy of school intervention in which consultants work in coalition building, coalition maintenance and active efforts on behalf of particular social changes. Such effort requires a clear and committed belief that a particular social change is necessary and desirable. A power or financed base which permits performance of such activity without interference is imperative. Dr. MacLennan describes a multiple level strategy of intervention which yielded mixed success. As crises begin to wane, fragile *ad hoc* coalitions begin to fail. A coalition finding success in obtaining social change may suffer from its own achievements.

Dr. MacLennan makes a plea for an expanded concept of the role of the community psychologist, emphasizing schools and social action. She suggests that, in addition to the skills traditionally provided to the clinical psychologist, a healthy sampling of the skills belonging to other professions is necessary for an adequate community oriented professional. The philosophical, political and ethical considerations inherent in a social activist consultation role are only hinted about. It should be obvious from this example that this kind of consultation and social intervention is neither for the naive nor the innocent.

COMMUNITY MENTAL HEALTH PROFESSIONALS

ASSIST IN SCHOOL DESEGREGATION

Beryce W. MacLennan
National Institute of Mental Health

The first question you may ask is why psychologists and other community mental health professionals should be concerned with school desegregation.

Each year we learn more about the strong influence which pervasive environments have on the development and functioning of individuals. Headstart children, for instance, do not maintain their gains in traditional schools. Psychological counseling with individual adolescents very often cannot withstand the effects of destructively provocative families, teacher expectations of failure, or the lack of employment opportunity.

Children spend a quarter to one third of their lives between the years of 4 and 18 in school and receive a great part of their social, moral and emotional, as well as cognitive training there.

A school environment which is not congruent with the basic values of the larger society creates confusion and conflict in the children who grow up there (Miel and Kiester). An environment which does not expose the children to the problems of the larger society and help them cope with them, will not graduate well-prepared adults (Rousseve, 1969). Consequently, we believe that a school in a heterogeneous society should teach its students how to know and relate to others of different origins, beliefs, and behaviors.

It is important for children to learn that all kinds of people are human, to accept different cultural groups with different values and ways of behaving and to respect and enjoy these differences (MacLennan, 1968). When children get to know each other well, stereotyping and irrational fears are reduced. If they are kept apart, they cannot deal with each other realistically.

Thus all children are shortchanged by segregation. Perhaps most importantly, when one group in a society rejects another group and refuses to allow their children to associate, the message of contempt and the demonstration of unacceptability fundamentally damages the self-esteem and self image of those rejected, creates feelings of bitterness, anger and despair, and splits and corrodes the fabric of society.

It is also now recognized that a school environment which includes a reasonable number of children who are curious and eager to learn and who are already trained to educational cues is an important condition for learning. The enthusiasm of these children infuses the climate with excitement and stimulates all the children to learn. This means that socially advantaged and disadvantaged children should be combined in school together for if they are kept apart, the untrained children hold each other back.

A final dimension is the political one. Segregation is as much a rich-poor as a black-white issue, for most of the wealth and power is in the hands of white people. Those with money and power can ensure that resources flow into the schools which their children must attend. If only for this reason, in the past segregated black schools have been disadvantaged and deprived. A society that believes that all individuals should have the right to realize their creative potential through equal educational opportunity cannot support segregated schools.

COMMUNITY OPPOSITION TO SCHOOL DESEGREGATION

Taking into consideration these different dimensions, it is not surprising that school desegregation becomes a serious community and political issue.

1. Education in modern America is thought to be the key to adult success, bringing high earning power and important social ease. Consequently, parents are very concerned to have the best for their children. Opportunities for top level cognitive learning are highly prized and fought for.

2. Schools and particularly, it is thought by parents, secondary schools are places where children learn values, social behaviors and make desirable social contacts and lasting friendships. In adolescence, youth may make their first intimate heterosexual contacts there. Parents have great anxieties about whether their children will be contaminated and damaged for life by the relationships they make with other children in school.

3. Middle class parents fear the violence and antisocial behavior which they believe to be characteristic

of the poor. They fantasize that their children will
be attacked, beaten, shot, raped, doped in schools
where there are many poor children. This is true of
middle class parents of all cultures. It is further
true that white parents frequently expect of all minority group members what they expect of the poor.

Consequently, many well-to-do parents are willing to use
whatever influence and power they have in order to prevent
their children from being exposed to malignant influences. This
means that they will attempt to influence school boards, county,
state and federal governments; will lobby for segregationist
legislation; enlist the press to affect public opinion; appeal
to the courts; organize demonstrations; and even resort to private intimidation and public violence in order to maintain the
status quo.

OPPOSITION TO INTEGRATION WITHIN THE EDUCATIONAL SYSTEM

Opposition does not come only from the community, but from
the educational system itself. Educators are people. They have
anxieties, fears, prejudices, ambitions like everyone else.
They embody the values and mores of their world. In segregated
systems and even in many so-called integrated ones, black and
white teachers feel estranged from each other and from children
of different classes and cultures. Administrators too, often
don't recognize the biases which they express in their behavior
and in their regulations and policies. Boards of Education generally represent the powerful factions in their communities.

The students too reflect the prejudices of the culture.
Their attitudes are formed out of their needs to conform or to
oppose their elders, their self-esteem and security, or their
need to ventilate their frustrations, anxieties and anger
through attacking others.

A move to desegregate a school or an educational system demands community acceptance and internal accommodations. Both
create a crisis in the community and in the schools (Johnson and
Hall, 1968; Orent, 1970).

When we started to develop a community mental health program, we started to work with both schools and community--not
at first around community conflict--but later on with increasing
focus on the problem of school desegregation. We did not at
first have a well-formulated theory about how we should proceed
but rather responded to the changing demands of the situation.

THE SITUATION

Our County had been faced over the past ten years with a rapid change from a rural to a suburban and urban community. The County's population doubled during that time to more than 500,000 and it had one of the largest school systems in the country.

During the 60's the County had slowly and quietly been moving to desegregate its schools, and by the end of the decade only a few remnants of the old two-school system remained. In the year in question, HEW insisted that the last two black secondary schools, a high and junior high school. situated in a socially mixed black neighborhood, be integrated with students from neighboring affluent and powerful white communities. These communities had resisted integration up to this time through subtle behind-the-scenes manipulation of school boundary lines. In the summer of that year, the Board of Education achieved its first integrationist majority and the communities were faced with with the imminence of change. In a maneuver to stave off the inevitable, a model school program was established in the black high school to try and satisfy the demands of HEW and the black community. However, this was not successful and the date for desegregation was set for the following September.

The two black schools served a part of the County which included the largest concentration of black residents and a section which had been designated for a model cities program. Because population was expanding, proposed school changes included a new secondary school and involved altogether eight schools with a population of approximately 14,000 students. With the exception of the black students in the two black schools, all students had previously attended integrated schools. However, no other secondary schools were situated in a totally black neighborhood, and many white parents were anxious about sending their children into what they considered alien territory.

Two members of the CMHC staff were engaged in regualar school consultation with the black schools, and one member, a psychologist, who had a special interest in the community, had begun the previous year to work with the Mental Health Association on class and race relations. This organization had held an Institute entitled "Class and Color in the Changing Community," in the previous winter, after which it had set up a Committee for Improved Community Relations (MacLennan, 1968). Inasmuch as the overall trends in the County and in the country at large at that time appeared to be toward polarization, the members felt there was a need for an organization which would be visible and would attract those in the community who wished to maintain inter-race relations and to work for integration

Their first effort was to unite anti-segregationists and then
to interest residents who were more neutral. They decided to
try to identify areas of agreement, and to work for the development of coalitions and consensus which many people would
be able to support.

As school desegregation seemed to be the point of crisis
in the community, this committee decided to make this its prime
target and to concentrate on the communities involved in the
boundary changes.

A workshop on "Good Schools for Every Child" brought school
and community leaders together who had many divergent points of
view. These participants agreed, however, that they wanted
quality education for all and that quality education implied
truly integrated schools. There was less agreement as to how
this could be achieved. However, the community psychologist
and the committee were asked to work closely with the affected
schools and with the communities which were involved. They
began to speak at community meetings and PTA's and to work with
school officials in getting parents and officials together to
plan for the changes required the following year. They hoped
to obtain visibility in the press for these positive efforts
but found at first that they were not sensational enough to be
"news."

The Fall started off quietly. A desegregation plan was
agreed upon. The Board supported it. The Superintendent, who
had decided to resign at the end of the school year, was obviously cool to the plan and did not put much effort into working
out its implementation. The County Commissioners neither supported nor opposed it. The school officials and well-disposed
citizens slowly made some headway in considering what needed to
be done. Oppostion seemed minimal.

However, as mid-winter approached, a segregationist group
in the affluent white community began to oppose the plan vig-
orously. They obtained much publicity in the press and circu-
lated many leaflets urging action against the plan. They attracted considerable support.

The Mental Health Association committee, in the belief
that it was important to provide accurate and unbiased information, issued a mildly stated fact sheet. This was seized on
by politicians of both sides in a local councilmen's election
and the segregationists attacked the MHA. They accused the MHA
of interfering in politics and complained to the Community
Chest and the State Attorney General. This action had several
positive effects for the committee. It forced the MHA Board

members, some of whom had not been interested in this committee, to review their positions and decide whether this was a vital issued for the MHA. The discussions which ensued were very educational and resulted in the MHA giving much greater support to its committee. The complaint to the Community Chest also made it necessary for the Council of the Community Chest to take a formal position on school desegregation, which it had a- voided unitl now. The third important effect of the attack was that the MHA committee now became "news" and was able to have its activities reported more easily in the press. This gave visibility to the committee's efforts and attracted many additional supporters.

In spite of this, in the early spring, support for the segregationists was growing rapidly in the white communities and amongst some black militants.

Politicians preparing for an election year, sensed that this would be an important issue and began to give support to segregation. The segregationists filed suit against the Board of Education and some politicians introduced bills in the State Legislature to try and freeze the school boundaries. The Governor replaced a Board of Education resignation with a segregationist. The County Teachers' Association voted against the plan. It seemed as if a landslide shift in public opinion was inevitable. Furthermore, because of a feeling of uncer- tainty about whether the plan would be carried through, the school system's planning for the changeover had slowed down.

PLANNING INTERVENTION

Reacting to this crisis, the three community mental health consultants called a meeting of mental health professionals to review the situation and to discuss what should be done. This interdisciplinary and inter-racial group consisted of psychia- trists, social workers, public health nurses, social and clin- ical psychologists, socialogists, anthropologists and public health administrators. The situation, as it had developed, was presented. The group then brainstormed about possible strate- gies and interventions. In this analysis, attempts were made to identify, at State and local levels and in the school sys- tem, those persons and groups who were for or against integra- tion; to consider who made what decisions; who had power and influence and how people could be reached. They discussed what they themselves could do and how they could persuade others to become active in spheres beyond their influence or competence. At the end of the first meeting, all ideas were laid out on a blackboard and at a second meeting, decisions were made as to priority actions.

These actions included the following:

1. The creation of greater visible support for integration. This seemed essential if they were going to prevent the landslide and reversal of decisions. It was suggested that a coalition of important agencies be formed in the community to show that many thousands of votes could be lost by segregationist support and to create public pressure for more effective planning. This coalition was to include neighborhood organizations, business associations, and church groups, as well as social agencies involved with parents and students. Attempts were also made to obtain favorable publicity in the local and area papers, TV and radio for integrationist efforts.

2. The Board of Education was urged to speed up planning and reduce ambiguity to develop teacher training around desegregation. The mental health consultants working in the affected schools reported great anxiety expressed by school faculty and students regarding who would be transferred and who would stay. No one felt able to truly involve himself in planning for the fall because no one knew where he was going to be. Many staff and students, as well as parents, had feelings about race relations whcih were not being dealt with. There was uncertainty whether the principal in charge of the model school program at the black high school would be confirmed in his appointment for the following year. A new superintendent had not yet been chosen. Teachers felt incompetent to deal with black-white confrontations. Planning and training seemed essential.

3. Help to be given to students to organize for integration. Students were seen as key people in the changeover. They ultimately would destroy the plan or make it work. Some black and white students had already started to work together. Support should be given to extend these efforts.

4. Police Involvement. Students and community leaders expressed considerable concern about the way the police had handled previous incidents in integrated schools. It was recommended that police should be involved in planning and consideration given to how they presented themselves, how they were kept informed and who they should relate to.

Attention should be paid to the men's own feelings about school desegregation.

5. Implementation of the Plan. The community psychologist who was consultant to the Mental Health Association met with the committee and leaders of several important organizations, the County PTA's, the League of Women Voters and the Human Relations Commission. Together they decided to move for the formation of a coalition. They obtained the sponsorship of a national inter-religious organization which had strong business affiliations and experience in race relations and began to establish their organization, inviting many neighborhood and special interest groups to join them.

This Coalition obtained support from over thirty groups influential in the County. The School Board was represented on the Coalition. The coalition executive also met with the administrators of the school system and with the Board of Education. They pressed for effective planning and training and they worked for the organization of youth. The community psychologist represented the community mental health agency and consulted with the Coalition.

The Coalition was able to place articles in the local and regional press and by virtue of its numbers, was relatively newsworthy. The Mental Health Association committee was able to obtain radio time and also to report its activities in the press.

Efforts to gain support for the Coalition were educational in themselves. The MHA sent inter-racial teams to many groups in explaining the need for support. A team also met with the Community Chest and obtained their support for the Coalition.

Members of the Coalition were also influential in their own organizations and community groups and with the State and County legislature.

THE SCHOOL SYSTEM

The three community mental health consultants, joined by two others experienced in community organization and race relations, met with the new Superintendent as soon as he was officially nominated, although he did not take office until three months later. They pressed for speedy decision-making, for the creation of vehicles for working through feelings about desegregation, and for the structuring of the desegregation so that it could move easily.

Two of the CMH consultants were appointed to a special Superintendent's advisory committee which consisted of faculty and community leaders to plan desegregation: to develop procedures for student and teacher transfers and for the start of the school year, to obtain community, student and teacher support for the desegregation and for teacher training, and to design new curricula such as black studies.

The School Board set up an office to plan desegregation, and the community psychologist worked closely with the project director. The CMH consultants helped the director of special personnel to plan a training workshop for counselors and also agreed to participate in a training workshop for teachers to be held prior to school opening. This was later cancelled. The principals and program directors met regularly throughout the early summer to plan. Community leaders and police attended some of these meetings. Decisions regarding student transfers were largely completed by mid-April. The Teachers' Association reversed its decision and gave its support to the plan and decisions regarding teachers' transfers were mostly finalized by the end of May. The appointment of the principal of the black high school was not made until the end of the school year. For these reasons, it was very hard to persuade school staff and students to settle down and work through their feelings, needs and plans for the fall because no one knew where he was going to be.

However, the consultants met with the model school planners in the black high school and discussed the particular issues involved in the changeover from a black to an integrated school. Feelings about integration were mixed on the part of the black community and the black school's staff and students. On the one hand, most black residents disliked the segregated school system. However, these schools had been their schools. They grieved for their loss and now feared a take-over by white parents, students and staff. The blacks were also angry that it was to take integration to obtain for them many of the things they had requested for so long. They felt, which was true, that the school system was more sensitive to the needs and pressures of the white community then to their needs.

The consultants also worked with the Model Cities School Committee, which was pressing for greater community involvement in school affairs. This committee obtained agreement from the Board of Education to set up Education Action Teams in each school. These teams were to include the principal and representatives from the students, parents, teachers, classified and special personnel, and community leaders. The CMHC consultants were asked to participate in a training workshop for these teams. Race relations, as well as basic interpersonal relations, were a major focus of this workshop.

The consultants had worked throughout the year with the State Equal Opportunity in Education staff and the two teams had kept each other up-to-date. Now, at the Education Action Team workshop, the consultants also met the State educational facilities staff who, with their counterparts in HEW, were eager to support and finance a new kind of intensive planning workshop (a "charrette") which, centered on school facilities, in fact involved all members of the school and the community in planning program for the school. They wished to hold such a "charrette" at the black high school.

The Model Cities School-Community Committte seized on this idea but wished to include all 30 schools in the area, Ultimately, the Board of Education decided to involve only the eight junior and senior high schools most affected by the student and staff transfers. A week long workshop was held in June, which focused on short and long-term planning for each school. Groups from each school, consisting of 40 students, faculty, administrators, parents and community leaders, met to explore their feelings and problems regarding desegregation, to plan for a smooth transition and also to consider what kind of long-term education and educational climate they would be interested in. The CMH professionals, who included one anthropologist, one psychiatric nurse, two psychologists, three psychiatrists and one social worker, assisted in planning and acted as group leaders and resource persons for this workshop. Again it became clear that the problem of race relations was just one part of a central problem regarding interpersonal relationships within the schools. Students felt a longing for a more human, more personal school. They wished to be able to have more personal counseling and to have courses which were relevant to their concerns and their future life: courses on human relations, financing and budgeting, home care and child care and crafts for both boys and girls. Teachers expressed feelings of helplessness, loneliness and insecurity, and both teachers and administrators were anxious about loss of control. All seemed to wish to pass responsibility to the principal and to "give" the school to him. It was clear that the attitude of the principal was vital to the climate of the school. Principals varied very considerably in their attitudes and their willingness to involve themselves. At this charrette, detailed plans were developed for the start of the school year, and many recommendations were made for continued staff and student involvement.

At the end of the school year, many teachers began to request a seminar on school desgregation. The community pscyhologist offered to meet this need. University credit was obtained and a short 15 hour course was developed in collaboration with two members of the School of Education faculty at the University. Although in the end, only a few teachers attended, the course was received enthusiastically and membership and involvement increased over the five sessions. Much of the course was spent on the problems the staff had in relating to each other and to the students, in gaining support from each other and the administration, and in feeling that they had any power to make decisions and changes. The group was eager to understand the feelings of black and white colleagues and both black and white teachers indicated that they didn't fully understand the position of black militants or how to relate to militant students. The last meeting of the seminar was devoted to this topic, and militants with several different points of view were invited to participate. For the seminar a small reference library was assembled, and the teachers were able to borrow reading material directly from the classroom. Information for the planning activities and for the development of this seminar was sought from many sources, from the Federal and State offices of Equal Educational Opportunity, from experts in NIMH and other mental health specialists and from school systems, who had already experienced desegregation.

THE STUDENTS

Some black and white high school students from the affected schools had already begun to meet in the winter. The Mental Health Association (MHA) committee attempted to give them some support, but rivalries for leadership broke out and the group dissolved. The Coalition conducted a youth workshop for high school leaders from all the County schools in the spring to attempt to organize student leadership in the County.

In May, the MHA and the CMH consultants persuaded the Board of Education to allow them to hold a meeting of students from the affected junior and senior high schools to consider how they should plan to obtain student support for desegregation and how to maintain order and resolve problems in the schools. The incoming students met with the students who were to remain in each of the schools and began to plan. A committee was established for each school, and it was determined there should be meetings and activities in the schools throughout the summer in order to help students to become acquainted with their new schools and with each other in a more relaxed way. On the recommendation of this group, and supported by

the MHA and the Coalition, the Board of Education paid some students as student organizers and eventually appointed a counsel-
lor to assist the students. Two or three of the schools were
kept open for student activities throughout the summer. Students were encouraged to meet in each other's homes, and the
Coalition supported the students in organizing meetings and
one or two picnics.

In one or two of the schools following the charrette, the
principal continued to involve the students in planning for the
beginning of school, how the black and white students could mix
and get to know each other and how they would control friction
and disorder.

In all student programs, the lack of public transportation
was a crucial factor in limiting interaction.

THE POLICE

All parties who were involved in the desegregation were
concerned that the police play a positive role in maintaining
order. The chief of police or his representative was included on the Superintendent's faculty advisory committee and police attended many of the Coalition meetings. The MHA committee met with the police during this period to discuss ways
of improving police-community relations at the neighborhood
level. Members of the Coalition staff participated in police
training. The students, from their deliberations, made several
recommentations regarding liaison between the police and the
school faculty and students. They were particularly anxious
that if there was minor trouble, the police should not arrive
precipitously, misunderstand the situation and start shooting
indiscriminately. They suggested that the police should arrive
inconspicuously and be given a contact person from amongst the
faculty.

THE FIRST FEW WEEKS OF SCHOOL

In most schools, the first day started more smoothly than
usual because it was exceptionally well planned. Everyone
knew where to go and old students helped new students to their
classrooms. Teachers were prepared with a program for the day.
Only in two new schools, where the buildings were not finished,
was there any trouble. This resulted from the students having
nowhere to go and starting to mill around in confusion. Reinforcements of well-trained counsellors aborted this difficulty.

However, in the desegregated black high school, only
about two-thirds of the white students who had registered actually attended. About one hundred black and white students

registered in private schools ond other students and parents
continued to try and obtain transfers. An unfortunate decision
on the part of the Board of Education to sanction certain transfers stimulated an increase in this effort, so that students
and parents continued to attempt to evade the situation rather
than accept it. This created unrest throughout the fall.

Unfortunately, also, many of the recommendations made at
the charrette workshop were not put into practice so that there
continued to be no vehicle for the safe ventilation of feelings
or the working out of problems. For a time after the first
day, community interest waned. However, as tension began to
rise, concerned school officials, the Coalition, the MHA committee and the CMH professional again became active. All began
to press for staff training and student counselling. By mid-
year, a Human Relations Dept. with an advisory board had been
established in the school system and some programs here being
developed.

SUMMARY

This paper describes the activities of community mental
health center professionals in working with the community and
the school system to prepare for school desegregation in the
face of community conflict.

An interdisciplinary group met together to analyze the
support for opposition to desegregation and to plan how mental
health consultants could assist in a smooth desegregation.
Staff worked with community leaders, the School Board and administration, and with individual schools, teachers, and students.
They participated on committees and acted as trainers.

They found that the development of a visible community
group who were in support of desegregation was very helpful in
reducing polarization. They also found that, within the school
system, race relations was just one aspect of concern for more
human and respectful human relations.

As this situation developed, its dynamic nature became
very clear, and it was important to analyze the overall situation, to understand where the forces for and against desegregation lay and to decide what interventions would have most effect. This analysis was most important.

Secondly, it was very important to recognize that in community action and in the achievement of institutional and community change, it may be necessary to intervene at many points
in more than one way.

Thirdly, it was hard to mobilize interest and effort until a crisis ahd clearly developed, even though some people were working on the problem before. Again, after school opened without violence, it was hard to hold the groups together. The staff of the MHA and the Coalition and the CMH professionals were important in remaining in contact with the schools and in keeping their groups informed.

Fourthly, the CMH professionals, wherever possible, mobilized community groups of citizens to press for action. Their major function was advisory both with the Coalition and in assisting the school system to plan. They worked more directly only when their technical skills were required as in leading discussion groups and seminars for teachers.

We need to ask what competences a psychologist should acquire in order to work in school desegregation or other efforts for community change. Psychologists span a wide range of competences, more or less relevant. I believe that community psychologists need to combine the qualifications of developmental, clinical and social psychologists with a broad base of social science. To be effective, they need to understand individual, group, and family dynamics; to be able to analyze the structure and functioning of institutions and communities. They should know how to inform themselves about the values, mores, language of sub-cultures. They must understand as much as is known about how people learn, how change takes place, and about the strategies of power. They may have to play a number of different roles as counselor, consultant, negotiator, mediator, planner, organizer, trainer, educator, communicator, data-gatherer, writer and evaluator. They must have energy, courage and a capacity to get along with people. No professional group is now trained in all these skills. Pscyhologists have much of the basic knowledge and some of the skills. If they wish to work in this field, they must learn more.

REFERENCES

Miel, Alice with Kiester, Edwin, Jr. *The Shortchanged Children of Suburbia.* Institute of Human Relations Press, The American Jewish Committee, 165 East 56 Street, New York, N.Y. 10022.

Rousseve, Ronald J. Social Hypocrisy and Integration. *Integrated Education,* 7, No. 6: pp. 42-50, November-December, 1969.

MacLennan, Beryce W. Mental Health Issues in a Changing Community. Prince George's County 1968 Community Mental Health Institute "Class and Color in the Changing Community."

Weinberg, Meyer. *Desegregation Research: An Appraisal.* Bloomington, Indiana, Phi Delta Kappa, May 1970.

Johnson, Harold T. and Hall, Morrill M. (Eds.) *School Desegregation, Educational Change, and Georgia.* University of Georgia, 1968.

Orent, Iris. Black and White: An Old Issue, A New Perspective. National Institute of Mental Health, Mental Health Study Center, 1970. Unpublished paper.

Prince George's County Board of Education. Charrette - Summer, 1970. Upper Marlboro, Md.

SECTION IV

EVALUATION

14. MANAGING BEHAVIOR PROBLEMS

The chapter by Dr. Stachowiak provides a clear and good example of a systematic school intervention project. Based upon operant strategy several years inoperative, the program has produced substantial evidence of its success. The kinds of evidence reported by the author include lower referral rates to mental health services within the school system, several hundred anecdotal cases with specific and concrete data records, increased teacher satisfaction reported and some empirical studies conducted by graduate students.

The methods presented in this chapter should be appropriate to many University settings whose only existing form of contacts with schools is through courses offered to teachers in mental health and educational psychology. It was this vehicle that Dr. Stachowiak used to develop a concrete, broad and effective program.

TOWARD THE MANAGEMENT OF CLASSROOM BEHAVIOR PROBLEMS:

AN APPROACH TO INTERVENTION IN A SCHOOL SYSTEM

James Stachowiak
University of Kansas

Traditional approaches to dealing with the problem of mental illness are undergoing considerable change today as members of the mental health professions are becoming aware of the need for providing services to the community rather than simply for directing their efforts toward the amelioration of "illness." Attention is being focused also on the need for developing adequate conceptual models which will permit a shift in orientation from treatment of illness to its prevention and to the positive promotion of mental health within the community. Within this context, two major problem areas requiring immediate attention have been largely overlooked in planning and implementing comprehensive community-oriented service programs. The two areas are: (1) the need for innovation at the community level, and (2) the need for a strong emphasis on program evaluation and research.

Current recommendations regarding the setting up of priorities in comprehensive community service programs (e.g., Smith and Hobbs, 1966) place emphasis on the need for developing and refining new methods of intervention which are directed toward the problems of children. It has become painfully obvious that attempts at dealing with emotional and learning problems in children through providing them with individual psychotherapy administered by highly trained professionals will have about the same effect as attempting to hold back a flood by placing a finger in a gaping hole in the dike. As Albee (1959) has pointed out, "The number...who need help and the number of people prepared to give help are so out of proportion that time and arithmetic will not permit such individual face-to-face approaches to be meaningful from a logistics point of view" (p.254). Albee further stresses the need for the development of new techniques and methods which will permit more persons to be reached per professional person.

The purpose of the present chapter is to describe a program which was developed in an attempt to deal more effectively with

behavior problems in children through providing training and
consultative services to teachers and other school personnel who
work directly with children. The program is oriented toward the
goals of: (1) the development and refinement of a model approach to intervention within a social system, i.e., the school;
and (2) the development and refinement of methodologies for effective intervention services. The successful implementation of
the overall program has involved an integration of three component parts. The first involves the training of graduate students in clinical psychology to serve as consultants to school
personnel. The second involves the actual development and testing of methods for dealing effectively with behavior and learning problems in classroom settings which can be implemented
successfully by teachers. The third part is concerned with
building into the program a research component which provides
the opportunity for evaluating of program effectiveness.

DESCRIPTION OF THE PROGRAM

The Psychological Clinic

The Clinic is maintained by the Department of Psychology at
the University of Kansas as the primary intramural training and
research facility for graduate students in clinical psychology.
The Clinic is organized along the lines of a community mental
health center, with most of the client population consisting of
children, adolescents, and adults in the community of about
35,000 people surrounding the University. During any given year,
24 to 30 second and third year graduate students receive practicum training in the Clinic on a year round basis. The supervisory staff currently consists of five clinical psychologists who
are full-time members of the Department of Psychology faculty,
two full-time social workers and one half-time social worker,
and five part-time clinical psychologists. In addition to providing direct clinical services to clients, every effort is made
to provide the student with experience in consultation activities with members of other professions, e.g., teachers, mini-
sters, physicians, etc. As part of the program, a two semester
training seminar dealing with consultation theory and methods is
regularly offered each year for students who demonstrate an interest in, and an aptitude for, developing specific skills in
this area. The major emphasis in the training seminar over the
past five years has been directed toward the development of a
comprehensive program for providing consultative services to the
school system of the county in which the University of Kansas is
located.

The Target School System

The county school system for which the program was planned

includes 15 elementary schools, 2 junior high schools, and 1
senior high school. There are approximately 4600 pupils enrolled at the elementary level, 1800 at the junior high schools,
and 1500 at the high school. The total enrollment in the school
system, then, is close to 8,000 pupils. At the present time,
these schools are being staffed by 412 full-time teachers.
There is also one parochial elementary school in the county
which includes the grades from one through eight. This school
has been included in our plan for developing a consultation program.

Historical Development of the Intervention Program

The program was initiated five years ago when the writer
was asked to offer a course for teachers, counselors, and principals in the local school system. It was arranged to offer a
15 week course dealing with "Learning and Emotional Problems in
the Classroom." The class met once each week for a two hour
period in the later afternoon so as not to interfere with teaching responsibilities. The 50 member class meetings were divided into two parts, with the first half consisting of a lecture
and the remainder of the time being given over to working in
small groups of eight or nine participants. Since the writer
had initiated the consultation training seminar during this same
year, the five graduate students participating in the seminar
and the instructor served as discussion leaders, or "consultants," for the teacher groups. This provided the opportunity for
the instructor tnd the graduate students to function as a consultation team, with the added benefit of stimulating considerable feedback and interchange of ideas and experiences during
the training seminar sessions.

During the course of the semester, some of the teachers in
the discussion groups requested that their consultants make
visits to their classrooms, in order to better understand the
teachers' problems. These classroom "visits" were felt to be
beneficial, both from the viewpoints of the teachers and the
graduate students. The student consultants and the school personnel enrolled in the course viewed the experience as being
very helpful and personally rewarding. In an anonymous questionnaire, the school personnel rated the course as much more
beneficial than courses taken previously in education or psychology, and they also indicated a change in attitude in the direction of increased favorableness toward the idea of working
together with psychologists.

Following the favorable reaction to this first attempt at
providing consultation to school personnel, the program has been
expanded so that 18 graduate students are currently participating

in the training seminar. The increase in number of participating students and interest on the part of the school personnel has enabled us to develop an integrated, three level approach to providing consultation to teachers on a county-wide basis. The three major aspects of this approach may be described as follows:

(1) Lecture course. The course which was initiated five years ago has been offered each year for elementary and secondary teachers, principals, and counselors. The course emphasizes a presentation of principles concerned with the effective management of learning and behavior problems of children as these occur in the classroom. Techniques for behavior modification based on operant methodologies are described and examples are given, with emphasis placed on the importance of keeping behavioral records in order to evaluate results. The major class assignment involves having each class member select a "problem case," and plan, carry out, evaluate, and write up the results of an attempt at modification of the problem behavior.

(2) Problem-solving groups. We have continued to use part of the class periods for small group discussions, with graduate students serving as the discussion leaders. The discussions are designed to provide assistance to the class members in working out difficulties which may arise in connection with the planning and implementation of the modification of their problem cases.

(3) Direct consultation. The 18 graduate students in the training seminar were assigned, either singly or in pairs, as consultants to the elementary and secondary schools in the county system. With the exception of three elementary public schools, one or two consultants made regular weekly visits to each of the other schools throughout the school year. In order to encourage the development of stable consulting relationships, the student consultant was assigned to one school for the entire year. In the case of the three non-participating schools, it was felt that regular consultation was not as necessary, and the principals of these schools requested consultation when necessary. Each consultant is primarily responsible to the principal of his assigned school, and is available to consult with teachers about problems which arise in their classroom settings. Most of the consulta-

tion is carried out on a one-to-one basis, although at some schools the teachers have requested group meetings in addition to individual contacts. It should be stressed that
this consultation program is directed toward
assisting teachers to deal with problem behaviors, and the consultants rarely, if ever,
have direct contact with the children. Consultants are encouraged to make classroom observations, however, if this is agreeable to
the teachers.

THE CONSULTANT ROLE

Theoretical considerations

The training seminar is primarily concerned with consideration of the various "models" which have been proposed for the
consultant role, e.g., the consultant as an expert, as a resource person, or as a "trainer" interested in the consultation
process (Ferneau, 1954; Klein, 1964). In actual practice, of
course, a consultant often finds himself called upon to function
within the context of all three of these roles. Nevertheless,
we have conceptualized the primary role of a consultant for our
trainees as being that of a "trainer," or process consultant.
Thus, the major efforts of the consultant are viewed as being
"directed towards bringing about changes in his consultee which
will enable him to solve his problem himself and to handle similar problems more competently in the future" (Klein, 1964, p.1).

In contrast to the "pseudo-therapeutic" mental health
approach to consultation which tends to focus on the "personal
affective involvement of the consultees" (Altrocchi, 1964, p.2),
our approach can best be understood as being based upon a social-
psychological model. That is to say, the model is essentially
interactional and is derived from an ecological frame of reference. Following Rhodes (1967) we would view problem behavior
in school children as being the product of the reciprocity between an activator, e.g., a child manifesting disturbed behavior, and a responder, e.g., a teacher. While there may be a
community of responders (including teacher, principal, counsel-
or, parents, etc.) involved in any given case, as suggested by
Rhodes, in actual practice we have found that it is quite possible to bring about effective changes in the classroom behavior of children by paying primary attention to interaction between child and teacher. The consultant is thus trained to or-
ient himself toward the development of intervention methods
which are based upon an appreciation of the extent to which a
problem situation can be attributed to: (1) the activator, (2)
the responder, and (3) the divergent environment conditions

arising from their interaction (Rhodes, 1967).

An   adequate assessment of a problem situation arising within a classroom setting is dependent upon carrying out a functional analysis of activating and responding behaviors.   In the interaction between the activator and responder, each person's behavior bears a functional relationship to the other, and the child and the teacher can be seen as alternately taking the roles of activator and responder in a cyclic-fashion.   Since the interaction pattern is maintained (because of) its functional value for each of the interactants, changes in behavior will "depend upon the extent to which the functions of these behaviors are changed" (McAllister, 1968, p.50).

Method

The consultant's role has been conceptualized as a scientifically grounded, "problem solving" approach.   Primary emphasis is placed upon the utilization of techniques for the modification of specific behaviors and the amelioration of concrete behavior problems which arise in the classroom setting.   The consultant is trained in methods of effectively communicating this approach to the consultee teacher, and in providing appropriate social reinforcements which are aimed at encouraging the teacher to integrate the approach into his repetoire of teaching behaviors.

This specific approach employed in our consultation program is based upon an operant conditioning methodology (Bergan and Caldwell, 1967; McAllister, 1968).   In the assessment of a child's problem behavior, attention is focused on the events (or consequences) which follow the child's behavior.   These events may (1) accelerate the behavior, (2) decelerate the behavior, or (3) have no observable effect on the behavior.   Events subsequent to the child's behavior generally occur in an unsystematic manner.   The consultant assists the teacher in preparing for planned schedules of events to follow the child's problem behavior.

The consultant approach is derived from the clear and concise paradigm for changing behavior which has been developed by O.R. Lindsley (1967).   The plan includes the following steps: (1) pinpoint the behavior, (2) record the rate, (3) change the consequences, and (4) evaluate the results.

(1) Pinpoint the behavior.   The first phase of the change plan is concerned with the identification and specification of the problem behavior to be changes.   The initial complaint about a child's behavior is frequently presented in very vague and general terms, e.g., "He's lazy," or "He's impossible to manage,"

developed professional skills, as would be true in the case of the "mental health" type of consultant, which seems to require extensive training and experience in psychotherapy. This does not mean, of course, that the trainees are equally skilled in their abilities to "sell" the program to the consultee teachers. The method can only be useful and effective to the extent that the consultant becomes proficient in the arts of teaching and persuasion.

(3) Since the consultation program is part of a university training program in clinical psychology, it is oriented toward dealing simultaneously with needs for service and for training. In this respect it is directly concerned with the problem of arranging for the most effective and efficient use of profess- ional manpower. Thus, it should serve as a possible model for dealing with the pressures of staffing and meeting the urgent service demands which are so prevalent in present day community mental health center operations. Perhaps the direct traatment model as practiced by the three-man mental health team can begin to give way to the training of sub- and non-professionals as a means of reaching a broader segment of the community.

The foregoing account represents a description of the ini- tial phase in the development of a comprehensive program of in- tervention within a school system. During the first five years, we have directed our attention toward three main goals: (1) est- ablishing and maintaining collaborative working relationships with school personnel, (2) developing techniques for providing "concrete" assistance to teachers in dealing with problems be- haviors, and (3) developing methods for evaluation of program results. Our success in moving toward the realization of these goals has encouraged us to turn our attention toward further re- finement of methods and techniques, which should enable us to increase the overall impact of the program.

It is clear that dramatic changes in problem behaviors can be brought about quickly and effectively in a large number of cases by systematic application of social reinforcements by the teacher. Moreover, teachers who have been receptive to this approach have been amazed and "positively reinforced" by the extent to which they are able to modify and shape the behaviors of students through learning to control their own responses. Most of them view the method as a "common sense" approach, and there is every indication that successful applications will lead to further employment of the systematic use of social reinfor- cers in dealing with future problems. The extent to which tea- chers continue to employ this method will be investigated through follow-up contacts.

Now that we have demonstrated to our satisfaction that the

etc. At the outset, then, the consultant's major task is to assist the consultee to specify as precisely as possible the behavior which needs to be changed. Behaviors which are most frequently reported include talking out without permission, walking about the room, hitting others, and failure to complete assignments. In some cases, two or more behaviors are identified as requiring change. In such situations, a hierarchy of problem behaviors is arranged, with the behavior which is seen as the most disruptive being placed at the top of the hierarchy and receiving attention first.

(2) Record the rate. The next step involves obtaining a record of the rate (or frequency) of occurrence of the defined problem behavior. The teacher obtains a record of the baseline rate of the occurrence of the specified behavior over a period of time, and this record is most clearly represented in graphic form, i.e., plotting the rate per specified time period, e.g., per minute, per class period, or per day, depending on the particular problem situation. Such records can serve several functions. For one thing, they serve in making a judgment as to whether the problem behavior is occurring at a high enough rate to warrant the application of a modification plan, or if it only "seemed" to be occurring "all the time." Also, the keeping of records, in and of itself, appears to be a very effective means for bringing about changes in behavior. Thus, teachers and consultants alike have reported that the mere institution of recording procedure (providing that the child is aware of the procedure) has served to decelerate problem behavior in many instances. While we have no specific data on this observation as yet, it is quite possible that the teacher's recording of the problem behavior represents a change from what she had been doing, e.g., critically admonishing the child, and the cessation of this response serves to bring about a deceleration in the child's behavior. After an examination of the baseline data indicates that action is justified, the consultant assists the teacher in devising a modification plan.

(3) Change the consequences. The modification phase can be defined as beginning when an event is arranged to follow a specific behavior on a planned schedule (Bergan and Caldwell, 1967). We have focused most of our attention on the use of positive and aversive consequences (as emitted by teachers) as events which have considerable effects on children's behavior. If one makes classroom observations, it soon becomes evident that teachers spend a good deal of time and energy in providing consequences for child behaviors. For the most part, however, these consequences are provided in a very inconsistent fashion. Also, many "warnings" of aversive consequences are given, e.g., "You'll be sent to the office," or "You'll have to stay after school." Frequently, however, these aversive consequences are not put into

effect. Perhaps the most striking observation is that children's problem behaviors tend to receive a good deal of attention from the teacher, while "school appropriate" behaviors are
taken for granted. Thus, a child who is identified as a "problem" by a teacher because of his spending a good deal of time
out of his seat without permission is likely to receive a lot
of teacher attention (most of it critical, of course), for this
behavior. As a first attempt at modifying the "out-of-seat" behavior, the teacher might plan to ignore the occurrence of such
behavior, while providing the child with positive social reinforcement (e.g., attention, praise, interest in his work) for
time spent in work at his seat. For this example, it can be
seen that what is involved is planning for acceleration of one
behavior (seat work) which is incompatible with the behavior to
be decelerated (being out-of-seat).

Recording of the specified behaviors is continued during
this "change phase." In the example described above, graphs
would be kept indicating the rates of frequencies of "in-seat"
and "out-of-seat" behaviors. This provides an opportunity for
an on-going evaluation by the teacher and consultant of whether
or not the plan is achieving the desired effect.

(4) Evaluate the results. The "change plan" may be considered successful when the problem behavior "has been changed
in the planned direction and to a degree which remediates the
problem for the child and the teacher" (Bergan and Caldwell,
1967, p. 140). It should be noted that the particular choice of
a planned consequence may vary for different children and in
different situations. For example, it may be determined that
providing a particular consequence does not have the desired
effect on the child's behavior, or that the changes produced are
too gradual, or that it requires too great an expenditure of
time and energy on the part of the teacher. In such cases, an
alternate plan may need to be devised. It has been our experience, however, that most classroom behavior problems can be modified with lasting results. Teachers who have employed this
method during the past five years report achieving success on
the first try in over 80 percent of the problem cases, and if
three attempts are made, success is reported for 100 percent of
the problem cases. These results are in agreement with those
reported by Lindsley (as cited in Bergan and Caldwell, 1967).
In any case, the keeping of behavioral records provides a built-
in opportunity for a continuous evaluation of the effects of the
procedure.

EVALUATION OF THE PROGRAM

In attempting to evaluate the effectiveness of the program
described above, one could point to the continued support of and

participation in the program by school personnel and the consultant trainees. Both of these groups have given considerable time and effort in participating in the program. Teachers in the lecture course and problem-solving groups rated their experience as highly favorable. They also reported feeling "more positive" toward the idea of working together with psychologists after participating in the course. The course enrollment has also increased from about 50 members during the first year to a current enrollment of 75 members.

Such methods of evaluation have been widely employed in published reports of school consultation programs. They have been soundly criticised, also, on the basis of failing to specify the techniques, methods, or approaches employed by the consultant. Wilkins (1964) has pointed out that endorsement of a program by those who participate in it does not constitute empirical evaluation of the program. Similarly, MacMahon, Pugh, and Hutchinson (1961) have questioned the use of subjective feelings of consultees as being valid indicators of beneficial results, without attempting to correlate such ratings with observable changes in behavior.

In the light of such criticisms, we have been concerned with the need for building into our program an adequate evaluative research component. Thus, one of the "observable" effects of the program during the past five years has been a decrease in the number of referrals of school children to the Psychological Clinic. This is in line with our goal of attempting to deal with such problems more promptly and more efficiently in the classroom setting. Nevertheless, one of the primary strengths of the approach we have employed with respect to program evaluation is the built-in emphasis on obtaining behavioral records. Our approach to program evaluation has included the following components: (1) teachers' records, (2) consultants' records, and (3) controlled research.

(1) Teachers' records. As mentioned previously, teachers enrolled in the lecture course are asked to select a problem case, and, with consultative assistance, to plan, carry out, evaluate, and write up the results of their attempts at modification. Thus far, over 400 case studies have been completed by class members during the five years in which the class has been offered. These studies are currently being analyzed and integrated for presentation in book form. In addition to providing a large sample of behavioral reports of the success of modification attempts, the case studies are useful in assessing the extent to which the teachers have been able to learn the "method" and to implement it in dealing with classroom problems.

(2) Consultants' records. The consultants are asked to

turn in weekly records of their school contacts, which provides
an opportunity for assessing the overall impact of their consultation efforts on the school system in terms of number of teacher contacts and number of modification attempts initiated. In
addition, each consultant is asked to prepare a case study on a
problem arising in consultation, in which he attempted to modify
some aspect of consultee behavior.

(3) Controlled research. The acceptance of the program by
teachers and school administrators has made it possible to initiate controlled research studies. In a recently completed doctoral dissertation, McAllister (1968) describes an experimental
demonstration of the use of social reinforcers by the teacher of
a low-track high school English class. Serving in the role of
consultant, McAllister collaborated with the teacher in devising
a plan which proved to be successful in the modification of deviant behaviors which were occurring at a high rate in the class
taken as a whole. Measures of these same behaviors were obtained in a "control class" also, in which the modification program
was not applied. No significant changes in the rate of the deviant behaviors were noted in the control class. This study is
especially noteworthy in demonstrating that the approach applied
in individual cases can be modified for use with entire classroom groups.

CONCLUDING REMARKS

One of the major aims of the program described in this
chapter has been to proceed toward the development of a "model"
approach for effective intervention at the community level.
While we have chosen to direct our attention toward intervention
within a school system, the basic approach should be applicable
within other community subsystems as well. The consultation
program has several unique aspects which should be emphasized:

(1) The focus of attention is directed toward the "front
line" worker, i.e., the teacher, rather than the upper-echelon
of the power structure, as is so often advocated in the literature on planning for change in a social system. It is our con-
tention that, at least in a school system, changes which have a
direct bearing on pupil behaviors can be implemented most quickly and effectively by working directly with teachers. We have
also found that the feedback which teachers provide to administrators has much more impact on the formulation of policies
concerning teacher-student relationships than that provided by
outsiders, e.g., psychological consultants.

(2) The approach is based upon a method which can be easily communicated, both to relatively inexperienced consultant
trainees and to teachers. It does not rest so heavily on highly

classroom management of a large proportion of problem behaviors is an attainable goal, we can begin to focus our efforts on the discovery of more effective methods of achieving generality of application among a broader range of teachers and school personnel. Not all teachers are ready and willing to embrace suggestions of change in their customary approaches to dealing with classroom problems, even though they may be quite dissatisfied with the results they are obtaining with these approaches. Resistance to change is a pervasive phenomenon which is manifested in an endless variety of ways. Frequently, a good deal of preparation, in the form of propagandizing and repeated demonstrations of successful case examples, is required before some persons can be persuaded to "learn new tricks." In any case, inducing change in a large social system is not accomplished overnight, except perhaps in certain instances requiring revolutionary tactics. Our "revolution" is viewed in a more orderly fashion, requiring the exercise of patience, persistance, and promotion. Thus, the next phase in the development of our intervention program will be concerned primarily with the development and testing of methods for enhancing the effectiveness of the psychological consultant in his role as an active collaborator in the educational process which seeks to promote change and evaluation.

REFERENCES

Albee, G. W. *Mental Health Manpower Trends*. New York: Basic Books, 1959.

Altrocchi, J. A conception of mental health consultation with groups. Paper presented as part of a symposium on the Role of the Consulting Psychologist in Community Mental Health. American Psychological Association annual meeting, Los Angeles, September 5, 1964.

Bergan, J. R., and Caldwell, T. Operant techniques in school psychology. *Psychology in the Schools*, 1967, 4, pp. 136-141.

Ferneau, E. F. Which consultant? *Administrator's Notebook*, University of Chicago, 2, No. 8, 1954.

Klein, D. C. Consultation process as a method of improving teaching. Boston University Human Relations Center, Research Report, No. 69, 1964.

Lindsley, O. R. Games children play. Presentation to the Groves Conference on Marriage and the Family annual meeting, San Juan, Puerto Rico, April 3, 1967.

MacMahon, B., Pugh, T. F., and Hutchinson, G. B. Principles in the evaluation of community mental health programs. *American Journal of Public Health*, 1961, 51, pp. 963-968.

McAllister, L. W. A demonstration of a consultation program using operant techniques for the secondary school classroom. Unpublished doctoral dissertation, University of Kansas, 1968.

Rhodes, W. C. The disturbing child: a problem of ecological management. *Exceptional Children*, 1967, 33, pp. 449-455.

Smith, M. B., and Hobbs, N. *The Community and the Community Mental Health Center*. Washington, D. C.: American Psychological Association, 1966.

Wilkins, L. T.   Approaches to community mental health: In
L. E. Abt and B. F. Reiss (Eds.).   *Progress in Clinical
Psychology,* Vol. VI. New York: Grune and Stratton, 1964.

15. CHANGE FROM WITHIN

When we first received Dr. DeCharms' chapter, we were both alerted to and intrigued by the title. We had planned a conference on school intervention and one of our invited contributors wrote a chapter saying that intervention was impossible. Well, Dr. DeCharms is both right and wrong. He correctly points out that lasting change requires both apparent free choice and commitment on the part of the person changing, and the term intervention traditionally is applied to unilateral and external action. Those two are incompatible, and thus intervention is impossible. Perhaps fortunately, we've all been using the term intervention quite loosely, and Dr. DeCharms has proceeded to redefine the term in ways that we can find useful. For Dr. DeCharms, intervention can be understood only in terms of change from within. Using his concepts of "pawns" and "origins," he takes a preventive mental health approach (our term) towards building into the classroom setting procedures to help make pupils more internally controlled and to help these pupils see themselves as masters of their own destinies.

Realizing that imposed intervention is bound to be sabotaged, Dr. DeCharms works deliberately with all levels of staff within the school system in such a way that these people will enhance their feelings of competence, self-motivation and self-control. Within this context he manages to conduct a rigorous research program which allows a thorough evaluation of his theoretical notion.

A notable feature of Dr. DeCharms' strategy is his decision to "intervene" at the level of teacher. Following acceptance by superintendents and upper level administrative staff of his ideas, Dr. DeCharms involves teachers in an open, flexible process whereby plans for origin-training of pupils are jointly developed. Uniquely, teachers developed increasing self-esteem, competence, or in Dr. DeCharms' terms, they become more "origin-like," the result of a procedure designed to increase the origin-like nature of the pupils.

In some ways, this can be seen as starting a benign cycle which ultimately is self-sustaining and self-reinforcing. Rather than creating additional dependence on the part of teachers

for experts or outsider assistance, the teachers become self-
sufficient, self-directed, and responsible. This is in pleas-
ing healthy contrast to increasing dispersion of authority and
diminished personal responsibility within its school system.

We can be especially excited about Dr. DeCharms' notion
that while intervention is impossible, programatic work within
the schools can develop an intervention strategy designed to
enhance the competence and adequacy of social functioning of not
only all pupils within a school but teaching and administrative
staffs as well. Mental health professionals interested in
school change, even though in formats different than those attempted by Dr. DeCharms can benefit from concepts of "pawn" and
"origin" and his sophisticated strategies for "intervention."

INTERVENTION IS IMPOSSIBLE:

A MODEL FOR CHANGE FROM WITHIN

Richard DeCharms
Washington University

Intervention is, at best, a dangerous game. We are learning this painfully in many parts of the world today and we can
look back on a long history of intervention in the affairs of
nations. Have we learned anything from this history that can
help us in school intervention? One thing, at least, is clear.
If changes are not desired within a country or an organization,
they cannot be imposed from outside without the use of some
kind of force.

I take it as my basic premise that to force changes in a
school setting is to endanger our major goal which is to improve the quality of educational experiences in the school.
The logic behind this premise is really quite simple. The
people who determine the quality of educational experiences are
teachers. When teachers are forced to do something against
their will, they do it badly. Chris Argyris makes this point
in a slightly different way. As he puts it, "unilateral action
cannot be taken without reducing the client system's free choice
and internal committment." (Argyris, 1970, p.83-84) Free
choice and internal committment are prerequisite to any lasting change in poeple.

The term intervention has always left me feeling uneasy
because it implies unilateral action or arbitrary external manipulation. To intervene in the affairs of others from outside
is to arouse hostility and resistance. In fact, in one dictionary I found, the first definition of to intervene was
"to enter or appear as an irrelevant or extraneous feature or
circumstance."

Given these implications of the term intervention and giv-
en the goal of improving the quality of the schools, I maintain that intervention to reach that goal is impossible as long
as we must work with the people who are now in the schools.

But we must work with the people in the schools. After all, we can't ship them all out to sea and replace them. We must work with them and some change must be effected. I refuse to say we must change them, but I'm willing to see the goal as change. Argyris says: "Change is not the primary task of the interventionist." (p. 21) But we must distinguish between task and goal. Change is the primary goal.

For purposes of communication, I shall discard my dictionary definition and define intervention as follows: To intervene is to enter into an ongoing system of people as a cooperative participant to help them in reaching their goals or to help them to clarify or change their goals.

So far I may be accused of setting up a straw man and destroying it, but I have done it to emphasize the point that there are two ways to effect changes in people. One is to force them by external compulsion. The other is to elicit internal change which they themselves initiate. I think there are good practical reasons (to say nothing of ethical ones) which preclude the first; therefore, let us concentrate on eliciting internal change which people in the schools initiate themselves. Let us concentrate on change from within.

In common parlance to elicit internal change is to get a person to want to change or, more simply, to motivate him. I have spent most of my professional life puzzling over the problems of motivation and for the past five years I have been trying to develop or increase motivation in school children. Suddenly I find that I am an interventionist. As unsettling as that thought was to me, I was even more shaken when I realized that I was being asked to present my **model** of intervention.

I guess I'm afraid of words but I find the word model very intimidating. What I shall here call my model is really a loosely connected set of thoughts based on my conception of what motivates people. I have been told that the test of a model is whether it is fruitful in spawning ideas in various areas, and this distinguishes it from a theory that should lead to testable propostitions.

Although I feel the word is too grandiose, I will try to do my assigned task by calling a few propositions about motivation my modest model.

The basic principle of the model for change from within is that behavior that is perceived by the individual as originating from within him is quantitatively and qualitatively different from behavior that is perceived by the individual as imposed on him from the outside. The relationship of this principle to stress on stimulating free choices and internal committment in the client system is very close.

We have found it useful to indulge in a bit of jargon to cut down on the verbiage necessary to describe this conceptually simple distinction between what Fritz Heider (1958) has called the internally vs. the externally perceived locus of causality for behavior. We call the person who feels that his behavior is externally determined a Pawn. He feels pushed around. He is a puppet and someone else pulls the strings. The Pawn may be contrasted with a person who feels internally motivated, who feels that his behavior is really determined by himself, who feels that he originates his own behavior. Such a person we call an Origin.

What I propose to do is to apply the Origin-Pawn concept of motivation to the implementation of school intervention. I will use my attempts over the past few years to develop motivation inducing techniques for elementary school classrooms to provide clarifying examples.

First, let us look at how to help a person develop his own motivation.

To help a person to be an Origin is to treat him as an Origin. It is to help him to achieve his goals by his own personal effort. A person who is seeking his own goals through effective action chosen by himself is an internally motivated person.

The steps in treating a person as an Origin are the same as those for helping him to develop his motivation and to become more effective in his life. First, he must know what his goals are. Second, he must have a realistic plan for attaining them. Third, he must know what he can do now and as each day passes to help him reach his goal. Fourth, he must take personal responsibility for doing what he has planned and for its consequences good or bad. Fifth, he must know how to evaluate his progress and the consequences of his behavior. Finally, he must have the confidence to persevere. For short-hand purposes, I refer to these six steps as 1. Goal Setting, 2. Realistic Planning, 3. Internally Determined Instrumental Activity, 4. Personal Responsibility, 5. Evaluation of Feedback, and 6. Self-Confidence.

This, then, is my modest model for motivation development that I want to apply to the problem of intervention. The model has a curious feature in that it works back on itself and ultimately I end up applying it to myself before I can help others with it. It forces me to consider my own goals, to plan, and

to go through all the other steps before I can start asking
others to do the same. In a sense I cannot tell you how to
apply the model to your problem (and in the spirit of treating
you as an Origin I should not try). All I can do is show you
by example how I use it. Somehow, it is all wrong to try to
tell you what to do.

My goal is to suggest to you the value of my motivation
model for intervention. I am realistic enough to know that a
hard sell won't convince you and that talking is only a minor
step. My plan is to present five general phases of intervention, describe a concrete instance where I tried to apply the
model to each phase and try to generalize from the instance.
Hopefully, I will be able to evaluate my success from discussions after this presentation.

The five phases of intervention that I shall discuss are
1) Conceptualization, 2) Entre, 3) Planning, 4) Execution,
and 5) Evaluation, all as applied to a project designed to help
develop motivation. Notice the curious fact that these phases,
themselves fit into the model although they were taken from a
preliminary outline of topics for this conference. Let me re-
peat them and translate. 1) Conceptualization: To me, Conceptualization is goal setting and clarification of your model for
intervention. 2) Entre: This involves both planning and reality
perception. 3) Planning: Must be closely related to the model
and, for us, it had to be maximally flexible and involve cooperative activities between school personnel and ourselves.
4) Execution: Is instrumental activity and as suggested by the
model should be internally determined. 5) Evaluation: Provides
feedback but as we shall see, it is also intimately related to
goal setting.

CONCEPTUALIZATION

We start with Conceptualization of the motivation development project that I have been directing for the past four years.
I have already laid the groundwork by stating the major premise
that change must come from within and by sketching the Origin-
Pawn conception and the steps for motivational development.
The primary goal of the motivation development project was to
increase the feeling of internal motivation in a group of elementary school teachers and children. We started with a basic
conception of human motivation elaborated elsewhere under the
title *Personal Causation* (DeCharms,1968). We set out to show
that increase in the feeling of personal causation will have
dramatic effects on behavior.

Probably the most important point to emphasize at the be-

ginning of any intervention project is built in flexibility.
A project's preliminary conceptualization must be flexible e-
nough to fit it to the people and the situation. Because we
were dealing explicitly with motivation this was obviously of
primary importance to us. If your aim is to treat people as
Origins, you can't preplan everything. You must engage them
in the planning.

I think the applicability of this principle is more general than may appear at first and I would say, every intervention
project should do everything possible to treat all the people
involved in the project as Origins. To do otherwise is to court
disaster through resistance and sabotage.

ENTRE

In order to gain entre to a school system, the interventionist must seek cooperation of the personnel or resign himself to strong arm tactics. The latter course was closed to
us. We were committed to treating people as Origins, and in
order to do this, we could not go to the school system as experts or start pushing people around. We could not force our
gift on them. We spent considerable time and effort presenting our basic aims to the Superintendent, his staff and the
principals of the eleven schools that would be involved in the
project.

At our first meeting with the Superintendent, we presented
our ideas briefly and tried to make it clear that we wanted to
show rather than tell him what we hoped to do. We wanted to
invite him and his assistant to participate in a short three
day training session similar to the training sessions to be
provided for some of the teachers in his district. At the end
of the first meeting the Superintendent and his assistant a-
greed to fly to Boston for a motivation training session to be
held at Harvard. This session, conducted by Dr. McClelland,
stressed achievement motivation and provided the groundwork
for our teacher training for Origin development.

As a result of the training session the Superintendent became very enthusiastic about the project and took upon himself
the responsibility for clearing it with the relevant officials.
From that moment on, the cooperation that we received everywhere
in the district was beyond our hopes. We like to think that it
was because we tried in every way to work with the administrators and teachers on problems that were important to them. We
tried to consider their goals first and to help them to reach
their goals while at the same time, we conducted our study. We
tried to do everything possible to treat each individual from
the Superintendent to pupil as an Origin.

After a careful study of the goals of the client, it is necessary to coordinate their goals with the goals of the interventionist. At this point the presentation of the planned intervention project concentrates on showing the school system administration or teachers what's in it for them. To be authentic the intervention agent must also be quite open in discussing what benefits he expects to derive from the project.

The general procedure that we used may be seen as starting at the top and working down, but it must not be confused with so-called "top-down goal setting." It was not our intention to seek the cooperation from the Superintendent so that he could pass along orders for those below him to cooperate. Once we had his blessing, we moved to the next administrative level and courted the interest and cooperation of the principals. The procedure was similar. We presented descriptions of our goals and demonstrations of our training procedures. Again enthusiasm developed quickly. Soon, the principals all wanted to have their teachers receive the training. Our worst problem was telling some of them that their school had been selected as controls.

As we moved down the ladder, our next step was the teachers. They constituted the major "target population" with whom we would work directly. Preliminary meetings were held with those selected (randomly) for training. Since our design was to conduct a field experiment we could not rely on volunteers. Some pressure was applied, I'm sure, by the administrators to assure attendence at our training session. I was most gratified to find that what ever the inducements were, they worked. We obtained 100% attendance.

PLANNING

Our plan was to share the planning. The value of this flexible approach became clear in our first contacts with the Superintendent. The contacts were made before we had definitely decided to try the experimental approach.

A very significant thing happened in our early discussions with the Superintendent that probably changed the whole complexion of the project. As careful researchers, we had planned to spend the major portion of the time finding what was "out there." That is, we had planned to engage in the observation and measurement of behavior and motives of the children and to use correlational procedures to analyze the resulting data. Finally, as a capstone to the investigation, we hoped to develop procedures to change things. In this last goal, we were far more conservative than the Superintendent. He encouraged us from the very outset to innovate. In essence he said, "We can't wait around for you to study longitudinal trends as they exist. What can you do now to try to shake things up and change things?" From a practical point of view, he wanted to get something done. He challenged us to apply the dictum, "If you think you understand something--try to change it ."

As a result of the Superintendent's encouragement, we began thinking of a change project from the outset and developed our design around the concept of introducing experimental innovations that would encourage self-initiated change in the teachers.

Once we had settled on an experimental design, we planned a two step procedure. The ultimate goal was to develop the motivation of the children in the schools, starting with sixth grade children. But contact with the children would be through their teachers and not direct. We would work directly with the teachers--they, with the children. Thus planning was in two stages. We planned to provide a week long residential Origin development session for the teachers. This would be followed by joint planning with the teachers of techniques for Origin development in their students. Again, the basic principle was sharing and combining our goals with theirs.

The general plan for working with the teachers was to treat them as Origins and so develop their motivation. We also accepted them as the experts on the children. The combination of their expertise with our knowledge of motivation enabled us to plan classroom exercises in motivation development, which the teachers were to implement in their classes.

The execution of the first step of the project was two fold: first, the teacher training week, followed by the planning with the teachers for the project's second step. Actually, this planning occurred throughout the school year in long Sunday afternoon sessions. Here, the university project staff would suggest a goal for a classroom exercise and would sketch ways to achieve it. With that much of a start, the teachers would take up the problem, mold it, change it, suggest concrete procedures and discuss its feasibility in general. By the end of the afternoon, the teachers and staff usually had a series of procedures with which they were comfortable and which the teachers were eager to try out in their classrooms.

The general principle here is obvious. The planning of intervention should always be jointly carried out by the "interventionist" and those who are expected to implement it.

IMPLEMENTATION

During the first year of the planning sessions, the teachers and the staff developed four classroom motivation training units. Each unit lasted for approximately ten weeks and most were designed in a way that called for a daily activity in the classroom. I will confine myself here to presenting the general underlying concepts that the units were meant to convey. The four concepts were 1) self-study and evaluation of personal motives, 2) achievement motivation, 3) goal-setting and 4) the Origin-Pawn concept.

The units designed to convey these concepts were presented by the teachers in their classrooms. (The contact with the children was always through the teachers.) This stage, when the project's effects were finally directed to the children themselves, formed the implementation stage of the project.

The details of what the teachers actually did are not as important here as our orientation to how they went about doing it. Each teacher had, as far as possible, been completely involved in developing the units. It was of the utmost importance to us that she feel the units to be, in a sense, partly her creation. And since she had helped develop each unit and was thoroughly familiar with the goal of the unit, it seemed reasonable to allow her some freedom to innovate even in the final stages of its execution in the classroom. Although we drew up a set of instructions and guidelines to insure some standardization, the teachers were explicitly told to follow the spirit rather than the letter of the unit if the two, for some reason, were incompatible. Thus, to make the point in a more meaningful way, ficticious incidents or stories developed for the units were often replaced on the spot by real incidents known to the class and teacher.

The teachers used feedback from the children to modify the units. Sometimes this was done by changing procedures after a lengthy discussion at a staff meeting. In one case, an initially accepted unit became boring before it was scheduled to end. Since the teachers felt it had served its purpose, it was terminated two weeks early. The opposite happened, also. One unit, in the form of a game, was so popular that many teachers incorporated it into their regular schedule and used it once a week for the rest of the year.

To generalize from our experience, it seems to me that the actual execution of intervention in the classroom, at least, is best handled by the regular teachers if they can be trained and involved in the development of procedures. But they must become internally committed to its success and not submit to doing it as a Pawn to outside pressure.

This procedure is applicable, of course, to other school
personnel for other problems. In general, the people in the
schools must be counted on to see the goals of intervention,
to accept them as their own, and ultimately, to participate
and even initiate the implementation of change.

EVALUATION

The final step in the process is evaluation. Here we meet
some of the most difficult problems of all. The problems of
evaluation can be roughly divided into reactive problems and
technical problems. By technical problems, I mean the problems
of measurement, design, adequate sampling, etc. All the basic
problems of methodology become compounded if you are attempting
to derive generalizable evidence in a field setting.

Reactive problems derive their name from the reactions of
the people being evaluated. It is the reactive problems that
are the most difficult to solve in a way that is compatible
with treating people as Origins and at the same time with good
technical practice.

We are tying a millstone around our neck just before leap-
ing into the pond, if we enter the school while talking about
evaluation. People don't like to be evaluated and they will
resist it from the outsiders. If, on the other hand, intervention from within is stimulated but good results are demanded,
the school people will give you good results even if they have
to cheat to do so. Frankly, the pressure from governmental
agencies is so strong for the school to show success that they
have very little alternative. Can we expect to learn much
about school intervention if the pressure to demonstrate "success" is so great? Think how much you would trust the results
of the experiments of doctoral dissertations if you knew that
the students were told they must produce positive results before they received their degree.

A scientific experiment or any inquiry procedure designed
to produce knowledge must have built into it provisions for
the possibility of producing unexpected and even undesired effects.

Another problem of concern is who does the evaluation. At
the highest level of inquiry, where the researcher's goal is
to produce new knowledge, the only person competent to collect
and evaluate results is the researcher who designed the project in the first place. The reason for this is obvious. From
the very beginning, the techniques and instruments of measure-

ment must be designed into the procedures. The precise goal
of the inquiry or intervention dictates the means for evaluating the attainment of that goal. The person who defines the
goal is the one who knows best how to evaluate progress toward it. Most often, too, he cannot and should not spend years
tinkering with people's lives only to have some outside evaluator come in at the end and show the effects. Feedback must
be continuous and must feedback to the agency or person who is
running the experiment. Too often, I have seen people conceive
of projects of change, implement them, but then ask someone
from outside to evaluate them.

Before I get down off my "evaluation" sopabox, let me simply say that from an inquiring or scientific point of view,
evaluation as it is most often practiced is all wrong. It is
too often intended to demonstrate whether something is "good"
or "bad." Because finding positive results is so often reward-
ed with large amounts of money, unbiased evidence rarely results. What's worse, neither does real committment to doing
some real good for the children. In such a situation, what
counts is the scores, not the kids themselves. The governmental agencies' penchant for accountability and the recent
spate of performance contracting tends only to aggravate the
difficulties involved in this area.

But let us look at some more basic problems. In the motivation project, we faced enormous technical problems and a
very significant reactive problem. First, let's start with
the technical problems.

Our design was experimental based on the simple notion
of randomization. Nevertheless, even in the first year, several teachers selected to participate in the experiment were
shifted within the schools in a way that was out of our control.
Worse yet, by the second year of the project, although we had
planned to follow the same children and extend the training
for the experimental groups, the children had changed schools.
Half of them had been moved into one large school that accomo-
dated only seventh and eighth grades. No need here to go into
details, but both of these events could be turned to our advantage. I'll just give one example. Our design the first
year was a simple experimental-control design. After about
half of the children changed schools for seventh grade, we
found it easy to select and train new teachers in a way that
gave us maximum comparisons. The result was a 2 X 2 factorial
design that produced evidence about two years of training for
some children, either the first or the second year for others
and no training at all for controls. The point to be made
here is simple but important: With a little ingenuity, evaluation of intervention can often capitalize on unforseen events.

Another technical problem that we faced was directly related to our major goal. It is here that I think the close relation between goals and planned evaluation can be seen. We set out to increase Origin feelings in the children--but at the outset we had no measure of the Origin-Pawn variable. The technical problem was to develop this measure. The measure that resulted was an outcome of careful observation of the children's behavior, something that probably could not have been done nearly so well outside the project. In general, the measure was developed to assess the crucial variable, namely the Origin-Pawn measure. Other measures were used also, of course, and they were of the kind most often used, sometimes irrelevently, in evaluation, i.e., I.Q., academic achievement, etc. By a loose chain of reasoning, one could deduce that increasing Origin feelings should increase motivation and this might increase academic achievement. Although changes in academic achievement were not our primary goal, they were important to the school people so we measured them.

Let me give you the results in a nutshell. The project worked. In the sense that it produced significant changes in both motivation measures and school behavior, it may be said to have been successful. Although we have results on many measures such as achievement motivation, attendance, grades, etc. which give a consistent picture; let me simply show you results on our Origin measure and on the Iowa Test of Basic Skills (Lindquist, 1955).

The crucial question is: Did the measures reflect differences between trained and untrained pupils in the classroom?

Figure 1 gives the answer. Displayed here are the means on Plimpton's Origin scale (1970) for four groups of students measured at the end of each year in fifth, sixth, and seventh grades. In the lower right hand corner, we see the group that received training the first year but not the second. The mean Origin score increases from about 5 to 12 the training year and does not decline significantly during the second year. At the top right we see the expected effects of training the second but not the first year. Finally, top left shows effects of both years of training. In every case where training intervened the mean Origin score increased significantly (p. < .001 in every case). In no case where training did not occur did the mean differences even approach significance.

Does the effect carry over to other behavior? Figure 2 shows that on all four subscales of this test there are significant differences favoring the trained students.

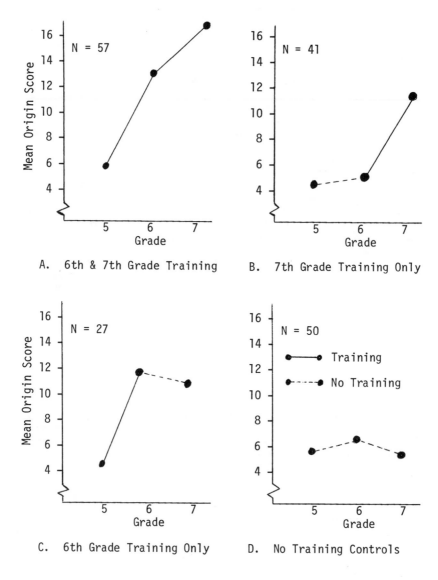

A. 6th & 7th Grade Training   B. 7th Grade Training Only

C. 6th Grade Training Only   D. No Training Controls

Fig. 1. Mean Origin Score Before and After Motivational Training (Longitudinal Data, Plimpton, 1970).

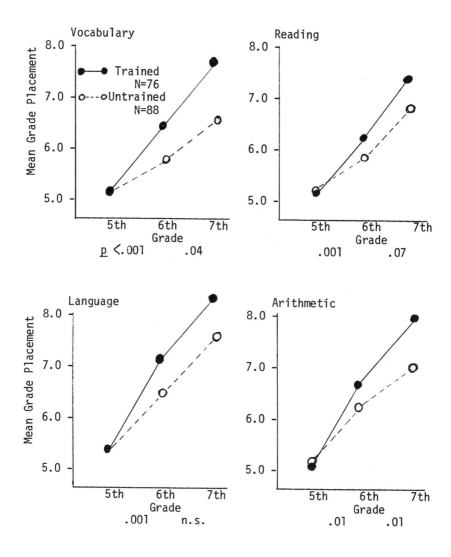

Fig. 2.   Mean Grade Placement on Iowa Test of Basic Skills
(Self-Contained Classrooms).

We have data on the children, but it is often argued that our major effects were on the teachers. Where are the data on them? This raises our second type of evaluation problem: namely the reactive problems.

If we had measured teacher behavior in any obtrusive way, we would have been out of business before we started. Most carefully developed measures of behavior demand that the teacher respond to instruments such as a questionnaire. To use such measures would be to treat the teachers as Pawns, i.e., to counteract the effects of our independent variable. With teachers, it is especially important to maintain this. To measure their teaching behavior or anything related to it is to threaten them severely, and to reduce them to the very restrictive classroom behaviors that we were trying to help them to overcome.

Measurement need not make Pawns of people, however. We set out to obtain valid but unobtrusive measures. Thus, without imposing controls on the teachers, we could, after three years, gain evidence of increased motivation in the trained teachers. We did this through a follow-up analysis of the activities and positions of the trained and untrained teachers. We found that a significantly larger number of trained teachers had subsequently been advanced within the school system than of the untrained, randomly selected, control teachers.

I have indulged myself in presenting some data, but let us now try to summarize the problems of evaluation in intervention. The technical design and measurement problems demand the most flexible and sophisticated methodology available. Most often, techniques may need to be developed specifically for the project and the design must bend with the viscissitudes of the practical situation. I like to tell my students in a methodology class that they must know all the rules of methodology so well that they can defend themselves when they break them. The design, implementation and evaluation must be intimately connected. Anything that tends to separate them will tend to invalidate the results.

But our biggest problems are the reactive ones. Intervention, to be successful, cannot make Pawns of people and this is precisely what a threat of evaluation most often does. My best suggestion here is to use measures with great discretion and whenever possible use unobtrusive measures.

I have talked about the effects of treating people as Origins--effects on the teachers, effects on the students. But I have left out what may have been the largest though unmeasured effect. The effect of the teachers on me. When you set out to treat people as Origins, be prepared to change. If you really try to relate your goals to theirs and to help them to internal committment, you will learn an enormous amount about them and they about you. For me, this was a most rewarding and, at the same time, humbling experience.

In conclusion, let me try to capture the spirit of treating people in the schools as Origins. The very first premise is "Let us be infinitely modest." This is a quote from the aviator-journalist Antoine de Saint-Exupery writing in another era about another problem. His concern was how Frenchmen outside France could best serve the enslaved French of the Second World War. Without pressing the analogy too far, let us conceive of ourselves as the lucky few who are outside the classroom trying to intervene in the lives of those inside the schools. Let me paraphrase Saint-Exupery further, translating his words and substituting the Educational Interventionist for those outside France trying to help.

Let us be infinitely modest. Our theoretical discussions are the discussions of ghosts; ambitions among us are comic. We do not represent the schools; all we can do is serve them. And what ever we do we shall have no just claim for recognition. For there is no common measure between the freedom to theorize and bearing the crushing weight of teaching... The people out there in the schools are the only true saints. Even if we have the honor of taking part in the battle, we shall still be in their debt. There, in the first place, is the fundamental truth. (Saint Exupery, 1965).

REFERENCES

Argyris, Chris. *Intervention theory and method; a behavioral science view.* Reading, Massachusetts: Addison-Wesley, 1970.

deCharms, R. *Personal causation.* New York: Academic Press. 1968.

Heider, F. *The psychology of interpersonal relations.* New York: Wiley. 1958.

Lindquist, E.F. & Hieronymous, A.N. *Iowa test of basic skills.* Boston: Houghton-Mifflin. 1955-56.

Saint-Exupery, A. *A sense of life.* New York: Funk & Wagnalls. 1965.

Plimpton, F. The effects of motivation training upon the Origin syndrome. Unpublished doctoral dissertation, Washington University. 1970.

SECTION V

SUMMATION AND RECOMMENDATIONS

SUMMATION AND RECOMMENDATIONS

Discernable within the chapters contributed to this volume
are four implicit intervention models undergirding the specific
programs. One model is based on the premise that mental health
work should be left largely to professionals, but that the
school presents an ideal place for detecting problems and referring children for treatment. A second model contends that the
school, itself, should be a mentally healthy system and professionals should work diligently to aid a school to function for
positive mental health for itself as well as for its members. A
third model suggests that mental health workers should train teachers to be paraprofessional mental health technicians in addition to being teachers. And finally, a fourth model looks at
the school as but one aspect of the larger community, and postu-
lates that in order to have a mentally healthy community, there
must be a mentally healthy school system. Clearly, the premise
adopted will determine the nature and direction of an intervention program.

More diverse than the underlying philosophies are the assumptions about what produces positive mental health. Traditionally, mental health is thought to result from a private therapeutic relationship between the professional mental health worker and his client. Consequently, mental health in the schools
is produced by making appropriate referrals, with teachers responsible for diagnosing the problems. If the teacher lacks the
requisite skills, special mental health experts can do the early
detection work. Improved mental health for pupils can then be
accomplished by traditional client-centered or case-centered consultation.

More recent approaches for creating a pre-mental health social environment for an individual child, a class, or an entire
school involve contingency management or other behavior modification techniques. Moreover, a school interventionist can suggest new programs (buddy systems, foster parents, helping teachers, etc.) to facilitate the development of a mentally healthy
child, or work for open communications and organizational development in the school system as a whole. Finally, if mental
health suffers because of problems in society, social action involving schools may be the desirable tactic.

An important variable discussed in each chapter is the target of the intervention. Some authors advocate working with principals and administrators while others suggest working with teachers or with the children. Not confined by the boundaries of the school, several authors indicate that contact with parents and allied facilities and resources is essential for a successful mental health program. Service can be direct or indirect; professionals can be paid or volunteer. They can be invited on terms set by the school or they can be actively working at their own consultation relationships. In each case, the differences among these dimensions produce differences in the kinds of relationships that the consultant develops with the school personnel. The individual relationships that evolve from personal, informal contact are a major determinant of the success of a program.

Several suggestions generally applicable to all interventionists or prospective interventionists have been abstracted and briefly summarized below. In the chapter of its origin, each suggestion is made in context with elaboration and examples where appropriate.

1. Be authentic. The issue of authenticity can be translated into honesty and responsibility coming from "knowing what you are doing." The intervention business is not a game for amateurs; it is not something that can be done casually. Considering the ethical dilemmas constantly faced, the choices for action are difficult. A consultant needs to be responsible and able to carry out plans and pledges. He should understand his motives for wanting to become a consultant and the implications of these motives on his behavior.

2. Think and plan. Poorly articulated or thought-out plans are not likely to succeed. The use of "management by objectives" provides one method to clarify goals and to assess progress toward achieving those goals.

3. Up the organization. The value of an effective organization with demarcated responsibility, differentiated staff skills and provisions for supervisory feedback is evident. Whether the organization be one person clearly keeping in mind all of the facets of his job or that of a complex, multilevel staff, relevant guidelines, such as those illustrated by Townsend (1970) should facilitate good results.

4. Know your limits. An accurate assessment of the relevant skills possessed by the consultant is a prerequisite for success. Too many of us have plummeted into consultation relationships assuming that whatever our training was, it would serve in good stead. Clinical training may not always provide

the necessary skills, and the prospective consultants should actively work toward developing those skills.

5. <u>Be up front</u>. Open and effective communications are essential to any kind of organizational work. The consultant needs to have accurate and clear communication with all of the people with whom he works; he needs to be able to analyze conflicts and sources of difficulties, and to confront and resolve them.

6. <u>Listen to the audience</u>. Many mental health specialists harbor the delusion that they know best in every situation. Even if true, consultants need to be able to hear and understand the basic questions, and implicit assumptions of the consultees. An effective consultant cannot operate egocentrically.

7. <u>Know the territory</u>. Understanding of the ecology is essential to make uniquely suited, effective interventions. The chosen strategy should depend upon an assessment of what will work where.

8. <u>Don't tread on me</u>. A reminder for every consultant: understand the survival needs and the goals of teachers and other school personnel. They have to exist beyond and between interventions. They will work for their own survival even if this means sabotaging consultants.

9. <u>Clear it with the boss</u>. If as a consultant you decide that the level of effective intervention is with the teacher, and work hard to cultivate a teacher relationship, don't forget the boss. Superintendents and principals, with their responsibilities will need to be informed of your plans and to acquiese. The opposite mistake is possibly worse: do not get the superintendent and principal to agree and impose the solution on the people you intend to work with. Pawns don't usually make dramatic moves, but can get in the way.

10. <u>Build coalitions</u>. A competent consultant makes the best use of the available resources. A careful melding of family, school, church and other community resources should enhance an effective mental health maintenance program with many long-term benefits. Things impossible for the individual can be accomplished by joint effort.

11. <u>Start benign cycles</u>. Change comes unpredictably enough. Consultants should assure themselves that their strategy of intervention produces, in addition to its desired consequences, more positive organization and conditions fostering mental health of the participants. Intervention should be aimed at stimulating self-sustaining, positive change, as well as eventual elimination

of the need for the consultant.

12. <u>Evaluate</u>. Whether it is hard data, rigorous research data, impressionistic and anecdotal data obtained from teachers, parents, administrators, or the kids themselves, the only way a consultant knows about what he has done is by evaluation. Evaluation helps correct mistakes, suggest future directions, and provides the basis for justifying increased support.

A dozen rules for a model interventionist do not substitute for the substance of an intervention program based on sound theory. A review of programs described in these chapters provides helpful illustrations, but readers will need to adapt these ideas to their unique setting.

School intervention, as represented by the chapters in this book, covers a wide range of efforts. The factors tying these together are the choice of the school system as the point of entry and a shared commitment to preventive mental health. The authors represent a diverse group of individuals who have pursued unique ways to perfect their strategy of intervention. It is our hope that their successes and failures will serve as useful guideposts in the evolution of the readers' strategy for school intervention.

REFERENCE

Townsend, Robert. *Up The Organization*.   New York: Knopf, 1970.